Voices of Michigan,
An Anthology of Michigan Authors

Volume IV
2002

~~~~~~

Foreword by Dale Hull,
Executive Director of
Crooked Tree Arts Center of
Petoskey, Michigan
serving
Emmet, Charlevoix and Antrim Counties

Voices of Michigan,
An Anthology of Michigan Authors
Volume IV

Copyright©2002
First printing May, 2002

Published by
MackinacJane's Publishing Company
Box 475
Mackinac Island, Michigan 49757

ISBN: 0–9667363–46
Library of Congress Control Number: 2002103133

Printed in the United States of America

Cover painting – Marta Olson
Cover Design – Robert Roebuck
Pen and Ink Sketches – Misha Dodge, Tyler Finkel, Kaylee
Knickerbocker, John Tyler and Sam Winsor,
Typist and Typesetter – Jane Winston
Editors – Jeaneene Nooney
Michelle Cowell
Michael Patterson

Foreword

Winter didn't arrive in northern Michigan until Christmas Eve last year. The fall was long and golden and unusually warm. So when the northwest wind finally blew on December 24, it swept across the open waters of the Lake and emptied its lacy load all along the western Michigan shoreline. Another Michigan winter began and my wife, Ruth Ann, and I were snowbound north of the 45th parallel. Why do we continue to spend our days in the drifts of winter?

The answer came for me on an evening between Christmas and New Year's Day. We joined a very small audience at the Crooked Tree Arts Center in Petoskey where I serve as the Director. The program was an evening of storytelling by two men of the Odawa tribe. The men, accompanied by wood flute and drum, sat around a stage—crafted fire and told creation stories to distinguish their people and their culture from all others. These were the voices of the Anishnawbe and we heard them.

Contemporary people of Michigan, including the Anishnawbe, have a distinctive voice as well, and you will hear it resonating within these pages.

Most of you who are opening the leaves of this book for the first time are doing it with a level of anticipation and excitement that only this particular exercise offers. We are the legion of language lovers who look forward to this publication with a simple joy. Because inherent in the reading of a new short story or poem is the promise of a shared intimacy by one of our own tribe—in a voice we clearly recognize as our own. There are many shared intimacies in Volume IV of **Voices of Michigan**, and when you have finished reading it, you will know better what distinguishes us as a people.

There is a notion in some segments of the arts world (especially among actors), that the oral tradition is *real* literature and the written word but a poor substitute. It's a shallow deference to our linguistic heritage...a tribute to the fireside storytellers of antiquity. But for those of us living in the state of Michigan in the 21st century, the impact of the written word on our culture is unmatched by any other art form. The written word is our chronicler, biographer, family historian, political expressionist; our song of self, scribe of imagery, siren to the imagination, healer to the soul. And those who deliver the written word effectively make a contribution to our collective culture that is of infinite value. They deserve our gratitude.

Why do we continue to spend our winters here? Because we are richer for having braved the elements and become a part of what makes the Michigan experience so wonderfully unique.

And so, fellow readers, on your behalf as well as my own, let me say that we are grateful to those who have made a contribution to **Voices of Michigan.** Without them, our only opportunity in a snowbound winter in northern Michigan might be to gather around a fire listening to voices in the more literal form.

~~~ Dale Hull

Acknowledgement

As the publisher of **Voices of Michigan, An Anthology of Michigan Authors,** I feel privileged and fortunate to be engaged in a project for which I have great love and passion. This well–received writing project, which began seven years and four volumes ago, has given me extreme pleasure.

MackinacJane's Publishing Company is owned, operated, and run by only two folks, Jane and John Winston. Clearly this Anthology you hold in your hands would not be possible without the support of former and new–found friends. This is my time to send hugs and to say thanks!

We enlisted the help of three talented and well–qualified editors this year. **Jeaneene Nooney** served as the lead editor and proofreader while **Michael Patterson** and **Michelle Cowell** edited the three genres: poetry, nonfiction and fiction.

Marta Olson, whom I knew when she was a young child at Fort Mackinac many summers ago, painted the wonderful scene used for the cover of the book. Michigan school children competed for their artwork to find a space in the Anthology, and the following young folks' works were chosen: **Tyler Finkel** and **Sam Winsor** are middle school students on Mackinac Island, Michigan; **Misha Dodge** is a high school student in Kalamazoo, Michigan; **Kaylee Knickerbocker** and **Tony Snyder** are elementary students in Grand Haven, Michigan. **Robert Roebuck,** of Atlanta, Georgia provided the cover design for volume IV.

**To learn about the editors, artists and reading judges, please see the appendix of this volume. **

Thanks to Dale Hull, the Executive Director of the **Crooked Tree Arts Center** of Petoskey, Michigan serving Emmet, Charlevoix and Antrim Counties, for once again sponsoring our book signing party in honor of the authors and artists of the fourth volume of **Voices of Michigan.** Additional thanks to **Debra** and **Sandra Orr** of Mackinac Island, Michigan for serving as book signing sponsors on behalf of their Mackinac Island businesses: the **Orr Kids' Bicycle Rental**, the **French Outpost Restaurant** and the **Internet Café.**

A special thanks also to **Victoria Lee**, a secretary in my department at Fort Valley State University, who helped with typing. Also thanks to **Jo Richards** from Bath, Michigan, **Pam Finkel** of Mackinac Island, Michigan, Linda **Barlekamp** from Kentwood, Michigan and **Juanita Smith** of Warner Robins, Georgia for their support and assistance in a myriad of ways.

And without those who served as reading judges there would be no Anthology. Thanks **Joy Brown, Pam Meier, Nancy Martin, George Corba, Carol Douglas, Gary Cusack, Stefanie Lassiter, Debra Frontiera, Jo Richards, Joan Schmichael (Roth), "Bud" Mansfield, Mary Rupe, Peter Olson, Sharon Frost, Tracey Koperski, Judy Bartholomay** and **Glen Young.**

~~~Jane and John Winston

Voices of Michigan

Contents

Fiction:

Non–Fiction:

Youth authors:

Appendix

Voices of Michigan

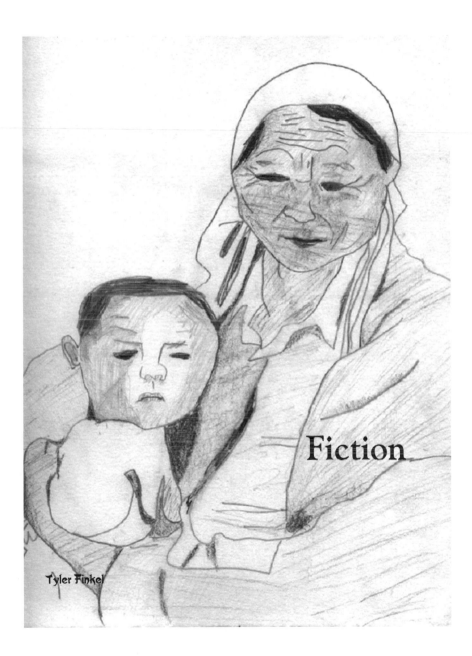

Fiction

Tyler Finkel

Voices of Michigan

Parallel Walker

Kathryn Fritz Kniep

I don't remember the first time I saw Lake Huron, but I am certain it must have been in the rain. My mother loved the rain.

Not the gentle, steady, springtime rains, although she liked those too, in a different way. The rains of summer. That rain that comes on in mid afternoon, so slowly you can feel it coming, smell it coming and yet convince yourself for an hour or more, even as the thunder begins to rumble at the horizon, that it will pass. You tell yourself that you still have options, some semblance of control, can still get on with the summertime plans for your day.

I think she liked the respite the rains provided from the steady stream of tourists in and out of the little grocery she and my father ran, there on Main Street. More than that, I think she liked their inevitability. The rain, looming ever closer, the first fecund drops beginning to pockmark the pavement, falling faster and faster until they became a steady, roaring downpour.

Summer rain falls straight down, and at its epicenter comes in great, pouring sheets, like the central drop of a waterfall. When it hits like this, there's not a great deal one can do about it. Life stops, ceases its hectic forward motion for a little while. The rain provides a small, brief spot of white sound in a world otherwise cluttered with the static of plans.

City people have a funny reaction to rain, at least when it has the temerity to fall on their vacations. They act as if it were

> **Kathryn Fritz Kniep** lives in Harrisville, MI with her husband Arthur and daughter Katrina. She writes a weekly newspaper column, "Putting on the Fritz." Kathryn is the author of two collections of poetry and co–author of a young adult novel. *Parallel Walker* is excerpted from a work in progress.

3

dangerous, made up of something far more sinister than simply water.

At the harbor, boaters deck themselves in expensive yellow slickers, made in Maine and sold to Lake Forest and Grosse Pointe. In the State Park, campers find themselves either filled with self–congratulation for selecting the best tent—the one with the waterproof over fly tarp—or with despair—huddled in the car with three antsy children and a damp, smelly dog.

The summer folk run around their cottages, frantically shutting windows and doors as though any amount of additional dampness could increase the constant mildly mildewed air that inhabits these places before they arrive and after they're gone. Tourists are people who travel north armed with an L.L. Bean catalog of huge umbrellas, fancy boots and waterproof English walking hats against something as harmless as summer rain.

Natives are more pragmatic. Those who can, stay inside or stand on porches or under eaves for particularly impressive displays. Those who can't, pull up the hood on their jackets—if they have jackets—and get wet.

There's a posture particular to the Northern Michigan native in bad weather. A hunch, a tucking of head and curving of shoulders, a placement of hands in pockets that comes of walking one's way through the wind and cold of February. It will certainly see you through a summer shower. It is so universal it could be trademarked, and such a gesture of habit that there are winters when it's warm and well into April before the locally hunched recognize it and begin, slowly, to uncurl.

If my mother hated the winters, she celebrated the rain. Let an afternoon tempest begin to rumble and plop, let the first stranded tourists begin to take restless, unhappy shelter in doorways and under awnings, and she slipped out the back door to the shore. She rarely spoke on those occasions, but sometimes she inclined her head in a way that let me know I could come along.

4

Thus, I have a hundred childhood memories of storms. The steady, drumming rhythm of windshield wipers is still the most soothing sound I know.

Most often, she drove to the overlook at the crest of the harbor hill or to the State Park's deserted swimming beach. There, we sat in the family station wagon, windows open to the damp, promising odor of wetness, silently watching the broken shards of lighting hurl themselves into the water and, my childhood self thought, surely through the earth to the place where the 45th parallel continued on its opposite side.

I've never been certain if the rain validated the anger and melancholia that filled her so, or washed them, for a little while at least, away.

I only know that it remains a piece of my small inheritance, the celebration of rain. I love best the amazing thunderstorms that come so late on July nights that it is almost the cusp of morning. When I can toss off my muggy, tangled sheets and lie flat in the very center of my bed, watching the crackles of lightning illuminate the room, then pitch it back into blackness, listening to the drum of raindrops pounding the earth and replenishing the lake.

In those early, formative years, we were not "on the shore." We lived in a cheerful white house with a garden, west of the business section of Main Street. There, my mother—like Lennon's Eleanor Rigby—put on a face that she kept in a jar by the door. A drawer, more precisely, below a small mirror that hung in the hallway. She never, once, went out that door to clerk at the store, attend church or PTA meetings or to the other social and civic events that made up her life, without inspecting herself in that mirror.

She lived almost half her life, almost twenty years, in my little town and she never came to like it. But she never greeted it without first pulling out the drawer below the mirror, removing the tube of Revlon Red and applying a fresh coat to her determined, if slightly down–turned, smile.

5

When people speak of her to me, they unfailingly say that she was a true lady, always so gracious, so soft–spoken, such a gentlewoman. I'm never certain, even now—when she's been gone for thirty years—if they believed the cheerful, whitewashed life she invented for us in that cheerful, white–painted house, or if they're too polite to say.

But then, I'm not objective. I was the one who shared her rain.

Up North people are a forgiving lot, at best. We gain a gentle amusement, at times, from the actions of the tourists. Still, we are even kinder to those who live among us. As the true native absorbs the concept that Lake Huron does not care, and thus, cannot save you, we also understand that there are people who are not, and cannot be, of here. We grant them the benefit of the doubt in a simple, three word colloquialism that explains away a multitude of errors, behaviors and sins: They are "not from here."

My mother was not from here. That, I think, was the absolutely unbridgeable difference of the multitude of differences between us. Three years and two young sons into their marriage, my father moved her to a place she viewed, always, as a cold and miserable backwater wilderness.

Two years later, in what she frankly described not as an accident, but as a mistake, she became pregnant. She gave birth to me in the bleak month of November, during a blinding snowstorm, in a little maternity home that looked out onto Lake Huron. I may not remember the first time I saw the lake, but her wild nor'easter lakesong must have been one of the first sounds I ever heard. Of my entire family, I became, on that bitter windswept night, the only one who was truly from here.

Always, even on the days when I do not have occasion to pass this way, always, because of this place, this apocryphal line, this old green highway sign that reads "45th Parallel," I have known precisely where I am. And who.

I am on the parallel. Halfway between the equator and the North Pole. If you begin at the top of the earth, that places me halfway to halfway to halfway around the world, and very near to nowhere. As to who I am, that much has been clear to me from the time I was old enough to know it and too young to comprehend. It is only now, maybe halfway through the time I've been allotted here, that it comes in words: I am a parallel walker. Let me explain.

When you spend your formative years in upper, lower, right–hand Michigan, you come to know it (and yes, the pun is intended) like the back of your hand. Here, you can walk a thousand miles of empty, suntanned shoreline without seeing another human soul, and never for a moment be alone.

The great, rolling liquid expanse that is Lake Huron comes to be as real a presence to you as any you may have known and loved. More so, perhaps. Love, after all, comes and goes, while the lake remains faithful, day after day. Always beside you, due east, until you no longer consciously hear her rhythms, but live them.

Which is not to say, if you know her, that you believe the lake loves you back. To grow up on Huron is to learn, very early, that some loves are ever unrequited. The lake will be there, every morning and every night and all day long between. Eternal, integral, more a part of you than the blood in your veins or the pulse in your ears, it would be easy to believe that you are as important—as beloved—to her as well. You are not.

The first lesson of the lake is that she does not care. She cannot care. Some will tell you that is only logical, because she is a large, only semi–animate body of water, void of emotion, incapable of feeling. I prefer to believe that in some first primordial night, she lost her heart to the moon, hanging full and round above her, and she has nothing remaining to share with mere mortals such as you and me.

To know her—really know her—is to understand at that very bottom line of existence, that the lake does not care. You learn this the first time you participate in a dragline—the macabre, silent ritual in which volunteers form a human chain, stretched out across an expanse of water. Walking slowly, an arm's length apart, toes gripping the lake bottom, legs alive and electric beneath the waves. Praying that it is not yours which encounters the drowned body the line seeks.

I was fifteen the first time I walked a dragline. It's not done much anymore. Radar and depth finders and other technology have taken over that sad seeking. I don't know how the young people today learn this essential lesson. But I do know you only need one silent march through the solid, dragging liquidity that, hours before, had seemed a playground to reflect that truly, this lake does not care.

If you are of here, you understand. It is precisely because she does not care that the lake cannot be blamed. Huron does not take revenge, doesn't exact a price like some goddess demanding burnt offerings. She accepts what is. What happens, happens. It does not concern her. She is unaware of you.

And yet...and yet, those of us who are of here, we stay here. Whether it is the lake or the pull of the parallel, or both, we simply cannot go, or not for long. Some of us leave for a while, some for years—most often for love or money, or both. But those of us who are of here, stay here.

There were so many differences between us. Everyone says of my mother that she was a beautiful woman. It is only for wont of a more adequate word. So slender she appeared taller than she truly was, she had, in my childhood, fine, long auburn hair which she brushed a hundred strokes before sweeping it into a simple, severe bun which brought out her chiseled cheekbones.

She had the opalescent, thin Irish skin that literally glowed when she was happy and large, slightly slanted eyes of a hazel so near to yellow that they had a cat–like quality. Her fine, narrow nose turned up infinitesimally, and the corners of her mouth turned down, even when she was smiling. So did the corners of her eyes, and in them were always the faintest clouds of sadness, which made people wish, I think, to banish them, to blow the clouds away and let the eyes sparkle unimpeded.

Those eyes, with clouds, are the only feature she passed on to me intact, although mine—like my lake—range from that cat–like yellow to green to a borderline cerulean when I am ill or far away.

The rest of me is "bracky," a word my mother may have coined. I am shorter, more squat than she, less willow–like from years of perfecting the Up North hunch. My hair is brindle, an odd mix of auburn and mouse, wavy and unrestrainable, perpetually on end from running my fingers through it.

At 45, my freckles have faded, and my skin begins to show some mild effects of sun and wind, but it was always thicker and less fragile than hers and it rarely occurs to me to add lipstick or any other makeup to help things along. My nose is pug. I am, on the outside at least, mostly a mess, and I never knew my mother to look upon that mess without finding it wanting.

That was only the beginning. My mother was, after all, a creature of rain, who brandished shards of lightening. She went through life convinced that, somehow, its rules did not apply to her. She was so beautiful, so gracious and so charming in her passions that they rarely did. She would have appreciated, admired even, a daughter who was an unruly, unmanageable firebrand.

Instead, she had a parallel walker. Parallels run to infinity, over rough and smooth terrain, never coming a fraction of a centimeter closer or farther apart than they initially are. I learned my lines flawlessly for the historical plays my mother authored each year for my grade school class to perform. Secretly, I envied those friends whose mothers' talents were limited to writing the names of their classmates in white icing on perfect sugar cookies for the reception that followed.

My mother's plays always received great public acclaim. I never knew if that was because people failed to see the lost and disorganized pages of scripts, the late night, hysterical last minute rushes to completion, the great, swooping liberties of poetic license she took, or if they attributed to her some brilliance they simply didn't understand. She was, after all, not from here.

I saw her as far too vivacious, too affected, somehow less than honest in the way she drew, demanded, attention. She saw me, I suppose, as far too passive, too disappointingly mule–ish, somehow less than totally alive.

I loved her, and I recognize, finally, that she loved me every bit as deeply. But she was the jagged zigzag of lightening across the sky, while I was the one–foot–in–front–of–the–other, straight–line march along a magnetic field. From time to time, it was inevitable that she struck.

I see her bent to look into my six–year–old face, a five–dollar bill clutched in her hand. She has caught me sliding out the door with a handful of cookies to share with the gang of children playing down the street.

"Look," she is saying, "I will give you this whole five dollars" (a fortune—nearly a year's allowance) "to tell those filthy urchins you don't want to play with them." I look resolutely at the toes of my dirty white Red Ball Jets, shake my head. "Mama," I force out, "I can't. I don't want to. They're my friends."

"Friends," her voice is not loud, but it is dipped in acid. "You won't get far in this world, needing friends. Needing people. Strong people don't need others. They stand alone. Anyone can buy friends." She lifts the five–dollar bill again. "Be strong," she says, "If you can't do it for yourself, do it for me. Learn to walk alone."

Dumbly, I shake my head, refuse to meet her eyes, wriggle beneath the hand on my shoulder. She sighs, straightens, tucks the bill into her skirt pocket and turns away. She does not say that I can go and I wait until I hear the screen bang before I walk away.

Throughout that afternoon, we run and swing and play at pretending and throughout I feel overshadowed, as if I am doing something wrong. I feel the wordless condemnation of my mother's sigh.

Maybe she was afraid the children were too tough for me, that they would tease me. Maybe she was afraid, later, that they would break my heart. Maybe it was only the black side of her Irish

10

nature. I never knew. I only knew I was not a strong person. I didn't know how to walk alone.

To her credit, she never once stopped trying to fix me. Her fine, slender fingers reached, always, to tidy a collar, calm a cowlick, tap a fingernail away from my gnawing mouth. She took me to her hairdresser regularly, to "her" stores in the city twice a year. There, she tucked labels, straightened belts, determined that my colors were green and brown, and ultimately made her choices.

It must have been dispiriting, given my relative lack of enthusiasm. For while I loved the time together, loved watching the initially haughty salesladies come to eat from her hand, it was not my element. Ultimately, what I saw reflected over and over again in the dressing room's three angled mirrors was not good enough, standing before a slightly frowning, sad–eyed perfection.

I was better at manners, if not grace. Exquisitely sensitive to her nuances, the slightest lift of an eyebrow signaled to me that when the guests were gone, we would have something to discuss. The rules in this arena, the only rules that never chafed her, were so absolute, so etched in the stone of society, that they appealed to the likes of me. Children were more seen than heard, and I learned to be clever and then quiet. I was a quick study and a good mimic and got by nicely by saying what I knew would please her, in a subtle imitation of her faintly unidentifiable, not–from–here accents.

I did well enough in school, sliding by on good behavior and excelling at things written. On paper, my heart could relax and sing and soar and my teachers often read my work aloud to the class. I never did, would have sooner died. It was years before I found my own voice.

The one gift my mother fully succeeded in giving me was her own love of the written word. She read to me, from the time I can remember, and later shared with me the books she herself was reading. She managed to convey, if not the keys to style and carriage, the deep, resonant chords that poetry and prose touched in her being, and mine as well.

11

Each Monday morning, from the time I was ten, she taped a list of words and their definitions to the bathroom mirror, where I could study them while brushing my teeth, then use them ten times that day, thus making them mine. She was little impressed with other efforts—a watercolor on which I'd labored weeks drew, "Oh Darling, why do you waste your time on what you do so poorly?" Words, however, properly and beautifully assembled, drew her warmest praise.

She taught me that a lady is judged by her shoes and her hands, that one never wears a hat after six, gloves to dinner or white shoes after Labor Day. On entering a room, you pause, take a breath, lift your chin and walk in as though you own it. "For heaven's sake, don't sidle in along the wall, darling, as if you don't really believe you've been invited."

And she told me, over and over again, that true completion was found in not needing others. Early on, she told me in her faintly arid, instructional way. "Be independent my darling. Hold on to your freedom. Don't belong to anyone. And never, ever, to any man."

Later, when her sky grew darker, when the impending rain began to loom, she used stronger terms. "Slut," she hissed at me, as I hurried to get ready for an outing, a dance. "Run after them like a bitch in heat. Show them just how grateful you are for their too little, too late invitation.

"My god, will you never learn? They only keep on wanting you if you keep on turning them down. You need people too much." And then her greatest damnation, shouted at my retreating back, "You'll never walk alone."

Finally, in her last, classically dramatic act, she forced me to learn what she had been unable to teach me. That first, dreadful dragline I walked, my fifteenth summer, the body we were searching for was my mother's.

She had taken to leaving more and more in the year leading up to that July day. She spent days closed in her darkened room, lying in her bed, staring sadly at nothing. She erupted periodically

12

in unreasonable, irrational, black bouts of anger, followed by days of silence.

It wasn't raining that final afternoon when we realized she was missing. The sun shone warm upon me the entire time I walked through that leaden, tugging water, white–faced and tight lipped, but dry–eyed.

My father and brothers insisted that I should not be there, were horrified when I stepped forward to take my place as a link in the human chain. They did not, however, move to stop me. I was my mother's child, after all. They didn't dare. They stood together on the shore, while I walked back and forth, back and forth across the lake bottom. Finally, they turned and walked away. I understood that. They were not from here.

It was hours later that they found her, a little way into the woods behind her white house, lying beside a patch of violets she had planted there.

I should have known she hadn't drowned. In all my years, I had never once seen her in the lake. The closest she had ever come was one extremely hot afternoon while she watched a much younger me paddle in the shadows. On that day, she lifted the long hem of her brown and white checked skirt and walked a little along the edge of the shoreline. She never, in my experience, actually entered the water. It was cold enough, she said, to stop one's heart.

She stopped her own heart by walking into the woods and swallowing the contents of a bottle of pills prescribed for her haunting insomnia. Apparently, she'd driven to the hill first— perhaps for one last look, perhaps to lengthen the time until she was discovered—parked the car, walked home, taken the pills from the bathroom cabinet, freshened her lipstick at the hallway mirror and walked out into the woods. That time, she did not incline her head for me to follow.

They tell me she was just lying there, beautiful and quiet and looking very, very peaceful. I'm not certain I believe them. After all, they had never really known her. She wasn't from here.

In the days that followed, I exercised my only option, that of putting one foot in front of the other. I served the casseroles and cakes and Jell–O salads people brought to the door or left on the porch, washed the pans and bowls and returned them.

This was my little lakeside community, taking care of its own. I returned the dishes, sure that their generous owners would not upset or disturb me or make me uncomfortable. They pressed my shoulder, smiled sadly, told me I needn't have worried about that, and left me to the silence of my thoughts. They watched, but they let me learn to find my own way.

I didn't, couldn't, wouldn't, cry. Not then. Not when they found her or examined her, declared her dead, searched fruitlessly for a note. Not through the viewing or the service, the internment or the dinner that followed.

I walked the beach, endlessly, for the balance of that summer, spending whole days huddled between two large boulders out near the point, where visitors seldom came. There, the sun baked some of the rawness from the pain.

Only once did I give voice to the emotions that rocked within me, one hot August night when a massive thunderstorm raged through the air. I woke to the first hard drops, slipped out the back screen door and walked to the harbor. I sat on the hill and watched as it built into a downpour.

At its apex, I cried and sobbed and howled and keened while the lightning crashed into the lake, into the ground. Into the ground which had, inexplicably, claimed my mother. Where through some huge cosmic error, they had placed my vital, incredible, amazingly alive mother. Through it all, the lightning crashed about me, but never came near. I like to think it kept its distance out of respect for the loyalty of the woman I mourned.

When it was over, when the last thin blue–white crackles lit far out over the lake and the trees wept softly onto my hunched back, I stood up and walked back home, with the lake on my right and the parallel running beneath my feet. Almost, but never entirely, alone.

A New Year for Laura

Joan Roth

The road ahead curves left then takes a small dip into the schoolyard. Maybe that's the "ridge" in Red Ridge School. There doesn't seem to be any other ridge around. Beyond the school are flat fields covered with snow, not a sign of the bright green of spring, not a single cornstalk to show where hide–and–seek is played in summer. It's January, months to go before warm weather comes again.

I trudge up the walk to school. A blast of warm air invites me in. Red Ridge School, with the Christmas decorations gone, looks exactly the same in 1936 as it did in 1935. It even smells the same, of chalk dust and wet wool, a smell that includes my snow–covered coat, which I hang on the coat rack outside the sixth grade classroom.

Don't you think a new year should bring something new? Take me, Laura Grey. I still have skinny arms and legs, pointy nose and frizzy, dishwater hair, but this year I'm wearing new snow pants. And, I almost forgot, I have new books from Old Mrs. Lockgaar. The books are funny. Not funny to laugh at, for goodness sake, but funny that they don't make sense. Take **A Tale Of Two Cities**, where this man says it's a better thing that he gets his head chopped off. He should keep his head. It's a story, after all. If I were a story, I'd give my father a job and us indoor plumbing. See what I mean?

"Good morning, class."

> **Joan Schmeichel**, writing under the name **Joan Roth**, lives in Kewadin, Michigan with her husband Neill. Before a recent retirement she worked as a development officer at the University of Michigan. She enjoys writing about Laura, featured in *Kisses For Laura* and in a *New Year For Laura*, and intends to continue the series about Laura and her friends.

I make it to my seat just as Mrs. Praeter, my teacher, comes into the classroom.

"Good morning, Mrs. Praeter," we sing out.

"Class," Mrs. Praeter continues: "I want you to welcome a new student to our school."

New? My ears perk up.

Mrs. Praeter turns to the door. "Eldora, come in, please."

Something comes through the door. It's wearing a ruffled dress and a hairbow like a cluster of giant butterflies. Eldora, our new classmate, is a creature of arms and legs skinnier than mine, straight, dark hair cut like a mixing bowl, round silver glasses, and freckles like red reflectors running up and down her nose.

She takes a stance behind and to the side of Mrs. Praeter.

"Class, this is Eldora Francis Fairfield." Eldora sticks out her tongue and rolls her eyes. "She comes to us from Cincinnati, Ohio." Eldora pushes her nostrils up with two fingers and pulls her eyes down with the other two. "Her father is the new owner of the Red Deer Tavern." With this, Eldora carries a make–believe glass to her lips, gulps it down, wipes her mouth with the back of her hand and looks happy but cross–eyed. "I know you will make her feel at home."

The class, wide–eyed, mumbles hello. Eldora walks surely and smugly to a seat in the front row, the vacancy arranged by God, I think.

Eldora knows everything. Mrs. Praeter beams, and Heidi grimaces, as Eldora answers every question. At recess, to the horror of the girls and red faces of the boys, Eldora tells embarrassing things about animals. She refuses to play fox and geese, everybody's favorite winter game.

Nobody knows what to think of her. Except me. I stay away.

Rosemary, the most popular and nicest girl in sixth grade, gives her a welcoming pat and a warm smile. In response, Eldora scratches her belly like a monkey. When Heidi, who thinks she's the smartest girl in sixth–grade but who's just the most stuck–up, brags about her father's feed store, Eldora neighs like a horse. The boys make faces behind Eldora's back but hang on every word.

A week passes and Eldora's the same. In class she reads aloud better than Mrs. Praeter and is the last one standing in arithmetic drills. During recess she thinks up games to play and crazy things to do. At times she ignores everybody.

One day after a heavy snowfall and a rejection of "fox and geese" in a nasty way, Eldora walks to the corner of the school and starts a snowman. It's going to be a giant. I eye it with interest as she works all recess and after lunch. From my stance by the door I try not to let her catch me watching. She packs snow in one place and carves it out in another. I cast gleeful looks, barely able to keep from laughing. It's Mrs. Praeter, for goodness sake, pigeon shape and all.

Eldora stands back to admire her work. She cocks her head right and left. Satisfied, she heads straight for me. What have I done? Go away, I want to yell. I see Florence and decide to be friendly. But Florence is hard at work cleaning her nose and wiping it on her jacket. I walk away, feeling guilty. I always feel guilty about Florence.

Eldora's almost up to me. I turn to the door, like there's something interesting there.

"How come you have your nose stuck in the door?" Her voice hits the back of my head like a hammer. "You look like a dog at a meat market. Come help me with my snowman."

My scalp prickles and my hands feel sweaty. I see red spots. What business is it of this strange girl from Ohio where I stick my nose? I yell I'd rather be a dog than a monkey because that's what she is, a chicken–headed monkey.

Is this me? Me, who never calls attention to myself?

My vision clears and I see Eldora standing with her mouth open and the freckles on her nose bouncing like drops of water on a hot stove. "Besides," I add. "It's not a snowman; it's a snowwoman."

Eldora's expression turns from astonishment to delight. Her glasses fall to the tip of her nose. She jumps up and down and flaps her arms. She pokes me with her elbow. Before I can stop myself, I poke back. Eldora clucks like a chicken. For some reason I bark like a dog.

Next thing I know, Eldora's running off flapping like a chicken and I'm chasing her barking like a dog. We run smack in the middle of "fox and geese." The players kick snow at us and we kick back. By the time the bell rings, everybody's covered with snow, but laughing. Amazing.

All the way home, with the wind and snow practically blowing me off my feet, I think about Eldora. What a funny girl she is. I want to tell somebody about her. But nobody's home. The house is dark and vacant, my mother cleaning offices in town and the rest of the family off earning money some place.

Everybody in my family works. Except me, that is. And my father, who hasn't worked in four years. He looks a lot, though. The rest of my family is Benjamin in twelfth grade, Thomas in ninth grade and Elizabeth in tenth grade. Tonight, I'd settle for Elizabeth. Elizabeth's problem isn't that she's got red hair and a temper; it's that she's way too grown–up for me. She's even more grown–up than my mother! Just ask her, she'll tell you.

The next morning when I arrive at school, Eldora's waiting for me. "We'll track rabbits today," she says, her twitching freckles making her look like a rabbit. "I study animal tracks."

Surprised by this sharing of information, I try to think of something interesting to say. As usual, my brain isn't working. Eldora waits a minute, then gives my scarf a jerk and walks off.

At recess, we tramp around the school, looking for tracks long since smeared by boots from kindergarten through twelfth grade. Eldora won't give up. She insists we try after lunch.

Eldora's father comes by and takes her to the Red Deer for lunch every day. I eat in the kindergarten room with other students who live too far to go home. Mrs. Rostenveld, the kindergarten teacher, supervises lunchtime. She hates crumbs. I

18

mean really hates them. You'd better not leave one crumb around. If you do, you have to eat off the floor. I never have, but I know it's true.

After lunch, Eldora leads me to a nearby field filled with snowdrifts as tall as we are. We make a nest in the snow. With a gleeful laugh, she pulls a thermos bottle out of her fur muff. The sweet smell of cocoa fills the air. We take turns sipping the hot, syrupy liquid.

Eldora's a real person, I decide right then and there. Not like me, for goodness sake; who would want to be like me. But she's a real person in some other strange way, a person who wears party dresses to play in and fur bonnets and muffs to dig in the snow.

"My father buys all my clothes," Eldora says suddenly, like she knows what I'm thinking. "He orders everything from the Montgomery Ward catalog: dresses, coats, galoshes, hairbows, even underwear. You should see my underpants. They have the days of the week embroidered on them." She giggles. "Sometimes I wear Thursday on Sunday." She takes a sip of cocoa and hands the cup to me.

Amazing. Eldora's not afraid to talk about anything, even underpants.

One Saturday in March I decide to go to Eldora's. For weeks she's been after me to come, saying she had something to show me. But her house is two miles from mine and in winter two miles is like two million. This morning, though, a streak of sunlight makes it seem almost warm.

Before leaving, I stop by Mrs. Willie's. Sometimes she pays me to watch over Violet. Violet's big but her brain's small. Mrs. Willie's big, too; so big she hangs in horizontal folds all the way to her ankles. I guess she'd be six feet taller if you stretched her out. She answers my knock, telling me Violet doesn't need watching today.

I head for Eldora's the same way I go to school, by following the creek. At Oakwood Road, I climb out. Eldora said to take

19

Oakwood for a half mile and then left on Parker for another half mile. If I angle through the woods behind Oakwood, though, I can cut the distance in half.

The woods look inviting. Sunlight sparkles on the snow and diamond trickles of water slide down dark tree trunks. I decide to take the shortcut.

Animal tracks keep me company as I walk. The deeper into the woods I go, the more tracks I see. Deer, rabbit, dog, mixed together, so I can't tell one from the other. Suddenly I come across tracks I do recognize, those of man–size boots. They circled from the deep woods, where the Klewickis live. I shiver, thinking of the Klewicki boys, my brothers' worst nightmare.

Suddenly, it seems I've been in the woods a long time. I stop to listen. The wind has picked up. It whistles through small branches overhead and creates shadowy fingers on the snow. The woods aren't friendly any more.

My mother feels strongly about the woods. But my mother feels strongly about a lot of things: school; my grades; my messy hair; Mr. Barren, who knocks his wife around; the Klewicki boys, who knock my brothers around. I try not to get her feeling too strongly. I won't tell her about the woods.

But what if she finds out when they bring her the sad news of her daughter? Shut up, for goodness sake, I tell myself, and start running.

"It's not far," I yell, in case anybody's listening. I feel silly even as I do it. There's nothing to be afraid of. The sun is shining. The woods are filled with light. I tighten my scarf and pull my hat down.

Running is a good idea. It just doesn't work. Broken branches hiding under the snow grab my feet. They threaten to send me flying. Strange crackling and rustling sounds fill my ears. The noises are mine, I know. Yet, I run faster, not sure I believe it. My eyes and nose fill with snow. Blood pounds in my ears, drowning out everything but the thumping of my heart. I stumble and grab a tree. Gasping and fearful, I try to run faster.

Suddenly, with a sharp crack, a dead branch snaps under my feet. A jagged end flies at my face. I scream and cover my eyes. Seconds later I crash into a pile of broken branches and dead leaves, the sound deafening in my ears.

The noise fades away and I lie still, listening. Do I hear something? I stop breathing. I try to squeeze my heart into silence. Yes, there it is. The sound of running feet! Someone——or something—is coming!

"Leery! Leery!"

Sheldon! I try to hold back tears. The tracks must have been his.

"Leery! Are you all right?" He emerges through the trees, a shotgun in one hand and an empty gunnysack in the other. "I saw you running awhile back and wondered." He sets his sack and gun down. "Is something wrong? Are you hurt?" He kneels and tries to brush leaves and twigs from my hair.

I want to die from shame. How can I let this big, dumb boy know I was afraid of the sounds of my own feet?

"I got snow in my eyes and up my nose," I tell him. "I was tracking a rabbit, if you must know, a big, white one," I lie. "And now you've probably scared him off."

Sheldon looks at me, questioningly. "Well," he says, with a smile. "If you see him again, let me know, will you? I've been huntin' rabbits all morning and haven't seen a one. We were hopin' for rabbit stew for supper, too."

He picks up my hat and beats the snow off on his arm. "Where you headed? To that dodo Eldora's?" He doesn't wait for an answer. "I'll walk with you, since you seem to see all the rabbits."

"I can find my way," I tell him. "Just give me my hat."

He holds it out. "You can have it if you give me a kiss."

"You're disgusting, Sheldon. I'll never give you a kiss!"

"You want your hat or don't you?" he asks, tossing it in the air, daring me to catch it.

21

Sheldon's always after me to kiss him. I can't think of anything worse than kissing boys, especially Sheldon.

"Leery, Leery, give us a kiss. Pucker up and do it like this." He makes a face.

I reach my foot back to kick him. He jumps out of the way and I grab my hat.

He doesn't seem to notice. "Come on. I'll walk you to Eldora's."

"You'd better catch your rabbit dinner instead," I tell him.

"Rabbits are good to eat," he wants me to know.

I shiver, thinking of Peter Rabbit in Sheldon's stew. But I guess that's not much different than skinning Peter to make Eldora a muff.

We reach the edge of the woods and Eldora's house. I can see Parker Road in front. Sheldon tells me he lives nearby on Digby's Road. He hunts a lot, especially in winter when work on the farm is slow and he can follow animal tracks in the snow.

"Don't you ever read books?" I ask, curious about this boy who kills rabbits and always wants to kiss me.

"Not unless I have to," he answers. "It's too much work. It's not like tossing hay or workin' the plow. That's fun."

It doesn't sound like fun to me. I head to Eldora's back door, skirting a broken dog house in my path.

"Don't chase any more rabbits today," Sheldon yells.

My face burns. I wish I had stayed buried in the leaves.

I knock on Eldora's door. A woman dressed in a bathrobe peers out at me. She doesn't say anything, just disappears. I'm wondering what to do when Eldora comes to the door.

"I'll be just a minute," she says, not inviting me in.

I'm disappointed, having hoped for a chance to warm up.

Without so much as a hello, Eldora says: "Follow me." She leads me into the woods behind her house. After a short walk, she stops and points to a giant of a fallen tree. Between the tree's trunk and one of its branches sits a small building. I can see most of the dog house in it.

"Our fort," Eldora proudly tells me. "The minute I saw the tree I knew it was perfect." She climbs on the trunk. "You have to get in from the top," she explains, folding back half the roof. We drop inside and pull the roof back.

The fort is about the size of the doghouse. I hope there are no fleas. Eldora lights three candles stuck in cans. I see a wood floor, a throw rug that looks suspiciously like Eldora's coat and two stools. Books and candle stubs sit on a box in the corner. The room feels warm and cozy. Eldora hands me a cinnamon roll frosted with pocket lint. We sit on the stools, eating and spitting.

"I read books and study about animals here," Eldora says, between bites and spits. "Mostly I stay away from the house."

She doesn't say why and I don't ask. People are entitled to say only what they want to, I figure. They shouldn't be pushed into saying more. I know there are a lot of things I never say to anybody.

"What are you going to be?" Eldora asks. "I want to be a scientist, but if I can't, I may just dig ditches."

"I won't dig ditches, " I tell her, knowing that right off. My father dug ditches once and every night he came home with mud up his nose.

"Maybe you'll get married and have babies," Eldora tells me. "I'm not going to get married."

"I wouldn't like washing all those dirty diapers," I tell her. The stories I read don't talk about diapers; they only talk about living happily ever after.

"Have you noticed how Heidi's getting all the answers right?" Eldora asks, not interested in the marriage talk any more.

I had noticed. "She seems to get smarter every week."

Eldora laughs: "Must be all those oats she's eating." Then she gets serious. "She's cheating. I don't know how, but I know she's too dumb to be so smart."

A horn blasts through the woods. I jump up and hit my head on the roof. Eldora nods. "It's a boat horn," she explains. "Papa's home for an early dinner."

We lift the roof off and walk back to Eldora's. I take the road home.

Monday morning, Mrs. Praeter announces an arithmetic drill. "I told you on Friday," she reminds us. Groans and moans, carefully hidden behind raised books, greet her words.

"I think I know what she's doing," Eldora whispers to me as I pass her desk. "Wait until recess."

She? Then I remember what Eldora said about Heidi.

During morning drill, Heidi doesn't miss one answer. Eldora looks back at me and smiles. It's not a nice smile.

At recess I hurry outside to see what Eldora's up to. "Watch," she whispers and pulls something from her snow pants.

"Oh, Laura," Eldora calls in a loud voice. "Help me get these answers written." She pretends to scribble for a minute. Then, as the entire sixth–grade watches, she snaps open a pair of bulging pink bloomers covered with arithmetic answers. They flap in the breeze like a flag on the Fourth of July.

"Want to borrow these?" Eldora asks Heidi. "They hold more answers than your stockings."

Heidi's eyes pop and her face breaks out in purple and red blotches. She grabs at the bloomers. They rip down the middle, sending half a bloomer sailing across the school yard and into a waiting puddle. It floats there, a pink blob, until Sheldon walks over and plants a rubber wader right in the middle of it.

"You're just jealous," Heidi yells at Eldora. "You're jealous because I beat you." She sticks her tongue out. "And nobody likes you. You think you're so smart all the time!"

As there's some truth in the last, I look to Eldora to respond. But Heidi's not finished.

"My ma says if your daddy didn't sell sinful whisky to everybody, your ma wouldn't be drunk all the time!"

Eldora's freckles stand out against her white face. Her hands clench into fists.

"Mama and Papa are none of your beeswax, cheater," she tells Heidi coldly. "You're a dumb cheat. Half the time you get the answers wrong anyway."

"Heidi! What a rotten thing to say about Eldora's mother!" I wait for Eldora's sharp tongue to pick up where I left off. But she's silent.

Everybody stands around not knowing what to do until Rosemary mops up the quarrel with smiles and pats and licorice buttons. I take a button, feeling disloyal, but Eldora takes one, too. We leave the others and sit on our haunches beside a puddle where we send stick boats out to sea. Neither one of us speaks. Eldora licks her lips with a charcoal tongue and shoves her glasses aside to rub a mittened hand across her eyes. Eldora shouldn't cry! I feel afraid for her and spit out the black button.

"I hate her," whispers Eldora.

"She's just a cheat, and a big mouth," I tell her. "Don't let her make you feel bad."

"Not Heidi, she's dumb." Eldora looks up at me. "It's Mama I hate." She wipes her glasses and puts them back on. "I hate them both. Papa's to blame. He should make her stop drinking."

I want to say something comforting, but can think of nothing.

"I have to finish school and get away to college so I don't have to live with them anymore," Eldora whispers as we head back to the classroom. Her words make her seem both young and old at the same time.

After that, I see Eldora's mother drunk once. It's a terrible thing to see.

Eldora's usually careful, but one day she invites me in to pick out books to take home. I'd just finished when I see Eldora's eyes fly to the door of her room. She looks away, as though by not looking, what she sees will disappear. It's Eldora's mother, leaning

25

against the doorway. She's young, I think, younger than my mother. It's hard to tell, though, because her long brown hair is matted around her face.

"Home so schoon, Dor?" she says, sounding like her teeth are missing. She weaves back and forth, then slides down the doorjamb, easy–like, as though somebody pulled the stays from her corset. She shoves her hair aside.

"I shlipped a little," she comments.

Eldora doesn't say anything until her mother pulls herself up and staggers off. "See what I mean," she says then.

"Drunk as a skunk all right." There doesn't seem to be any other way to put it.

We don't talk about Eldora's mother after that. We talk about the end of the school year and our plans for summer. We talk about expanding the fort, turning it into a real house. Eldora's making a drawing.

When there's only three weeks of school left, Eldora announces that she's finished her drawing. If I come in early Monday morning, she'll show it to me. She knows that getting to school early is not something I do.

But Monday morning comes and I'm here, waiting by the coat rack. I've been waiting a long time, too. Finally, I give up. Maybe Eldora forgot. Her desk is empty, as I knew it would be. Eldora doesn't forget.

When I walk in the room, everybody stops talking. Then they look away. Everybody but Heidi, that is, who's standing by Rosemary's desk watching me and looking smug. Sheldon's sitting on the window ledge, staring at his shoes. No one seems to want to talk to me. Even Florence has her back turned. I feel funny.

Finally Rosemary comes over. "The door of the Red Deer was found open Friday night," she says.

Heidi follows her, eager to tell: "Constable Martin found Eldora's mother inside. She was hanging from the ceiling light."

My scalp prickles.

26

"Constable Martin cut her down before she," Heidi lowers her voice, like she's saying dirty words, "before she killed herself."

I want to slap her. But I feel too sick. I run to the lavatory and lean over the sink, trying to throw up. I can't. "Oh, Eldora," I whisper.

Rosemary comes in and asks if there is anything she can do. I wish she would go away. She looks so unhappy I feel I should try to cheer her up somehow. Finally, she leaves, but not before giving me a soft pat on the arm. I fill the basin with water and bury my face in it. I wipe the water away and go back into the classroom. There's nothing else to do.

The class is quiet when I return, the only sound that of pens scratching back and forth across coarse theme paper. Mrs. Praeter gives me a sympathetic look.

The rest of the day is endless. I feel I should be some place else, doing something else. But there is nothing to do and no place to go. I can't go to Eldora's. I just have to wait.

At lunchtime Florence invites me to her house to eat. I refuse, forgetting to say thank you. But she's not through. Florence has something else to say.

"Leery," she offers. "They's better now, the class, than tafore." She hangs her head, letting her mousy hair hide her face. "You ken what I'm sayin'?" she asks.

I nod. Yes, I "ken" what she's saying. Has Eldora made the difference, or are we just growing up?

The last weeks of school, I stumble through class. School isn't fun without Eldora. Finally, Mrs. Praeter tells me if I don't pay attention, she's going to send me to the principal. I'm trying, for goodness sake, I want to tell her.

Finally, the last day arrives. I open the heavy front door and drag myself through. The teachers let us out at noon today. Mostly all we do is clean desks, pick up leftover papers and write notes to one another. The teachers don't seem to mind.

I walk down the hall. Halfway there I stop. I see a cluster of butterflies by the coat–rack. Eldora's back! I start to run to her. Then I slow down, suddenly feeling shy. Maybe Eldora won't be the same.

"Mama's quit drinking," Eldora tells me flat out, like we had been talking about her mother five minutes ago. "The doctor says with the medicine he gave her she's going to be fine."

Eldora's not finished. Her eyes sparkle with excitement. "Guess what?"

I can't guess and she doesn't want me to.

"Papa decided to sell the Red Deer."

That's probably a good thing, I'm thinking.

"And," she takes a deep breath. "Guess what else?"

Tell it before you explode, I want to say.

"Heidi's father wants to buy the Red Deer! But he can't afford it. So," she pauses and I want to shake her. "He's trading Papa his feedstore for it!"

My mind goes blank. What did Eldora say? She gives me a nudge. I wake up. I giggle. Eldora whoops. We hug one another and jump up and down. We poke one another with bony fingers. We gasp for breath and let the tears roll down our faces. Still holding back giggles, we go into class.

Everybody welcomes Eldora back. Everybody but Heidi, that is, who ignores us both.

"Quiet, class," Mrs. Praeter interrupts our chatter. "Next year you move upstairs, to Miss Olaf's seventh–grade classroom. You have completed the elementary level of your education. This means you are no longer children but young girls and boys. You will be expected to behave in a much more grown–up way." She stumbles over her words and pulls out a hanky. "Make me proud of you," she finishes.

I gulp, surprised to find that Mrs. Praeter will miss us. And even more surprised to find that I will miss her.

After her short speech Mrs. Praeter dismisses us and we take our leave. Before I go, Eldora and I make plans to meet at the fort. I head for the creek and home. As I walk by Florence's house, I see her and yell: "See you next year." Maybe next year I'll be friendlier.

"Hey, wait up, Leery." It's Sheldon. "What were you and Eldora whooping it up about?" he asks.

What we whooped about belongs to Eldora. "None of your business," I tell him.

"We'll see about that," he shouts. In two bounds, he's picked me up and headed for the creek. "Come on," he whispers, his blue eyes too close to mine. "Tell me, or I'll drop you in." He swings me back and forth.

"Sheldon, you nincompoop," I yell. "Put me down."

He grins and stands me up on the edge. "It's no matter to me; anyway, I just figured it was a good way to rile you. I like to rile you, Leery."

"Sheldon, you're hopeless." I'm not mad, though. Funny how I'm not mad at him anymore.

"You get riled easy, Leery. Like this." He ruffles my hair. I yelp and he grins. "I'd walk farther with you, but I have to go. There's always a mess of chores around the farm in spring." With a wave, he's off.

I continue the walk home, the sun warm on my back. I flush a red–winged blackbird from a bush beside the creek. Overhead a batch of starlings swoops across the farm fields looking for seeds leftover from spring planting. I think of the long summer ahead and happiness seems to bubble right up out of me.

Voices of Michigan

The Lion

Glen Rothe

In the evening after supper, when Mrs. Gerber would retire to the parlor and raise her swelling ankles on the ottoman in front of the television, Mr. Gerber had gotten into the habit of hurrying through his nightly chores. He would give the kitchen table a cursory wipe and quickly clean the dinnerware. When he was done he would hasten down the basement stairs and into the tiny cubby which he proudly referred to as his office. There, in front of the computer, the little man with the thickening middle and thinning hair would become The Lion.

> Glen Rothe was born and reared in Milwaukee, WI. He and his wife have lived many different places in the world, but Michigan isn't one of them. They have, however, a long history of spending wonderful times in Michigan. The Rothes currently operate a bed and breakfast in Albany, WI.

Leo was uncomplicated, and the only technical accomplishment that he had ever achieved was using his outdated computer to prowl the worldwide web. On most occasions he would start by checking the bulletin boards dedicated to his only visible passion: stamps. Leo Gerber was a philatelist, but on recent journeys down the information superhighway, stamps had become merely an excuse, a justification for connecting online.

It started one day when Leo received a cryptic message in his e-mail inbox that both intrigued and flustered him. The message simply said: *Visit privately with naked women.* Following this curt introduction was a worldwide web address. Being Leo Gerber, and not yet The Lion, his inclination was to delete the message and to move on to others sent by fellow philatelists from around the world. But something within Leo wouldn't allow him to delete the intriguing message. It sat in his inbox for days, buried under new e-mails arriving daily from philatelist friends in exotic locations; places which were tangible to Leo only as cancelled or uncanceled brightly colored square, rectangular and triangular stamps.

Each time the message *Visit privately with naked women* surfaced, Leo intended to delete it from his inbox. But he didn't. One evening, nearly faint with anxiety, and perspiring from anticipation, Leo could resist no longer. He typed the web address into the web browser—and The Lion was born.

The address www.privatenakedwomen.com was, for Leo, like opening a door leading to the kind of place that never in his wildest imaginings would he have considered visiting in the real world. But sitting in his little cubby there was no turning back. Leo Gerber was committed. When he entered the address, a screen offering brief instructions was displayed, and Leo was requested to enter an alias, a name by which he would be known within this new world of Private Naked Women. Without hesitation, Leo typed: The Lion.

Suddenly displayed on the screen were small thumbnail–sized portraits of a dozen women, each in states of partial undress, clad in exotic clothing. Leo could feel his blood begin to race. Not only had he never experienced something such as this before, Leo Gerber had never even imagined such things existed. But soon, the directions for how to navigate this exotic web site were being rapidly—almost hungrily—read. The Lion was impatiently wrestling with Leo for control of the keyboard and the mouse.

It was really quite simple. Clicking on any of the pictures would immediately whisk the operator to a fantasy room where a conversation (or at least the keyboard equivalent of a conversation) could be held with the room's willing occupant.

Left to his own devices, Leo Gerber would have remained frozen, worrying over the decision to actually proceed or not. Even having made that decision, another lengthy deliberation would have followed to decide which room to enter. The Lion had no such uncertainty. The image of Miss Scarlet on the computer's screen had caught his attention. Blonde and buxom, reclining en déshabillé on what appeared to be a bright red velvet chaise, Miss Scarlet was beckoning. The Lion clicked on the postage stamp–sized image of Miss Scarlet and he, along with a reluctant Leo Gerber, was ushered into another world, as almost magically, a little window on the computer's screen slowly filled with the image of the beautiful Miss Scarlet. A vision in red, adorned in silk, filmy lace and sequins, the young woman was reclining on a small mattress, with pillows, blankets, cushions and covers—all red.

In less than a minute the little window on the computer's screen went dark, replaced by a message which stated: *Miss Scarlet is in a private session. If you too would like to visit with this exciting woman in private, just click on this message, and you will receive detailed instructions for opening a confidential and personal account with www.privatenakedwomen.com.*

Uncertain of what to do next, and with the screen remaining blank, Leo terminated the connection and turned off the computer. He switched off the small globe light in the cubby and exited, making his way upstairs to rejoin Mrs. Gerber, now long since sound asleep in the double bed they shared in the cramped but tidy first floor bedroom.

In the weeks that followed, Leo Gerber's routine became set. Once in the basement cubby, he would quickly examine the philatelist bulletin boards and his stamp related e–mail messages, wanting only to go rapidly through these motions to clear the way for entry into the world of Private Naked Women. Once there, The Lion would emerge—again in control.

A month into this routine there had been a momentary battle of wills between Leo Gerber and The Lion. Leo balked at setting up an account with the Private Naked Women Internet service. He would be required to divulge personal information, particularly pertaining to his precious credit card. The Lion, however, had no such apprehensions. The account in the name of Leo Gerber was established, and it was really only a matter of time before the desire to visit in private with the stunning and exotic Miss Scarlet became overwhelming.

Private visits ensued. That's not to say that anything untoward or unseemly was requested of Miss Scarlet in private. Even without the restraining, repressive conservatism of Leo Gerber, The Lion had too much respect for the sensitive beauty to request anything but conversation.

But it was clear that what went on with others in these private sessions was not so proper. Once, through some technical glitch no doubt, the little window on the screen had not gone dark while a private session was underway. Leo had wanted to avert his eyes, so as to not witness the degradation to which Miss Scarlet was subjected. But under The Lion's prodding, he had been unable to look away.

With increasing frequency, The Lion, with Leo's reluctant assistance, would examine the Gerbers' finances in order to determine if it was prudent to allocate money for fifteen minutes of private conversation with the mysterious Miss Scarlet. If there was an unplanned expense, such as when a plumber had been called to fix a broken pipe, or when a handyman had been required to clean the gutters after a backup of leaves resulted in an overflow nearly flooding the basement cubby, then there were no private sessions. But barring anything unforeseen, a decision would be made to pay for another fifteen minutes.

Upon entering Miss Scarlet's room, The Lion would always politely introduce himself, then engage the vision in red in staid conversation. While in private session, The Lion would use this brief time to eliminate any vestige of Leo Gerber; portraying himself to the clearly world–wise young lady as a well–traveled, financially secure and erudite man of the world. Sensitive about his thickening middle, thinning hair and short stature, discussion of physical appearance was avoided.

And each time, following a private session with Miss Scarlet, Leo Gerber would find himself more strongly identifying with The Lion. Occasionally he would feel sufficiently motivated to quickly make his way back upstairs. Then, not making his usual attempt to avoid waking the sleeping Mrs. Gerber, he would change into his flannel pajamas, and in an uncharacteristically bold fashion, climb into the double bed, cuddling close to Mrs. Gerber, laying his small arm across her silently rising and falling bosom.

For her part, Mrs. Gerber couldn't possibly miss the change in tempo and tone of the ordinarily quietly considerate Mr. Gerber. Without fail she would rise to the occasion, saying, "My goodness, Leo, aren't you the frisky one! I don't know where you get such ideas!" This would always be immediately followed by girlish giggling and muted bedroom noises.

On a day early in summer the invitation to the International Philatelist Convention arrived, sealed, of course, within a colorfully fashioned commemorative first day cover. In years past, these annual invitations had been quickly discarded. This time something caught Leo's eye. The convention, attended by a world audience of stamp aficionados, was going to be in Las Vegas, Nevada. Reading the invitation, a charge soared through Leo. Although his private sessions had yielded little else of a personal nature, he had learned one thing. Miss Scarlet resided in Las Vegas.

That evening, nearly unable to contain himself, he rushed the clearing of the residue from dinner even more than usual. In his haste he dropped several pieces of the resilient melamine onto the kitchen floor, earning a scolding from the always–alert Mrs. Gerber from where she was already perched with her feet in the air in the parlor. Nevertheless, the dishes were soon back in the cupboard, and Leo, under the insistent prodding of The Lion, was soon connected online, with www.privatenakedwomen.com on the screen.

It would have been an impossible feat for Leo Gerber. However, under the direction of The Lion, in private session, Miss Scarlet had soon agreed to a personal meeting in Las Vegas.

Leo sat in the passenger waiting area of Detroit's International Airport, staring out the window at the gray and red airplane standing at the gate. He listened hopefully to the messages coming over the airport public address system. Leo

Gerber had never before been on an airplane. Right now he was longing to hear the message that Northwest Airlines Flight 1191 from Detroit to Las Vegas had been cancelled. But through the massive windows it was apparent that the summer day was beautiful. The air was clear and calm, and deep down Leo knew that nothing was going to intervene.

Past the DC10, which was now loading at the gate, Leo could see a runway with a steady stream of jets landing and taking off. Each time a plane would touch or leave the concrete, Leo could feel a shiver, starting in his brain and not stopping until it tingled in every part of his body. He was just going to have to proceed to the podium and tell the attractive young lady checking in passengers that he wouldn't be requiring his seat to Las Vegas today.

That day, if it hadn't been for The Lion, Seat 12D on Flight 1191 would have been returned to the airline's inventory of available seats. But The Lion wanted to go to Las Vegas. The Lion was going to go to Las Vegas. And if Leo Gerber didn't want to go along, well then he could damn well stay here in Detroit and wait for The Lion to return.

Leo would later remember nothing of the flight; only the shiver radiating through his body as the wheels of Flight 1191 left the ground at Detroit; and again as the wheels touched the runway in Las Vegas.

"Shit!" muttered Melanie Blaeske as the last remaining eye on her last remaining conservative white brassiere pulled out. The pressure from the hook had caused the eye to give way under the strain of her enlarged breasts. "Shit! Shit! Shit!" she exclaimed, louder this time. Loud enough to wake the baby who was napping in the portable playpen that doubled as his bed in the untidy bedroom the two of them shared, far from the Las Vegas Strip. Jesus Christ, she thought to herself; if her damn breasts got any damn bigger, there wasn't a damn brassiere in the whole damn world that was going to fit her anymore. Then hearing the infant beginning to wail, she bent over the crib and lovingly picked him up. Seeing Melanie's unfettered breasts, the baby, who had been fed only a half hour earlier, tried to again attach himself to an exposed nipple; habit not hunger driving him.

With the baby semi–attached, Melanie again rifled through her lingerie drawer in the oversized dresser which took up an inordinate amount of space in the little room. Tonight's "date," she thought, was a colossal mistake. Nothing was going right. She didn't want to be wearing one of her sequined or see–through show bras when her escort showed up to take her to dinner. In fact, the more she thought about it, the more she hoped he wouldn't show up at all.

She should never have agreed to the "date" in the first place. She wasn't in the habit of meeting her Internet clients in person. She had only tried it once before, and that time, she was certain, it had nearly cost her her life. That time, the brute, probably not wanting any evidence left in his car, had tossed her purse out onto the highway after her bruised body. Somewhere in the dessert between Las Vegas and Henderson, searching and crawling on her hands and knees in the dark, she had found and been able to use her cell phone to call Stick. When he got there, after pulling her into his car, Stick had slapped her around a bit, just for good measure. Then he had forced a promise that she would never again attempt to see one of her cyber–johns, as he called them.

And she wouldn't have. But Stick was hitting her up for more money; the Harley needed another new carburetor. And last month she had been notified that the bills for the delivery of the baby had been turned over to a collection agency. Now, to top things off, if her usual clockwork period could be relied upon, she was pregnant again. Jesus Christ, she thought to herself, as if her breasts hadn't grown enough with the last baby, all she needed now was another kid. She already felt pretty much like a walking, talking breast.

In spite of Stick's warnings, and even with the temper that would be turned on her if he ever found out, she needed the thousand dollars. That was the going Las Vegas rate for an all night date. A thousand dollars was more than two week's commission check from the agency paying her only a dollar per minute for the private sessions she solicited on the internet web site.

Rummaging through the Charmin toilet paper box in the corner which held a disorderly pile of discarded clothing, and which she, thank God, hadn't taken to Goodwill as she had been planning to do for months now, she found a modest white brassiere. It was a nursing bra, but not so heavily padded that it couldn't pass for everyday wear.

She quieted the baby enough to place him back in the playpen, and was just struggling to stuff herself into the dowdy bra and fasten all of the hooks and eyes when the doorbell signaled that someone was at the apartment door. "Jesus Christ, that better be the babysitter and not The Lion, or whatever his name is," she muttered to herself, as she slipped on her most demure blouse and checked to make sure that the baby had not been wakened again by her too loud muttering.

Mercifully, when she opened the door, she saw that it was Mimi from down the block, here to look after the baby. As she was ushering the teenager in, she noticed the little Geo Prizm pulling up in front of the apartment building. Normally, Melanie Blaeske wouldn't have known a Geo Prizm from a Sherman tank. But last year she had driven a "hot" Prizm to Elko for Stick, and as she watched the car being carefully parked at the curb, she was pretty sure that this was a Prizm. Seeing the cheesy little car, she had a very bad feeling about this "date." Then, when she saw what looked to be a gnome, dressed in the most unlikely green suit she had ever seen, getting out of the car with a bouquet of flowers, she knew that it was going to be a very long evening indeed.

What first struck The Lion when he got to the door and greeted Miss Scarlet, was how tall she was. After all, the little two–inch by three inch window on the computer screen, which had been his only image of her till now, didn't exactly provide a true point of reference. As he extended his open hand to introduce himself, he couldn't help but notice that he was head high to one of Miss Scarlet's overripe breasts.

"Hello, Miss Scarlet. I'm Leo Gerber," he said, too late realizing that he had neglected to use the alias by which she would know him.

"Honey, if we're going to be spending the night together, I think you better call me Melanie," responded the tall woman. Melanie, in truth, was so stunned by Leo's appearance that she hadn't paid attention to the name, or noticed that Leo Gerber was not the same name as The Lion. She took the bouquet and threw it to Mimi, who was still gawking at Leo from the doorway, not having moved since arriving.

"Stick these in some water, babe, will you? Don't expect me back too soon. Leon here is going to show me the town tonight. Aren't you honey?" said Melanie, turning to Leo.

As they got into the miniature pinkish–tan car, Melanie turned toward Leo, who, because it was a Geo Prizm, seemed nearly to be sitting in her lap. "You got my thousand bucks, honey?"

Although Leo had forgotten just how expensive this evening with Miss Scarlet was going to be, The Lion hadn't. He reached into the breast pocket of the new suit jacket he had purchased just for tonight, pulled out the slim beige envelope containing ten crisp one hundred dollar bills, and coolly handed it over to Melanie. He couldn't help but notice that she suddenly appeared to have a much relieved look on her face.

Left to his own devices, Leo might have taken Miss Scarlet to Applebee's, or perhaps Country Kitchen—Mrs. Gerber's favorites. But The Lion, already painfully aware that he should never have left details of the car rental to the discretion of Leo, had given dinner considerable thought and research. He had made reservations at the American Steak House at the Rio Hotel. This was reputed to be the home of the best beef in Las Vegas. With

Melanie giving directions as he drove, The Lion was able to make the long trip to The Strip with hardly a wrong turn.

Dinner was, she thought, amazingly comfortable—even pleasant. She wasn't used to the company of charming men. And Leon Gruber, or whatever his name was, had definitely charmed Melanie Blaeske. After dinner, she was pleasantly surprised to find that Leon, or The Lion, as she had now begun to think of him, had made reservations for a show as well. Although she had been living in Las Vegas for nearly four years, Melanie had never seen Siegfried and Roy. Sitting in a wonderful seat right at the front edge of the stage, watching the remarkable animals appearing and disappearing in a variety of fantastic effects and illusions, she even had a warm thought or two about what life might have been like had she encountered a gentleman earlier, instead of latching on to Stick when she was just a kid.

After the show, with the time nearly 11 P.M. clearly visible as they passed the clock tower in front of the Venetian Resort and Casino, The Lion's night was complete. There was nothing more he desired. He would need to hurry, however, if he was going to catch the midnight flight back to Detroit. He had reserved this quick turnaround flight when making all of the other arrangements two weeks earlier. Plans had never included a hotel room.

As the Prizm pulled up in front of Melanie's apartment, she couldn't believe what was happening. Not only had The Lion, or whatever his real name was, treated her like a lady; but he was bringing her home without insisting on the usual quick flop at a hotel. For a second, she was afraid that he was going to ask for some of the money back, this not being an all night "date" and all. Briefly, she even thought about offering to return some of the thousand dollars on her own. Wasn't that what a lady would do? But then, thinking about Stick and the carburetor, the doctor and hospital bills, and her missed period, she quickly put this thought out of her mind.

The Lion opened the driver's door, got out, and quickly crossed behind the car, hurrying to open Miss Scarlet's door. He hastily walked her to the small porch fronting the apartment, and there, under the bare bulb, which emitted a very unromantic, intense light, he reached for her hand, brought it to his lips, and placed a light kiss on her knuckles.

An unexpected rush of warmth surged through Melanie as the chubby little man in the ugly green suit reached for and then kissed her hand. She knew herself well enough to realize that a steady diet of this kind of romance would soon leave her numb with boredom. But for tonight, it seemed just right.

Before The Lion could turn and begin the walk back to the Prizm, the tall woman standing with him on the porch bent down, lips parted. The Lion turned his cheek, to give her easy access, but she grabbed his chin, turned his head, and planted her lips fully on his. He was taken aback, but pleasantly surprised. When he felt just the tip of her tongue touch his, he almost fainted from shock.

The trip home was a blur. The rental company was closed when he attempted to return the car. Unconcerned about the consequences, The Lion left the little Prizm at the curb in front of the terminal. Walking rapidly down the concourse, he arrived just in time to board the flight. He never noticed the wheels leaving the ground, and when the plane arrived in Detroit, he didn't notice, or was indifferent to, the touching of the wheels on the concrete runway.

It was early morning and still dark when he pulled his nondescript eight–year old sedan into the carport alongside the little bungalow in suburban Detroit. When he quietly entered the house, it was apparent that Mrs. Gerber was still asleep.

Not really attempting to be quiet, but also not wanting to abruptly awaken the sleeping Mrs. Gerber, The Lion decided to forego the flannel pajamas. Quickly climbing into the double bed, he cuddled close to Mrs. Gerber, laying his small arm across her silently rising and falling bosom.

Mrs. Gerber, who had heard every move since he had entered the house, simply said, "My goodness, Leo, aren't you the frisky one! I don't know where you get such ideas!"

41

He decided not to correct her. Knowing that Mrs. Gerber took to change slowly, there would be ample time for her to get comfortable with The Lion. For the moment, he was simply happy to enjoy the girlish giggling and the muted bedroom noises.

Halloween Witches

Linda Barlekamp

Halloween has always been one of the best days of the year for my friends and me. It's the day for dressing up, running around, collecting treats, playing a few tricks, and going out — not in — when it is dark. Afterwards, we laugh and talk about it for weeks; that's what makes Halloween so much fun. But this year it's different. It can't help but feel different when you're lying on your back in the hospital and all your friends are out trick–or–treating without you. But then, things started to change about a year ago.

"Suzy, when you're done with lunch, I need you to go with me to Mrs. Jancovich's house," Ma said, as she set a bowl of vegetable soup in front of me.

Stunned, I stared at her. Had she lost her mind? No one ever went in Mrs. Jancovich's yard, let alone near her house. "Why you going there?" I asked, swallowing hard.

"Mrs. Jancovich had a stroke not too long ago, and, now that she's home, all the ladies in the neighborhood are taking turns bringing her food and visiting for a while."

"Why doesn't her family take care of her?"

"They are, honey, but her sons live out of town, and it's the neighborly thing to do since she spends so much time alone."

"She's scary." I didn't know any polite way of saying it. Besides, I didn't understand how it could be the "neighborly thing to do" when Mrs. Jancovich was anything but "neighborly". If you ever set foot on her property she'd come out on the porch waving a

> Linda Barlekamp and her family live in Kentwood, MI. *Farewell*, a non–fiction piece written by Linda, was published in Volume II of *Voices of Michigan.* A summer resident on Mackinac Island, Linda and her husband, Bob, share ownership of Shell Cottage on Woodbluff with her sister, Karen, and her husband, Keith Loren.

broom and screaming at you in some language no one understood. My friends, Katie and Deb, and I joked about her a lot and had even shortened her name to Mrs. Vich, which later became Mrs. Witch. Around the schoolyard, her house was known as the witch's house.

But if the truth were told, we were sufficiently scared of her so that we stayed away from her place; except for one night a year. That night was Halloween. We couldn't resist repeatedly running up to the porch, ringing the doorbell and yelling "trick or treat." Of course, Mrs. Witch never gave us a treat. But then, maybe we were lucky that she never gave us a trick either.

Half the fun of Halloween night was staying up late so we could run to her door, sight unseen. Katie, Deb, and I would take turns daring each other to run up to the porch and ring the bell. She'd never turn on her porch light. That way, she could make it look like she wasn't home and hope the kids in the neighborhood would stay away and not come begging for candy. Of course, we knew differently. We'd sneak all the way to the porch and climb over the wooden railing on the side. From there, we could see the light on behind the drawn curtains. Oh, she was there, all right.

"Hurry up and finish your soup before it's cold. I've got a few more things to pack in the boxes and then we'll leave."

I didn't want to go to Mrs. Witch's, and I certainly wasn't going to set foot in her house.

Well, Ma and I drove down the street to Mrs. Jancovich's house, even though you can see her driveway from ours. It's within walking distance, but it was cold and snowing and Ma's packages were too heavy to carry. As we pulled into the driveway, Ma got stuck in the snow that had already accumulated into a drift, and she had to gun the engine while I pushed from the rear to get the car to move. Climbing back into the car, I could barely see over the hedges lining the left side of the drive. I could only imagine the dark, shade–drawn rooms filled with antique, smelly furniture. The house looked eerie and lonely and only confirmed my decision that I wasn't going in. I was certain Mrs. Witch would recognize my face from all the doorbell ringing over the years, and I had visions of her chasing me out of there, waving her broom, while Ma stood by in stunned silence.

I helped Ma carry the packages up to the porch and set them down, desperately trying to figure out a way to keep from stepping into the house. And then, I spotted it—the snow shovel.

"Ma, I'll shovel the end of the driveway so we won't get stuck when we leave," I volunteered, grabbing the shovel from its perch.

"What a thoughtful idea, Sue. Mrs. Jancovich will be very pleased. She isn't up to going out in the cold, let alone do any shoveling."

I didn't care how pleased Mrs. Witch would be; I was just pleased with myself for having figured out a way to remain outside. As my mother rang the doorbell, and a yippy, little dog approached the door, I picked up the shovel and trudged down to the end of the driveway. I'd only planned on shoveling the end, but it seemed like my mother stayed in the house forever, so I continued shoveling until the entire driveway was done. When I finally finished, I leaned the shovel back against the house, and, even though I was shivering, I looked around wondering what to do next. At that moment, the door opened and I shrunk back around the corner. Relieved to finally see Ma come through the door and hear her say good–bye, I hurried to the car and climbed in. And that's how it all started.

Ma went back to Mrs. Witch's house the following week and dragged me along, so once again I shoveled the driveway. Two weeks later, I was feeling bored on a cold and snowy Saturday and couldn't stand being inside with my younger brothers, so I went for a walk and ended up at Mrs. Witch's. Seeing the shovel in its usual spot, I went over and started shoveling. I looked up once and saw Mrs. Witch watching me from the window. I didn't look up again.

In spring, the city held a neighborhood clean–up day. Ma and the neighbors decided to form a street clean–up committee, and she added my name to the worker list. I was assigned Mrs. Witch's hedges to trim. Mrs. Witch came out several times and offered the people working in her yard glasses of ice tea and some candy. When she held out the candy dish to me, I picked out a couple pieces of Bit–O–Honey, my favorite candy. Mrs. Witch patted my hand and smiled at me. She said something that sounded like "goot girl." Later that night when I was falling asleep, I wondered what Mrs. Witch, an old lady with false teeth, was doing with Bit–O–Honey candy.

In the spring and summer Mrs. Witch would come outside and work in her garden, but I still kept my distance. She never said very much, though I knew she was watching me. It's a good thing that she didn't talk to me, because I don't think I would have understood her. I once asked Ma what the strange language was that Mrs. Witch spoke, but Ma said she sounded funny to me because she came from the "old country," which really didn't make much sense to me, because the way I had it figured, every country was old. Ma explained it as "broken English," and said that's why I was having such a difficult time understanding her. Mrs. Witch certainly looked like she came from another country. She wore long, ugly housedresses and she always seemed to have a plaid scarf on her head. Ma had a word for that, too. She said it was a "babushka."

One thing was certain. I found out that summer that Mrs. Vich baked the best cookies and grew the best flowers and vegetables in town. Not that I'd admit that to Ma, you understand. The first time she handed me a basket of tomatoes I tried to give them back to her, telling her I didn't like them. But she insisted, saying, "For you mooder." Well, I took them home and even tried one. It was the best–tasting and juiciest tomato I'd ever eaten. After that, I didn't turn down anything Mrs. Vich offered me, especially the pieces of Bit–O–Honey she'd pull out of her dress pocket and put in my hand.

Like I've been telling you, I went back a few more times that winter and shoveled; and in the spring and summer I trimmed

Mrs. J's hedges and did some weeding. The first few times I went to her house because Ma told me to, later it just seemed like a good way to kill some time, and, for some reason, I felt good afterwards.

Well, that brings me to this Halloween and me lying in a hospital bed. It certainly hadn't been my plan. Halloween morning, Deb and Katie were discussing who was going to be the first to ring Mrs. J's doorbell. I didn't feel like joining in the conversation. For some reason, running up and ringing her doorbell just didn't hold the same fascination for me anymore. So I took off on my bike and started thinking about my costume. I don't know whose fault you'd say it was. I certainly wasn't looking where I was going as I rounded the corner of Lincoln Street and slammed into the back of Mr. Fitzgerald's brown Ford, as he backed out of his driveway. Well, I came out on the losing end, and ended up on the ground unconscious.

I woke up in the hospital, Ma sitting at my side. She explained that I had a concussion and a broken leg, and would probably be spending the next few days in the hospital. My first thought was that it was Halloween, and I wouldn't be able to go out with my friends. When I tried to move, I discovered every muscle in my body ached; and when the room started to spin, I dismissed any idea of trying to convince my mother that I'd be fine by evening and could still go out trick–or–treating.

Later, when Ma was gone and the lights were out, I could still hear the hospital noises, and I couldn't sleep very well. With my arm resting behind my head, I leaned back and stared out the window, imagining my friends running up and down the streets, laughing and joking, filling up their bags with candy. A hospital bed was the last place I wanted to be.

That morning Ma was back bright and early, only this time she wasn't alone. She brought Mrs. J., wearing her blue plaid babushka, with her. Ma held her arm and they walked slowly into the room. Mrs. J. was carrying a tan train case. Slowly sitting up in the bed, I leaned forward as Ma kissed me on the forehead and asked, "How are you feeling, honey?"

47

"Okay." *Well, okay if you didn't mind a broken leg, a head that hurts, and the fact that I missed Halloween with my friends,* I thought.

"The nurse said you slept well."

I don't know how the nurse could say that since she kept coming in to wake me every few hours, but I just smiled weakly. There was no point in arguing. Curious as to why Mrs. J. had come, I watched as Ma pulled a chair over to the bed for her to sit. Once she sank back into the plastic chair, Mrs. J. held out the train case to Ma, but she looked at me and said, "Is for you."

Wondering what else Mrs. J. could have brought, except cookies or vegetables from her garden, I watched as Ma rested it on my lap to open it. I couldn't help but stare at its contents. It was filled with candy—lots of candy!

Confused, I looked up as Ma explained, "Mrs. Jancovich heard what happened to you, and, knowing that you would be in the hospital for a few days and would miss Halloween, she went around the neighborhood explaining what happened and asking for candy for you."

I didn't know what to say. Mrs. J. had left her house after dark and gone from house to house for me. Me—one of the kids who tormented her with ringing her doorbell every Halloween night. Chuckling to myself, I thought about how Deb and Katie had probably run daringly to her front door to ring the bell last night. Only this time she really wasn't home. I couldn't help wondering if she'd left the light on, but I didn't dare ask.

I looked up at Mrs. J., but my voice was a little shaky and all I managed to say was, "Thanks."

With a twinkle in her eye, she smiled and added, "I wear witch's hat." And I felt like sliding under the covers in embarrassment. She knew what we'd nicknamed her. Though, somehow, I'd long ago stopped thinking of her that way.

"You can't have the candy now," Ma said. "But, I'll take it home and put it in a safe place so your brothers won't get into it."

Reaching into the case, Mrs. J. took out two Bit–O–Honeys and placed them in my hand. "You keep two. They no hurt."

I smiled at her and tightened my hand around hers. Holding her soft and gentle hand, I knew this would be a Halloween I'd remember for years. I decided right then and there that none of my friends, nor anyone else's, would ever ring Mrs. J's doorbell on Halloween night again. After all, there weren't any witches living in our neighborhood.

My Lake Journal

Megan J. Murray

The sun was just beginning to set as I pulled onto the crushed stone driveway. As I opened my car door, my nose was met with the pungent aroma of the pines that surrounded the lake. The breeze was cool and damp...just as I remembered it. I smiled to myself as I fished around in my bag for the cottage keys. They were where all "important stuff" inevitably ends up—at the bottom of my bag. I walked to the front of the cottage. The lovely, rugged yard that I remembered from my youth was now more rugged than lovely. The wildflowers my grandmother so lovingly cared for grew haphazardly and looked weak. The signature geraniums that had once graced the grand porch looking out over the lake were no longer.

Megan J. Murray has a B.A. in English and Biology from Albion College. She recently went back to college to complete her teaching certification and looks forward to beginning a new career as a teacher in the year 2002. She lives in Albion, MI with her Beagle, Sadie, and a junkyard cat, Maddie.

"That's one of my first projects," I uttered out loud, surprising myself at the sudden break in the quiet stillness that surrounded me. My mind immediately traveled back to the smell of sun block and bonfires that were always so heavy in the air, and my grandmother's voice lilting from the porch, "I think that's the most beautiful sunset yet."

The whitewashed porch spread across the front of the creamy yellow, two–story cottage that looked out over the lake. The cottage itself sat on a slight incline, and years before, my grandparents had laid a brick walkway to the beach. It was a breathtaking setting. This was the place of my youth. I spent every summer at this cottage...from as far back as my memory would go.

I was an only child. My father was an attorney, a very busy one. My mother had many volunteer duties to keep her busy. I think my grandmother's willingness to take me for the summer was a reprieve for my parents. Oh, I think somewhere deep in the crevices of their lives, they loved each other, but it was never a deep, passionate relationship that I imagined marriage to be. Instead, it was a respectful, polite relationship that kept up the appearances of a happy life. I seemed to be their only connection.

Summers at this lake were delirium...I lived for the moment school was over. I think, in hindsight, my parents lived for it, too. For a few months every year, they could move along in their separate lives.

My grandmother was thrilled to have me. I took long walks with her, learning about butterflies and wildflowers and all manner of wildlife. She handed down to me her amazing eye for art and her immense talent and love for gardening. We spent hours in her wildflower beds, taking long walks deep in the woods to find just the perfect wildflowers for her garden. A passion for visual aesthetics grew within me, and I credit her with my success as a photographer today.

I pulled open the rickety screen door and stuck the key into the lock. The odors of damp and dust and Grandmother and lake rushed at me. It was always just my grandmother and me here for the summers. I couldn't recall my mother ever setting foot in this cottage. She was adamant about not coming. Her excuses were many and varied: too far away from her favorite cultural events; too many responsibilities for her various charities; too woodsy and rustic for her taste; being allergic to all the pine; or catching a severe summer cold that took her months to get over. I always wondered about that, even vocalized my curiosity once. "She has her reasons," my grandmother had said sadly. So, my father usually drove me to the cottage, and, when I was of driving age, I drove myself.

I threw my bag on the cane–bottomed chair that sat next to the door and began opening the shades. After my grandmother died, my father had come up to close the cottage. She had broken her hip the year before, and it was my mother's decision to move her down to my parents' home. She died almost a year to the day my parents moved her from her beloved cottage. Her death had been a great blow to me.

The furniture was covered in canvas drop cloths, and I sneezed as I began pulling them off. The giant dining room table stood to the right of the door. Opposite the table, the overstuffed parlor furniture was arranged just as it had always been around the huge stone fireplace. The black soot still stained the edges of the old fireplace.

Unloading all the groceries and clothing I had packed and dumping it all in the great room accentuated how road weary I was. I longed for the crisp linens that my grandmother always had ready and waiting for me on the old, white wrought iron bed. I walked into my old room. The bed was stripped bare; an old drop cloth covered it. I pulled the old canvas off the bed and tossed it in a corner. The crisp linens were, no doubt, packed away.

I grabbed the sleeping bag that I had had the forethought to bring and unrolled it, tossing it haphazardly on the bed. I was asleep almost before my head hit the pillow—thoughts of summers long since gone drifting in and out of my subconscious.

****

The morning fog still hung tightly on the lake as I made my way to the kitchen. I lifted the window over the sink and was met by the distant, mournful loon song trailing through the morning air. I grabbed a can of coffee from a box I'd shoved in the corner the previous night.

While I waited, I toured the second floor and discovered the storage place for all the old porch furniture. Carefully, I carried each piece down the creaky old stairs and put them in their rightful places. Grandmother's coffeemaker had seen better days, and so it was still chugging along when I decided to go back upstairs and poke around in the boxes that were piled in the four rooms that made up the second floor.

I found the boxes filled with linens and towels just inside the doorway and began shoving them into the hall. As I grabbed the last box, I discovered one with my name "McKendry's," written in my mother's handwriting. I was immediately puzzled. Mother never came to the lake; that is why the cottage had been left to me. I had always wondered how my mother, my grandmother's only child, must have felt at being overlooked. In the days following her death, I asked my mother. "That ramshackle old place! Oh good heavens, McKendry, why would I want that? Mother knew my feelings. She also knew your love for the place. It was given to the appropriate person, my dear." She kissed my cheek softly. It was a fleeting look, and it was gone before I recognized it for what it was. Still, as I think about it now, I am convinced that there was a sad longing look in her eyes as she turned from me.

Pushing the boxes of towels and linens out of the way, I grabbed the box labeled with my name and made my way through the short hall and down the stairs. I placed the box on the rag rug that covered the center of the sitting room and sat down next to it. It was taped tightly and after fighting with the layers of tape for what seemed like an eternity, I was finally able to lift the cover open. Black and white photos lay loosely on top. I picked them up and examined each one. A young, playful version of my mother smiled at me. She was standing on the steps of the porch, her hair blown by the lake breezes. She was laughing at someone, and she looked ecstatically happy. The composition was good, great in fact. It captured my mother in a candid moment in life. I picked up another photo. My mother stood in the lake, the water lapping at her bare calves; her Capri pants wet at their hem. She appeared unaware of the camera. A third picture was of a man, vaguely familiar to me, and yet a stranger. He stood leaning against one of the porch columns, his hand raised as if to say, "No, I don't want my picture taken." He was laughing. I turned the picture over—in my mother's handwriting was, "Liam, June, 1965."

I sat staring at this man on my grandparent's cottage porch, and I realized that my mother had had a life beyond my father, beyond me. At one time, she had come here to this cottage, had been very happy here, and had perhaps shared the same glorious summer memories, as had I. It hit me how little I really knew of my parents beyond their bland existence that had always revolved around me.

I placed the photos on the floor and pulled out a large, leather–bound book. It was thicker than I had initially thought, the leather flaking a bit from years of use. I opened the cover. In childlike handwriting were the words, "My Lake Journal, 1954 to ..." and then in more adult handwriting, resembling my grandmother's, "1993." I turned the first page. It was dated June 2, 1954, and in the same child's writing it read, "This is my tenth birthday! I got a lot of great presents, but the one I like the most is this Lake Journal that mommy and daddy gave me. It's got enough pages to fill up with all my lake stories. I can't wait to start." The pages following were filled with accounts of my mother's childhood adventures at the lake...stories of fishing with my grandfather, planting a garden with my grandmother. Her summers mirrored mine. As I flipped through page after page, I could feel a tinge of animosity toward my mother for having never shared these stories. I was also confused. How could she have loved the cottage as a child and grown to detest it so as an adult?

I continued to flip through the pages. An entry on May 7, 1963 caught my eye.

"Another summer at the lake, it feels so good to be finished with my freshman year. How I've longed for this place. I think memories of the lake are what got me through the exams and papers and the endless lectures.

We have new neighbors! I was walking, and I literally ran into their son! Dreamy does not begin to describe him. He is tall with broad shoulders that seem to stretch on forever. He has a wavy, almost curly head of hair that is the deepest chocolate brown I've ever seen. And his eyes, blue like the bluest sky...I know I am in love! I'm terribly afraid that I came across as a blithering idiot. I don't even remember what I said to him, but I remember his gleaming smile, and those eyes. His faint Scottish brogue was endearing...Liam McKendry is his name!"

My head shot up as I read my name. McKendry! As a child, I hated my unusual name. I was teased mercilessly for it, and I remember telling my mother how much I hated it. I still remember the pained expression on her face.

I flipped through more passages from that summer. My mother and Liam spent countless hours talking. By the end of the summer, it was clear that her affection for Liam was most certainly returned.

"August 23, 1963....
I leave for school tomorrow. I dread leaving the lake...I always do, but this time it has a stronger pull for me. Liam's here...our summer memories are here. My heart will be left here when I leave. Last night was bitter sweet. We sat on the porch watching the last bits of sun fall behind the horizon. I think we both felt it was a symbolic ending to our summer. In summers past, I've left this journal here. There never seemed any point to bringing it with me...but knowing that I will be away from Liam, I think it will be comforting to be able to read over our summer memories. I love Liam...."

Never had I witnessed my mother shower such affection on my father before. I felt jilted for him, reading these passages. My mother just didn't expose this part of herself, and it made me uncomfortable. I was saddened at the fact that my mother unabashedly wrote, "I love Liam," but had never uttered those words to my father in my presence.

> "October 23, 1963....
> Liam is coming this weekend! I can hardly contain my excitement. It has been exactly two months since we last saw each other, and I dare say it has been sheer torture. Only three more days...can my heart manage that long?"

> "October 27, 1963....
> How good it feels to be with Liam again! Having him near me, feeling my hand in his, it is as if we were back at the lake. The AXO girls were thrilled with Liam...all approved. Tonight was the big Sigma Chi dance. We had a wonderful time. Absence does indeed make the heart grow fonder— we were inseparable! We all went out afterwards to the FOOD SHOPPE and had lots of fun...until the talk of politics and Vietnam began. Liam said something that scared me...he told us he would gladly serve his country if called. I was very proud of him, but secretly, I'm scared...."

A black and white photo of Liam and my mother was included. They were standing in front of the Sigma Chi sign, arms around each other, obviously in love.

Much of the rest of the entries for that fall semester were of academics and sorority news. Beyond my mother's every day life were entries about Liam—the phone calls and letters they shared. There were entries on the Vietnam War—the worries on campus, the brothers, fathers, uncles, cousins, and boyfriends lost...and of course, there were the entries from their summer in 1964. Her devotion to Liam grew, as did Liam's devotion to my mother.

I flipped through some more pages until I came to an entry dated December 15, 1964. Pressed between two pieces of waxed paper were a withered bunch of daisies. Bits of the petals crumbled off and fell to the floor as I gingerly lifted them from the journal.

"Liam has asked me to marry him, and I've accepted!! In a few short months, I will be Mrs. Liam McKendry! I can hardly believe it!! It all happened so suddenly; I can barely breathe as I write this. He surprised me at the dorm. An early Christmas present, he said...a dinner at Marlowe's. He had daisies, my favorite flower...how he managed to get them in the dead of winter, I will never know! We laughed and talked, and I couldn't imagine being happier. After dinner, he handed me a small box...it held the most beautiful diamond I'd ever seen! "Would you spend the rest of your life with me, Emily?" "YES! YES, LIAM MCKENDRY, I WILL MARRY YOU!" However, news that Liam has volunteered for helicopter pilot training sobered our engagement. He has the spring semester and part of the summer, but by August he will be reporting for training. I almost gave the ring back! But I feel fairly certain he will be drafted anyway...it's only a matter of time. I think that is why he proposed to me now, rather than wait... Liam will most likely go to Vietnam. But we have Christmas, and we have this next semester—and we have the summer."

My mother wrote of the Christmas holidays, of her spring semester, of her wedding plans. It was to be at the lake as soon as school had ended for the year, on the steps of the cottage, my cottage. I looked out toward the porch, imagining my mother and this man. The image made my mind reel.

I got up from my spot on the floor and paced the room. I stepped out onto the porch, feeling the need for fresh air. I walked across the porch and leaned against a column, staring out at the lake. I looked at the steps, trying to imagine what the wedding had looked like. I was standing at almost the same vantage point Liam was in the photo that I was now certain my mother had taken of him in 1965. He would have been her husband then. I walked back inside, hoping a fresh cup of coffee would clear my head.

With my coffee and the journal, I settled into my grandmother's rocker. June 2, 1965 was the day of their wedding ...the entry was a short one; it read only, "I am now Emily McKendry...Mrs. Liam McKendry. I will love him forever."

The entries that followed were some of the most touching entries, and I felt somehow voyeuristic reading them. They were written by a young woman completely devoted to her new husband, and they explored the deeper levels a love reaches when one says, "until death do us part." I read only briefly.

It was difficult to not feel as though I was invading my mother's privacy. I flipped carelessly through the journal, trying to avoid the rest of 1965. A folded piece of paper fell to the floor. I picked it up, my thumb holding the page, dated January 20, 1967. Setting the journal in front of me, I opened the paper, a War Department telegram. I could only imagine the sickening feeling my mother had when she read, "we regret to inform you..." I looked at the date on the telegram, January 20, 1967. The entry in the journal was heart wrenching to read, the ink smeared and the paper warped.

"I can barely bring myself to write the words...Liam is gone...dead...my heart died with him..."

There were no more entries written in my mother's hand. The next entry was dated January 30, 1967, and it was written by my grandmother.

"Liam's remains arrived today. It sickens me to write it. Emily is heartbroken...she says she would have rather died with him in that God–forsaken land than to live this life without him. My dear sweet child...what can I do to help her get through this terrible grief. It seems so unfair how cruel this world is. Liam was just here at Thanksgiving. And now, he is gone."

"February 7, 1967 ...
Emily will have a baby! Due in August! My heart is full at the thought of a grandchild, tempered only by the fact that Liam will never know his child. Thankfully, Emily has a reason to get up each morning, although her grief is still very raw. She is refusing to go to the lake with us. She wants no part of the place, she says. I think she will change her mind; she just needs time. "

In a moment not unlike the grand epiphanies one reads about, I made the connections that for years had puzzled me. It was then I understood why I never really looked all that much like my mother and not at all like my father. I had always wondered where my blue eyes had come from and this deep head of curly auburn hair, a gentle mix of my mother's blonde hair and Liam's deep brown. My eyes were Liam's eyes. I was Liam's daughter.

I devoured the other entries my grandmother wrote, desperate, suddenly for more information. The pieces of my mother's life were falling into place, and with each new entry I read, I began to understand my mother. My father entered the scene in March 1967, when mother was hired as a temporary legal secretary, working for a young attorney, Michael Alistair, the man I had grown up thinking was my father.

"July 29, 1967...
Our sweet little girl was born today...a bit early.
She is Liam's child through and through with bright
blue eyes and a mass of dark hair. A precious angel
she is.   In honor of her father, her name is
McKendry Alistair."

There was one last entry in the journal, written by my
grandmother and dated July 27, 1993.

"My dearest McKendry,

You know the entire story now. Perhaps you didn't
know there was a story...perhaps you did. Even so,
I leave it to you...this journal is your legacy. I leave
this cottage to you, because it too is your legacy. My
happiest memories are of you here at the lake. I
recall those memories often when I think of you. I
have no doubt you will love this place as much as I
have, as much as your mother has, and as much as
Liam once did.

My love to you,
Grandmother"

The remaining contents were photos...mother and Liam's
wedding day, their last summer spent here, photos of Liam in
uniform. Tucked among the photos was a stark, white envelope
with my name written on the front, in my mother's handwriting. I
opened the envelope and pulled my mother's signature stationary
out.

"I wanted to tell you so many times, but in doing so,
I would have had to relive Liam's death all over
again, and I can't do that. Michael, the man you

61

call father, is a generous man. He loved me enough to marry me, knowing I would never love him as I had Liam. He has cared for you and has loved you as if you were his own. While I bitterly curse fate for snatching Liam from me, I will forever be grateful to Michael for what he has done for us. Michael gave you his name—you are his daughter. Liam gave you his life—you are his daughter as well. Never has a child been so loved.

If I believed in reincarnation, I would say Liam is alive in you today. I see him in the obvious: your curly mass of hair and those piercing blue eyes, your incredible photographic talent. I see him in the subtle, too: the lilt in your voice, the gestures you make, and your laugh.

He would have loved and adored you…"

I left the box in the middle of the room and walked out onto the porch. The pull of this place had always been so strong in my life. I never knew why until the journal. I walked along the porch, stopping at the column Liam had rested upon so many years ago. I leaned against it, pressing my face against its coolness.

I thought of my father and our travels to the lake. The sadness I saw flicker in his eyes as he said good–bye to me each summer was not because he would miss me—although, I knew he would. The pull at his heart was giving me over to the memory of a man that would never die in the hearts of those that knew and loved him.

Grandmother had been right. This place was my legacy. My legacy was a woman that loved and lost so completely—a man principled and strong who gave his life—but it was also a man so completely devoted to me that he gave me his name and his love …and he, too, gave his life.

The Race

William McTaggart

"Hey Jim. Want to go out to the raft?"

It was a hot day in July. We were at our cottage on Silver Lake and I had just spied the girl who lived on the other side of the bay walking out to the end of her dock. We had seen her out there, before, soaking up the sun. She looked to be about my age though I had never met her and didn't know her name. She wore a two–piece bathing suit and was about the prettiest thing I had ever seen. The raft was anchored half way across the bay. A lot closer to the girl on the dock than our cottage.

"Okay," Jim replied. Jim was eleven. He still didn't think much about girls. I was thirteen and I was thinking a lot about girls, especially that girl who lived across the bay.

William R. McTaggart is a retired lawyer who lives near Petoskey, MI. Since retirement, he has written five children's books, published by the Gramma Books Publishing Co. His most recent book published in the summer of 2001 is *A Tiny Pinch of Courage.*

We ran to our rowboat tied to the tree on the shore. Jim grabbed the oars. "Be careful boys," Mother called out from the porch, "Don't let your eyeballs fall out." I'd swear she could see out the back of her head. We couldn't get away with anything.

Jim was a good rower and we had soon tied the boat to the raft. After splashing around a bit for show, we climbed onto the raft. I pretended to close my eyes but I was really peeking through my eyelashes at the girl on the dock. She didn't know I existed. Jim was not interested and was looking back toward our side of the bay watching what was happening at the Williams' estate. We had been in the Williams' house only one time, two years earlier. A formidable chain link fence separated it from the neighbors.

Somehow, probably by mistake, we had been invited to Gerald Williams' birthday party.

The most direct path from our cottage to the Williams' house was across the yards of our neighbors and over the fence. Gerald's mother had caught us as we jumped down from the fence and made us climb back over. She told us polite boys did not climb fences. We were instructed to go back up the road to their front gate. What the heck, it was a lot easier to just climb over the fence but she told us if we wanted to come to Gerald's birthday party we would have to come to the front door like decent people. Then she watched as we walked all the way out to the road, down the road to their gate and up their curving drive to their front door. If we hadn't already put on our shoes and combed our hair we would have turned around and gone back home.

A maid with a silly looking lace apron answered the door. I guess that's the way they dressed at Gerald's house. Gerald was about my age, not a bad kid given a chance. I started calling him Jerry. That is until his mother heard me and told me his name was not Jerry, but Gerald. "Gerald Williams", she said, "and please don't forget it.'

We never got invited back to any more birthday parties at Gerald's house. I felt sorry for Gerald. There was nobody to play with except his uncle. Never could figure what the Uncle did for a living; I guess not much of anything. Anyway Gerald didn't come around and I had learned my lesson about climbing over their fence so we didn't chum around.

We could hear him practicing the piano and I guess he spent a lot of time reading, too. I figured he would probably grow up real smart but it was a heck of a way to ruin a good summer.

The Williams family had plenty of neat stuff for Gerald to play with; a shuffleboard court, a tennis court, an outboard motor boat, even a beautiful mahogany Chris Craft. They wouldn't let Gerald run any of the boats himself but his uncle let him ride along. Jim and I wouldn't have put up with that. It's no fun just riding along.

Anyway, while I was lying on the raft in the middle of the bay peeking through my eyelashes at the girl on the dock, Jim exclaimed, "Hey, look at the sailboat in front of the Williams' house."

Sure enough there was a brand new sailboat tied up at their dock. Gerald and his uncle were rigging it up to go sailing. As we watched, they pushed off and soon were sailing up the lake with, of all things, Gerald at the tiller. His uncle was telling Gerald what to do, but he was actually letting Gerald steer the boat. We watched them sail past and Gerald waved at us. We waved back, not very enthusiastically.

That evening at dinner when Dad had returned from his office in town we told him about Gerald's new sailboat. He thought about that for a while and said, "After you boys clean up the dinner dishes, let's take a look at our boat and see whether we might make her into a sailboat of our own."

I washed, Jim dried. It wasn't ten minutes and we were all down at the boat to see what Dad had in mind.

Dad was looking at our boat. Finally he said, "Well, maybe we can have a sailboat of sorts. But of course you boys know it won't be anything as nice as the Williams boat. That's a real sailboat. Maybe we can rig old Bessie here to sail downwind. You'll have to row upwind."

"That's O.K. Dad," I said. "Jim and I are real good rowers."

Two days later, Dad came home from his office with two sturdy bamboo fishing poles along with a big triangular piece of canvas. The awning company had bound the edges of the canvas and sewed in a series of eyelets along two edges to tie the sail to the bamboo poles; one pole for a mast, the second for the boom.

Dad bored a large hole through the front seat of the boat and nailed a two by four with a hole in it to the floor of the boat beneath the front seat. That would secure the bottom of the mast. He tied the canvas to the poles and erected the mast through the hole in the seat. He bolted a new oarlock to the transom to use with one of the oars for a rudder. It was magnificent! A real sailboat!

"Hop in," Dad said. "We're ready for our maiden voyage."

"Me, too," Mom said as she pulled off her shoes, stepped into the shallow water near the shore and climbed into the boat.

Fortunately the wind was offshore. None of us knew a thing about sailing and the only direction our sailboat would go was downwind. Soon we were in the middle of the bay.

In the excitement we had not noticed that Gerald and his uncle were already out in the lake skimming along on a starboard tack. As we passed close by them Gerald yelled out, "What do you call that tub, the Queen Mary?" Gerald's uncle laughed at his nephew's wisecrack. Dad and Mom smiled at the neighbors but said nothing.

Not my kid brother Jim.

"This is our new sailboat. My Dad made it and we can beat the pants off you any day of the week!" Jim shouted.

Gerald had turned their craft downwind to run alongside of our boat. "How you gonna do that smart guy? You can't even go upwind without a centerboard!"

"Oh yeah, well we can row faster'n you can sail!" Jim responded. "We'll take you on any time you say."

Mom and Dad were looking straight ahead, wishing their youngest was a little less feisty.

"O.K., wise guy," Gerald replied. "Tomorrow at 2 o'clock. My uncle will set up the course. Three legs. Up the bay starting from in front of our cottage to the first buoy. Then across the mouth of the bay to the second buoy. The final leg will end right here in front of this cottage."

Oh great, I thought, we were right in front of the cottage where the two–piece bathing suit lived. My big mouth little brother had talked us into a major disaster. Our homemade sailboat was no match for a real sailboat. We would be humiliated right in front of the girl of my dreams.

"You're on!" Jim shouted. "We'll be here."

Gerald and his uncle veered away to resume their upwind course. "See you tomorrow, suckers." Gerald called out over his shoulder. Both were laughing uproariously.

"Better get ready to do some pretty good rowing," Dad murmured.

By now we were close to the shore downwind from where we had started. There on the porch was the girl of my dreams, standing, smiling at us.

"Good luck!" she called. "We'll be watching." She had heard every word of Gerald's challenge. Dad and Mom waved while I tried to hide my face behind the sail. Dad turned the boat away from shore back toward the middle of the bay. He lifted the oar from the oarlock on the transom and handed it to me. I quickly thrust it into the oarlock at the side of the boat and began rowing upwind back to the center of the bay.

The next morning Jim and I were out in the lake early trying to learn how to sail. We gradually began to get the hang of it but without a centerboard there simply was no way we could force the boat to tack upwind. We decided to head for home to get some lunch. We would need all the energy we could muster if we were to row halfway around the course. At one o'clock we watched Gerald and his uncle head out into the lake in their Chris Craft to set up the buoys for the course. We watched as they repeatedly stopped to check the wind, doing their best to make every leg of the course as much upwind as they could.

As the hour approached Jim and I pushed our boat off from shore. A summer storm was brewing. Dark clouds had begun to form on the horizon and the wind had died to almost nothing. Gerald and his uncle were already out in the lake in their new sailboat waiting at the starting line in front of their cottage for the starting gun. They had arranged with their hired man to fire off a shotgun precisely at two. We looked around the bay. Word of the race had passed among the cottagers. Dozens of people were sitting on their porches waiting for the race to start. As we rowed into position at one minute to two, we saw Dad walk out onto our front porch with Mom. He had taken the afternoon off from work.

The shotgun boomed eerily across the lake. The air was heavy from the impending storm. There was no wind. None at all. I was in position at the rear of the boat holding the handle of the oar that was to be our rudder. There both boats sat, neither moving an inch in the still air.

But Jim had got us into this mess and he aimed to do his best to get us out. He grabbed the oar out of my hands and jammed it into the empty oarlock on the side of the boat. The other oar was already in place and he began to row madly across the starting line on the first course heading toward the first buoy at the mouth of the bay. Gerald and his uncle sat motionless back at the starting line, cursing the stillness. They had no oars, only a single paddle—without wind they were helpless. I jumped into the middle seat alongside my little brother and grabbed one of the oars. Jim was laughing and having a great time.

"Pull!" he yelled. And we pulled with all our might to the cheers of the cottagers sitting on their porches watching the race. We had reached the first buoy before the wind began to blow. And when it came it blew straight behind us pushing us toward the second buoy. I pulled my oar out of the side oarlock, thrusting it in the oarlock at the rear of the boat. Jim hauled in the rope to the sail and we went foaming toward the second buoy. Gerald and his uncle, now on a beam reach with the wind off their starboard side, were moving fast. They whipped around the first buoy just as we reached the second buoy and they were gaining rapidly. The final leg back into the bay had been deliberately positioned by Gerald and his uncle close along the shore. With the wind off our port side, we would be pushed into the shore without a centerboard to hold us on course. We felt the first raindrops. The wind was increasing and was gusting. Gerald's boat was rapidly closing the gap between us and we were being pushed toward the lee shore. Suddenly, miraculously, the wind shifted once again. It was dead astern and we were surging toward the final buoy. The buoy in front of the love of my life. I didn't know her name. But she had waved at us yesterday and she had wished us 'good luck.' There was a chance, just a chance, for a glorious victory.

The rain now began to beat on us in torrents as I strained to keep the boat on course toward the finish line. And there she was, on her porch waving excitedly, jumping up and down and cheering.

And then we crossed the finish line.

I looked back. Gerald and his uncle were not behind us. They had abandoned the race when they saw we were going to beat them and headed for home as the rain drenched all of us. We had won! I looked toward the shore. She had run through the rain to the end of her dock. There she stood soaking wet, waving and clapping her hands. The rain was drumming on the canvas but over the din I could hear her call out to us. "See you on the raft tomorrow afternoon!" Gosh, she was beautiful.

We turned our boat across the bay toward our cottage. The wind shifted once again pushing us toward home. Jim extended his hand, palm up.

"Give me five," he laughed and we smacked our hands together.

"Promise me one thing, little brother," I said.

"I know," he replied. "In the future, keep my mouth shut, right?"

"Right."

Unlikely Friends

Janet West–Teskey

"I'm late again," John muttered as he drove along the winding road. "Why do I always get behind the drivers that have all the time in the world?" he wondered as he swerved slightly over the centerline to see beyond the car ahead of him. He waited for two cars to go by, pressed the gas pedal to the floor, and flew by the white sedan. Traveling twenty miles above the speed limit to make up for lost time, he answered his cell phone on the second ring.

"Hello. Yeah hi, Bob. No, I didn't forget, just running a little late. The traffic is terrible. Start without me if you need to. I'll join you when I get there," he said with exasperation.

Usually the back road route was quicker than the expressway during morning rush hour. He was anxious to get to the office early to finish a report, but went back to sleep after turning the alarm clock off. He never seemed to accomplish much once his employees began arriving. The phone rang excessively and the interruptions were numerous. He sang along with the old Stones' song playing on the radio, making a quick turn onto Oakley Park Road. Sipping from his travel mug, he quickly glanced at the clock on the dashboard. Focusing on the road again, he spotted a figure up ahead. He lifted his foot off the gas pedal and squinted with furrowed brow, as he tried to determine what it could be.

"What the hell?" he said out loud.

It appeared to be a person in the center of the two–lane road, with arms waving in the air. As he neared, he realized it was

> **Janet West–Teskey** is a student at Wayne State University working toward teacher certification and a master's degree with a major in language arts. Janet is married to John and the mother of two sons, Jake and Daniel. They are her best critics and strongly support her writing endeavors.

an old woman. She apparently wanted him to pull over. He hesitated and considered going around her. Thoughts raced through his mind. He wondered if she was hurt.

He thought, "Maybe she's unstable. Has dementia set in and she doesn't realize she is in the middle of the road?" He was concerned as he pulled onto the gravel shoulder, but then watched as she smiled and approached his car. He pushed the button to lower the driver's side window and was startled as she quickly thrust her face near his. He immediately noticed the deep crevices running all over her face. He automatically pulled his shoulders and head back slightly, caught off–guard by her closeness. She smiled and displayed her nearly perfect upper plate with rosy red lipstick smeared on the two front teeth. He couldn't help but notice the perfect circle of rouge applied to each cheek and the sable brown eyebrows, drawn thinly over her eyes, that nearly met at the bridge of her nose.

"Hello, sir," she bellowed in a scratchy voice. "Thank you for stopping. I just need a ride to the coffee shop up the road a piece," she said as she pointed over the roof of the car in the direction he had just come from. She stepped back and opened the door, ready to climb into the back seat.

"Hold on! Just a minute," he exclaimed with surprise.

Turning in his seat to look over his left shoulder, he saw that she stood with her hand resting on the top of the open door, one foot already in the car. He glanced at the thick support hose and orthopedic shoe on her outstretched leg.

"Is there a problem? It's not far. Just a few miles, dear," she coaxed.

"Well, I don't know," he replied uncertainly.

"Should I drive away with this old woman in my car?" he asked himself.

"Where do you live?" he inquired, looking around at the farmland on either side of the road.

"Right over there," she pointed as she sat, pulled her left leg in, and slammed the car door. "I live in the big yellow house. I rent the third story. My daughters think the steps are becoming too much for me, but they're not. That's what keeps me young. Just turn around and take the first road on your left, then I'll give you directions."

It seemed to him she was already giving him directions. She fastened her seat belt and sat upright with hands folded primly in her lap. John sat for a moment, contemplating what he should do.

"Do your daughters live with you?" he asked, tipping his head to make eye contact with her in the rear view mirror. He was fishing for information. Someone might be looking for her. He questioned her mental state, although she seemed quite coherent and was dressed appropriately for the cool spring morning. For a brief moment, he wondered if it could possibly be a setup of some sort.

"Oh, heavens no. They are grown and have lives of their own. Grace, the oldest one, drives me to the coffee shop each morning, but she is in Jamaica right now and is having a grand time, too. She calls at least every other day. Boy, would she be mad if she knew I had taken a ride with a stranger. I've never done it before, mind you. I do have my sense about me. I know it isn't safe, but you look like a fine young man, and what she doesn't know won't hurt her," she said with a mischievous giggle.

Sighing, John rolled his eyes, checked his side mirror for traffic and made a U-turn, still uncomfortable with the situation.

"Just where is this coffee shop?" he asked as he made a left onto the street she had indicated.

Waving her hand haphazardly, she replied, "Oh, just keep going. I'll give you plenty of notice before you need to turn. It's not far."

John looked at his clock and thought, "Why me?"

"My other daughter lives in Vegas. Just moved there last year. I visited her last winter. Now, that's a city! I'd be in trouble if that one knew I'd stopped a stranger for a ride. I've never done this before, you know. Can't be too careful these days. What's your name? I'm Evelyn."

"I'm John, and your daughters are right. This is not very safe. I think when your daughter is out of town, you'd better make yourself some coffee at home. You might get in a car with the wrong person someday," John warned her.

"Well, while the coffee is good, it's my friends I would miss. All the regulars there are so friendly. They'd worry about me if I didn't come for a few days," Evelyn explained as she gazed out the window. "Besides, have you never heard the saying, 'Strangers are only friends you haven't met?' I guess I've lived that way. Haven't met too many bad ones either. Most people are generally good. Bet you can't guess how old I am," she challenged.

John glanced at her again in the rear view mirror and thought, "Great. I better guess low. I don't think I've ever seen a face with more wrinkles."

"Let's see," he said, "how about seventy five?"

Evelyn let out a loud chuckle. "Everyone always mistakes me for younger than I am. Had my eighty fifth birthday in March. I threw myself a party. It was a great day. Ain't never been afraid to tell my age. As a matter of fact, I'm proud of it," she explained. "Oh, turn right at the next corner. Where the party store is," she instructed him.

As John slowed down and turned right, he saw a small strip mall up ahead on the left just as she spoke from the back seat.

"Okay, pull into the drive. I'll just get out at the curb," she instructed.

John flipped his visor up so he could get a better look. He saw a dry cleaners, a small video store, an empty building, and Val's Coffee Shop on the end.

"Here you are," he announced. "Please don't try this again. Your luck may run out."

Evelyn opened her door, then placed her hand on John's right shoulder. "Let me buy you a cup of coffee for your trouble," she said excitedly. "I'll introduce you to my gang."

"No. No thank–you," he answered. "I have a cup right here and I am running quite late for work."

"What is it that you do?" she asked.

"I'm a sales engineer," he told her.

"Engineer. Humph. My husband worked for the railroad. Long time ago that was," she said with the door hanging open, but making no move to get out.

"Yep. Well, I do need to be on my way," he said, becoming anxious.

"Oh, sure you do. I know you're busy. Thanks again for the ride. I've never done this before, you know. Never can tell about someone just by their looks, can you?" she asked while maneuvering herself sideways in the seat and slowly placing her feet on the pavement.

"Speaking of that, wasn't that just awful what happened in Columbine last week! Just horrible. Those boys must surely have been disturbed. How could they do such a thing? And the poor parents of the injured and dead students. I can't stand to see their faces on the news. It just breaks my heart. It's too bad someone couldn't have seen it coming and helped," she said sadly.

"Yes, it was a tragedy," John agreed.

Sitting on the side of the seat, she snapped open the metal closure on the top of her purse.

"I'd like to pay you for gas," she said, fishing through the contents.

"No. That's not necessary. I was happy to help, but I really need to get moving now," he said quickly.

"Of course you do. I must be holding you up. Where is it that you work? Right here in Commerce?" she asked.

"No, my office is in Farmington," he answered, tapping his foot on the floor mat in agitation.

"Farmington. Now that's a city that has really changed. Friends of ours farmed there years ago before you were even born. I'll bet there isn't a bit of farmland left to be found. It's a shame, but time marches on," she said with a grunt and lifted herself from the seat.

Evelyn closed the door, but not hard enough to latch it completely.

"Oh, I guess I didn't get it closed. Hold on here a minute," she said, opening it and slamming it again with all her strength.

"I think you got it that time," John told her as the car shook from the force of the slam.

"Well, thank you again," she said, standing too close to the car for him to begin moving.

He nodded, smiled, and wondered why she did not move toward the coffee shop. They both waited, an awkward silence hanging heavy between them.

"Would you like me to wait and see that you get into the shop okay?" he asked.

"No, no, no, I'll be fine. I was just noticing the resemblance. Didn't notice when I first looked at you before I got in. You look like that guy in all the movies. You know the one. I think he was "Sexiest Man of the Year" in that *People* magazine. Harrison Ford. That's his name. No offense to you, but I don't know what all the fuss was about. I don't find him sexy at all. Guess it's all a matter of taste, though, don't you think?" she asked.

"I suppose it is, Evelyn," John answered with a chuckle. "It's starting to rain now. You better get inside," he told her.

"That I'll do," she said, turning to go. "Good thing is, this rain will bring all my tulips up out of the ground. My favorite time of year," she said with eyes twinkling.

John watched her back away, pulling the collar of her wool coat up around her neck. She pulled her purse up onto the crook of her arm, turned, and stepped quickly. She glanced back over her shoulder after a few steps and winked as she waved.

Pulling out of the parking lost, John picked up his cell phone and dialed information.

"Commerce, Michigan," he said in response to the operator's question. "I need the number for Val's Coffee Shop."

He waited while the automated voice gave him the number, then pressed the number one to have it dialed.

"Val's Coffee Shop," a cheerful voice answered while dishes clanged in the background.

"Hi," John said and then paused. "I just dropped an old woman off there who flagged me down in the middle of Oakley Park asking for a ride. I'm just a little concerned. I'm questioning whether or not I should have taken her anywhere," he explained.

Before he could finish, the woman on the other end laughed heartily. "Oh, you are talking about Evelyn. Got you this morning, did she?" she asked. "She's done this every morning for years. Thanks for bringing her in and caring enough to check on her. We always see that she gets home safely."

Grinning, he laid down the phone. He continued to smile as he drove south on the winding trail, recalling their conversation and scanning the road signs for one he recognized.

He tried to recall how many times she had told him, "I've never done this before, you know."

He laughed again, feeling like he had been taken advantage of, but finding humor in the situation. Finally, spotting a familiar road, he made a quick left onto Pontiac Trail and continued on to work.

Several weeks later, running late again and feeling stressed about the hectic day ahead, John traveled Oakley Park Road. He had passed the big yellow house numerous times since having met Evelyn, but hadn't seen her again. As he rounded a curve in the road, he noticed a car stopped on the shoulder of the road up ahead. He saw the elderly woman stooped over to talk with the driver of an older model Ford. He slowed down and saw that Evelyn was pointing back in the direction from which he had just come. John was sure she was soliciting a ride. He pulled up behind the green car and came to a stop. He got out and approached the vehicle.

He heard the young driver say angrily, "Look, old lady, I'm not taking you anywhere."

"Excuse me," John interrupted. "Evelyn and I are friends. I'll give you a ride this morning, Evelyn. Just let this young man be on his way," he said as he took her by the arm and guided her backwards away from the running car. The green car pulled away in a rush, throwing dust and gravel from behind as it did.

"I remember you," she said as he led her to his car. "You're the nice man that looks like Harrison Ford," she exclaimed.

John chuckled as he held the passenger side door open for her. "Yeah, that's me. Climb in and I'll get you to the shop," John said with a smile.

The Pickerel Creek Hunt

Douglas C. Dosson

Lisa looked up again at the big wall clock hanging in her living room, but the hands seemed to be frozen on seven–fifteen. If the pendulum hadn't been ticking back and forth, she would bet the clock had stopped altogether. She got up from the couch and anxiously moved to the rocking chair.

It was the opening day of the rifle deer season and, even though it had been dark for over an hour, Dad still wasn't back from his hunting trip. Lisa had spent other opening days waiting for Dad to return from the hunt, but never had it been as difficult as today.

She went over to the fireplace and stared up at the head of the mounted big buck that hung over the mantel. Lisa had only been five when Dad brought that deer home, but she still remembered it very well. She remembered how excited he was as he got out of his pickup and told his little

> **Douglas C. Dosson**
> lives at Higgins Lake, MI where he is the Probate and Family Court Judge of Roscommon County. Judge Dosson is a long–standing member of the Society of Children's Book Writers and Illustrators. His published works include *Cody's Wooden Whistle*, *Tricking the Wolves*, and *From Thin Air*. Many of his stories are written for or about his daughter, Lisa, as is the case with *The Pickerel Creek Hunt*.

daughter that he was going to win the $2,500 first prize in Conklin's Big Buck Contest. She remembered how he had lifted her into the box of his old pickup for a close–up view of the huge deer. Most of all, she remembered how her own excitement had quickly turned to sadness when she saw the beautiful buck lying lifeless on the bed of the pickup truck.

Lisa walked out into the garage and sat on the steps at the back door. Her little dog, Spike, put his head in Lisa's lap and she absentmindedly began to stroke his neck. Lisa really wanted to share Dad's enthusiasm for opening day. She and Dad lived a very modest life on their small farm and Lisa understood clearly that a freezer full of venison would fill their meat requirements for many months. There was also the $2,500 first prize money from the Big Buck Contest, which could turn an average year into a great one.

But Lisa's logical justification of deer hunting had vanished last spring when she had seen the magnificent whitetail buck she had named "Prince." On April sixteenth and she had gone for a walk in the woods after getting off the school bus. Where he came from, she didn't know. She had just stooped down to pick a wild flower and when she stood up, there he was, standing right in front of her. His velvet antlers were so big they would have been scary, but his dark eyes were soothingly gentle as he stared at her for a long time. When he finally moved, he didn't bound off in frantic flight, but simply turned and walked off as if he were called away by another task that just couldn't wait any longer.

Lisa had been rendered absolutely breathless by the beauty of this elegant creature and she hadn't been able to get him out of her mind since spring.

Headlights appearing out on the road suddenly interrupted Lisa's thoughts of the past. The lights turned into Lisa's long driveway and the rattling metal and squeaking springs left no doubt that it was Dad's old pickup. Lisa and Spike jumped up together and raced to greet him.

"Did you get a deer, Dad?" Lisa asked, with her hands nervously clenched together.

"Yep," he said. "A nice eight point! It won't win first prize, but I figure it's good enough for the $500 honorable mention."

Lisa breathed a sigh of relief. If it was only an eight point she knew it wasn't Prince.

"Want to see him?" Dad asked, motioning with his thumb to the back of the pickup.

"I'll look later," she said. "C'mon in. I have some hot soup for us."

Lisa and Dad went into the kitchen where the aroma of Lisa's soup filled the room. But as they sat at the kitchen table, Dad hardly touched his meal. He was too busy telling Lisa about the great day, hunting from his new blind near Pickerel Creek.

"I saw thirteen deer before noon," he said. "Finally, about one–thirty, just as I was eating a sandwich, here he comes—the biggest buck I've ever seen! He came up behind me so quietly that I didn't even hear him. When I looked up he was standing thirty feet from me—must've been at least a twelve point. But before I could raise my gun, he was gone. I had to settle for the smaller one that came along later. Too bad," he added. "That one would've won first prize for sure."

Lisa knew it was Prince that Dad had seen and, although she was relieved that Dad had not shot him, she continued to worry. There were thirteen days left in the hunting season and there were other hunters around. What if someone else shot him? Two things were certain: first, she must find out if Prince was still alive; second, she must figure a way to keep him alive.

As the rest of the hunting season went by, Lisa asked around to find out how many deer had been shot in the area and how big they were. She learned that none the size of Prince had been reported. So when spring came, Lisa went exploring in the woods in hopes of seeing him again. She often saw deer, but they were small or average size. Sometimes, though, she would find hoof prints that were so much bigger than the others that she knew they were Prince's.

Finally, Lisa saw him again. It was one very warm spring day when she had walked all the way to Pickerel Creek and found Dad's hunting blind. It was quite a simple structure, really; just old logs criss–crossed over two fallen trees forming a box. There were two seats inside, a big one where Dad sat and a smaller one Dad had made for the time when Lisa was old enough to go along.

Lisa got into the blind and sat down. It was a lovely, peaceful spot. It was on the edge of the thick cedar swamp, but the hardwoods behind let streaks of sunlight through. In the distance the gentle gurgling of the creek could be heard.

As Lisa sat perfectly still in her little chair, she imagined it was opening day. She could see the deer in her mind, cautiously weaving through the cedar trees. She knew that during hunting season the deer were extremely skittish and that they spooked at the slightest sound or movement. Suddenly, there was a deer—not an imaginary deer, but a real, live deer. Its thick neck and huge rack of antlers were unmistakable. It was Prince. He was browsing and he stopped right in front of Lisa to chomp on some tufts of swamp grass. Then he raised his big head and stared right at her. For several moments he stood still as a statue until, at last, he determined that she posed no threat to him and he walked off toward some low–hanging cedar boughs.

Lisa was glad she had come to this remote place, but she again realized that, come deer season this fall, Prince would be exactly the kind of deer every hunter would be trying to shoot—especially those who were competing in the Big Buck Contest. She wasn't particularly worried about the men who hunted the other parts of the county, but Dad presented a real threat to Prince. His blind was right here in the middle of Prince's territory, and winning that prize money was very important to Dad. Lisa couldn't stand the thought of agonizing through another deer season, worrying that Prince would be the next buck stretched out on the bed of Dad's old pickup. At that moment, Lisa committed herself to saving Prince from Dad's deadly rifle.

Although she knew it would not be an easy task, Lisa was confident that she understood Dad well enough to change his thinking. Within a few days she had a plan and she went to some of her teachers at school to enlist their help with critical parts. Mr. Patterson, the woodshop teacher, Ms. Morris, the journalism teacher, and Mr. Fralic, the photography teacher, all became enthused about the plan and agreed to help. Lisa invested all the money in her savings account and spent all her spare time on the plan. It was exciting to see things begin to take shape.

That summer was a very busy one for Lisa and her dad. In addition to the usual work on their little farm, Dad took on a part–time job as a night mechanic in town to make some extra money. This gave Lisa time to secretly work on her plan to save Prince. Dad knew she was spending a lot of time in the woods doing something special, but Lisa only described it as her "nature project." It was important that Dad not know all the details until it was convincing enough to show him. Generally, she couldn't believe how nicely things were working out. She just made sure that she got the mail every day, and she made it a point to go to the Pickerel Creek swamp at least twice a week to scatter kernels of corn, pieces of apples, and carrot tops near Dad's blind. Although she never actually saw Prince during that summer, his huge hoof prints among the other deer tracks let Lisa know he was frequently in that area.

Finally fall arrived. When Conklin's Sporting Goods mailed out the flyer announcing its annual Big Buck Contest, Lisa knew it was time to have an important talk with Dad. She put supper on the table and when Dad came in from doing the evening chores, Lisa could hardly wait for him to clean up and sit down before she began.

"Are you looking forward to deer season?" Lisa asked.

"Yep," he nodded. "If I can just get a shot at that big one I saw last year, I can win the prize money for sure."

"I know a way to make more than the prize money," Lisa said.

Dad reached for a slice of bread and then stopped. "How?" he asked.

Lisa took a stack of ads from the counter and dropped them down beside Dad's plate. "These wildlife magazines are paying good money for photographs of whitetail deer just like the ones around here. We could take pictures right from your hunting blind and make some of that money for ourselves."

Dad looked the ads over carefully. "But we don't even have a camera," he said.

"Yes we do. I bought it with my own money and Mr. Fralic taught me all about using it." Lisa spread a few professional looking photographs of flowers, frogs, and wild birds out on the table in front of Dad. "Look at these," she said. "I took these myself. This one even got published in the newspaper in Detroit."

Dad raised his eyebrows and looked at Lisa in disbelief. Then he looked back at the pictures. "These are beautiful," he admitted. "But I couldn't take pictures. All I know is hunting."

"I know, Dad," Lisa said, confidently. "That's why I had Mr. Patterson help me make this." She reached into the kitchen closet and pulled out the most unusual thing her father had ever seen. It was her camera, complete with a telescopic lens, mounted on a rifle stock. "See, Dad," Lisa explained. "Just put this baby up to your shoulder and take aim. When you pull the trigger you take a picture of the deer instead of shooting him."

Dad was very impressed with the clever contraption. He turned it over and over in his hands, studying it from every angle. Finally he turned back to Lisa. "Why have you gone to all this trouble, honey?" he asked.

Beginning with her first encounter, Lisa told him all about Prince and her desire to help keep him alive as long as she could. "I know how badly we can use that prize money, Dad," she said. "But with us working together, I know we can make more this way, and it can last just as long as there are deer in the wild."

Dad had always known that Lisa was a very serious and hard–working girl. But he had never seen her as intensely involved in any other project as she was in this one, and he could tell how important it was to her.

"Well," he said at last. "If I'm going to hunt with this thing, I'd better spend some time sighting it in."

Lisa was overjoyed and hugged his neck. "I'll make sure we have lots of film," she said.

When opening day finally came, Lisa got up excitedly and put on several layers of warm hunting clothes so that she could spend the whole day with Dad in the blind. They both agreed that this was the best day to see deer, since the hunters caused the deer to move much more than they normally do. They ate a big breakfast of eggs and potatoes, then climbed into the old pickup and headed for Pickerel Creek. The November air was cold and damp when they reached the blind. But the walk though the pre–dawn darkness had been difficult, and Lisa had worked up a sweat through her layers of heavy clothes. As she took her seat next to Dad, she knew she would be cool again in no time.

The first light of day appeared just before seven o' clock. Lisa and Dad sat very still, carefully listening for any sounds of approaching deer. After only about twenty minutes, the snapping of twigs and rustling of brush caused Dad to put his finger to his lips and point toward the cedars. He quietly put the stock to his shoulder and peered through the camera's sight. Then, as Lisa watched in amazement, a deer cautiously stepped into a spot where she could see it—a buck, with small gray antlers.

Dad was as still as granite with the camera held tightly against his shoulder. The deer silently took two more steps. Now it was close and could be seen clearly.

"Click z–z–z–ip," the camera said. "Click z–z–z–ip," it repeated.

Then the deer jumped and bounded artfully through the trees and into the swamp.

"Did ya get'im, Dad?" Lisa asked anxiously.

"Yep, twice! But I should've had my gun," Dad complained.

The rest of the morning went very well. A total of nine deer passed by the blind. There were big does with fawns, small does traveling together and one button buck. Dad snapped them all.

A little after noon the sun came out and sprinkled bright sunlight through the trees around the blind. Dad poured himself some coffee from his thermos but Lisa continued to sit very still, intently listening and watching for any sign of movement.

Suddenly, Lisa thought she saw something. She tapped Dad's leg to get his attention. As Lisa pointed in the direction of the movement, Dad slowly and carefully put down his cup and picked up the camera. For several minutes, both Dad and Lisa sat silently waiting for the deer to show itself.

Finally, it took one quiet step into the cover of some trees so that only its tail and back legs could be seen. There it remained, occasionally extending its nose out from behind the trees and sniffing the air. It seemed as if it would stay hidden in the trees forever. Suddenly, the deer bolted right in front of Lisa and Dad. Just two bounds, and it was gone. But in the brief moment that the deer had shown himself, Lisa had seen that it was Prince, with his huge antlers now polished from rubbing on trees and from fighting with other bucks.

"That was him, Dad," Lisa cried. "Did you get a picture?"

"I think so," Dad said. "I guess we'll only know when the film is developed."

Lisa and Dad stayed until after four o'clock, then slowly made their way to the pickup. Driving home, they passed a car with a deer tied on the top and a pickup with a deer in the back. Lisa kept looking down at the camera. She knew that she and Dad were bringing home lots of deer.

For several days Lisa couldn't quit talking about the day at Pickerel Creek. She told and retold the story to all her friends and teachers at school. Some of the kids found it hard to believe, but Lisa knew that the pictures would show exactly what she had seen.

When the pictures finally came from the developer, Lisa and Dad went through them eagerly. The ones that were taken early in the morning were a little dark, but the ones taken after ten o' clock were perfect. In every picture, Dad had the deer right in the center. By far the best picture of all was the one of Prince. Dad had caught him at the peak of his bound, the bright sunlight glistening off his huge white antlers. This picture was as good as any Lisa had seen in the magazines. Even Dad agreed that this was much better than bringing a deer home in the back of the pickup truck and hanging him over the mantle.

Lisa and her dad were able to sell several of the pictures. Just as Lisa had hoped, they made more than the $2,500. They even sold a picture to Conklin's Sporting Goods to promote the Big Buck Contest. As for Prince, he lived for many more seasons in the Pickerel Creek Swamp, and Lisa and Dad spent many enjoyable hours in the deer blind with their cameras, photographing Prince and other deer there for magazines. Although whitetails are generally shy and skittish animals, it sometimes seemed as if Prince were actually posing for Lisa. Maybe that was just his way of thanking her for saving his life.

Snowy Night

Lori Nelson

Julie Miller squinted over her steering wheel as she peered through the snow pelting her windshield at a sideways angle. The slight clicking noises it made heralded the presence of sleet mixed with the snow. She could barely see where she was on the road. Both hands gripping the wheel, she struggled to discern some semblance of lane markers as waves of snow moved like sidewinders across the highway. In some ways the lack of traffic was a blessing–at least she didn't have to worry about trying to see other cars as well as lane markers! On the other hand, every bone in her body told her it was past midnight. The isolation of the highway seemed to confirm that she was the only one crazy enough to be driving at this hour in such weather.

> **Lori Nelson** is a native of Munising, MI. who from an early age was fascinated with words. She works as a Speech–Language Pathologist in Marquette. Her interests include foreign travel, sign language, French and photography. She's currently rekindling literary aspirations that have been dormant since her high school days.

Julie had moved to the Upper Peninsula of Michigan eight months ago, back to the woods and lakes where her mother had grown up. Raising Julie in Rockford, Illinois, her mother had single–handedly eked out a living for them as a nurse. Julie's father had never been on the scene as long as she could remember. Her mother had rarely spoken of him. Now twenty–eight, Julie was used to being on her own. Her mother had fostered a keen sense of independence in Julie, a source of badly needed strength these days.

Julie's eyes blurred remembering the last time she'd seen her mother. That dim room in the nursing home, the narrowing of her mother's world after being diagnosed with an inoperable brain tumor, were memories that haunted her. Her mother had been thrilled to return to the U.P., had never felt at home in the big city. But the dream of a long retirement remained just that, a dream. Julie moved here to be with her mother those final months, taking a job as an obstetrical nurse at a local hospital. Even now, six months after her mother's death, it was still too painful to think about.

"Keep your mind on the driving," she muttered under her breath. Why had she stayed out so late? She hadn't really wanted to go out tonight but had forced herself. So much of her early months living here were spent dealing with her mother's illness. There hadn't been the time or the inclination to develop a social life. That changed now that her mother was gone. Julie felt she couldn't afford to pass up social invitations. It had been a toss–up...braving a snowstorm for a few hours of fun with some co–workers or spending a lonely evening watching videos in her small apartment.

She slowly made her way around a bend in the road that marked the halfway point between Marquette, where she'd been tonight, and her apartment in Negaunee, a small mining town ten miles away. Just past the curve, a new distraction took her attention from the relentless snow. A red light flashed on her dash. At the same time, her headlights and dashboard lights began to dim.

"Shit," she groaned in disbelief. Not now! As the lights went out, she pulled over to the side of the road.

"Now what?"

Can't get anywhere without lights, she thought, and she sat for a few minutes in frustration and dismay. It couldn't have happened at a worse time. Damn! She peered out into the white swirls of snow and tried to get her bearings. She'd noticed a side road off to the right just before the headlights went dead. A streetlight marking the turn–off appeared as a dim glow through the veil of snow. Wasn't that the road where she'd gone on the garden tour last summer? Wistfully she remembered the warm bright day when she'd gotten off work early and brought her mother to view one especially lovely garden on the tour. A spark of hope filled her. Maybe this was that same winding country road! A vision of warm houses with kind people and telephones appeared in her mind... she indulged that wish for a moment. Then, grabbing her purse with a sigh, she got ready to propel herself (if the wind didn't do that for her) toward the distant streetlight. The cold and wind assaulted her the minute she got out of the car. It took all her strength just to push the car door closed. The cold air hitting her lungs took her breath away and made her cough. Highly motivated to reach her destination, she headed off in the snow at top speed, head pressed down into her collar, gloved hands in her pockets. Surely the first house wasn't too far away!

It soon became depressingly obvious that the first house wasn't nearby. This was not the hospitable country road of her musings. Julie entered the side road, jogging blindly for a good ten minutes without coming across a driveway or seeing a light. The wind was a cold blanket wrapping around her and buffeting her every which way. Her cheeks and eyes were soon stinging. Blowing snow always made her think of sandstorms she'd seen in movies, sandstorms painted white. The fine bits of snow and sleet drifting across the ground made a chilling, eerie sound. Growing colder, Julie began to move more slowly, arms held stiffly at her sides.

"Not my idea of a fun Saturday night," she thought grimly.

At that moment, something glinted off to the side. Peering in that direction, Julie ignored the snow striking her wet face. There was a building! She could barely make out a driveway, its edges blurred by the drifts of snow. Her steps quickened to a near run as she approached the steps of what appeared to be a small one-story house. A glimmer of light shone from one of the windows, blinking a bit as gusts of snow blew by. Julie felt her way up the unshoveled stairs to a wooden door that rattled in the wind. Dreading to feel the raw cold on her icy skin, she peeled her glove off and knocked on the door with all her strength. No response.

91

Shivering, she tried again, each contact with the door painful to her chilled knuckles. The door suddenly swung open and she jumped. A man's shadowy silhouette greeted her. Dim light from a room behind him outlined his body while a musty smell emanated from the house. A hoarse, raspy voice invited her in. Julie's relief at finding shelter plummeted. She ventured a step forward into what seemed to be an entry shed. Old newspapers crinkled under her feet and rustled in the draft from the open door. Leaving the stinging wind behind, she heard a radio playing staticky country music somewhere in the house.

"My car broke down." Voice quavering, she held her hands to her cheeks to warm them. "Would I be able to use your phone?"

"Ain't got a phone," came the reply, matter–of–fact. It was hard to see the man very well in the dim entryway. The smell of garbage and cigarette smoke made Julie struggle not to wrinkle her nose.

"Well…" she stumbled over her words. Could this night get any worse? And who in this day and age didn't have a phone, for God's sake? "Do you have neighbors nearby?"

"Nope." That was it. No offers of help…nothing. As much as she hated the idea, Julie faced the thought of having to go back out into the wild storm.

"Where you heading?" The question shot out, in the dry cracked tone that made her wonder when this man had last spoken to anyone.

" To Negaunee. My car's out on US41, probably buried in the snow or run over by a plow by now."

The man stepped back into what appeared to be a kitchen. Julie reluctantly followed, stamping snow off her feet. A single bulb glared overhead. The harsh burst of light hurt her eyes, but the sight before her was even more painful. The kitchen was a low, square room that had been painted a dirty green color many years before. Too many years before. Spots and streaks of dirt and who–knows–what covered the walls. Piles of old newspapers and mail lay on the counter which was itself a scratched and stained Formica. It looked like it had been used as a cutting board. Old scraps of crusted food decorated the pile of dishes near the rust–stained sink. It held its own precarious tower of dirty plates, above which a pair of curtains that had once been white dangled in tatters. A skinny black and white cat lurked nearby brushing up against the yellowed refrigerator.

"You wanna cup of tea or somethin?" The question pulled her attention back to the man who had looked better in the shadows of the entry. Anywhere from fifty to seventy years old, his gray–streaked greasy hair trailed well over his collar. An even grayer beard grew in tufts to his chest, bits of food evident in its strands. She couldn't imagine that he'd washed in the past three months, noting other smells besides garbage and smoke in the room. Furrows etched into his forehead and along his cheeks. He had a slight wiry body, somewhat bent at the shoulders, legs bowed a bit. This made him appear shorter than his five foot six inches. His flannel shirt might have been ten years old and was dotted with stains down the front. An old pair of worn jeans sagged on him, covered in cat hair with a few cigarette burns scattered here and there.

"No thanks." The words came out a little too quickly, barely masking her real answer. She wanted out of here and fast. Comments by co–workers with home nursing experience sped through her mind. "I threw my shoes in the garbage after I left that house it was so bad," "I sprayed myself after every visit and left all my clothes in the laundry room the minute I came home," "The old man peed into coffee cans and emptied them out the window. There was no bathroom"...Julie quickly brushed these thoughts aside. Trickles of melting snow run from her hair onto her face. Maybe this was all just a bad dream.

"I mean, that's okay...I just need to get home. I'll try to find help elsewhere." As she turned, the cat brushed up against her legs. That they were frosty with driven snow didn't seem to bother it.   The word fleas entered Julie's mind and she repressed her natural tendency to bend down and pet it.

"That's Molly."   Hands in his back pockets, the man seemed oblivious to Julie's discomfort. "She likes company. Don't get too much of it around here. She come here about three years ago…just wandered up to the front step one evening. Been here ever since. Good company…cats."

"I have a dog, but I like cats too." Surprised by his sudden talkativeness, Julie felt she'd better make an effort to be pleasant, even though everything about this man and this place repelled her.

"Don't have no dogs here…too noisy and too expensive…costs too much to feed 'em. Besides, Molly here," pointing to the cat now perched amidst the clutter on top of the refrigerator "gets a little jealous, dontcha?" Thin bent fingers like twigs came out, picked up the cat, and scratched its black head. "Yep, she's pretty jealous." The dry cracked lips split apart to reveal a smile comprised of three long, yellowed teeth. The hooked nose nearly touched his upper lip as he smiled. The cat relished the attention, closed its eyes and began to purr.   For a moment, Julie forgot her discomfort.

Finally she ventured, "She really is a sweetie."

"Yep. My only company besides the T.V. and radio. Keeps me in line, dontcha girl? Wakes me up in the mornin' to feed 'er…better than an alarm clock!" He set the cat down and it streaked into the next room. Soon the sound of a small jingle bell could be heard.

"Playin' with 'er toys. Really likes 'em." With effort he slowly straightened up. With a movement of his head, he gestured into the room where the cat had gone.

"Take a look."

Julie wasn't keen to see another room of the house. She'd seen enough, but out of courtesy, glanced through the doorway into a small living room. Its sparseness struck her at first. There was nothing on the walls except a dingy beige paint and a few cracks here and there. No pictures or decoration of any kind.

Water stains showed on one portion of the ceiling from a roof leak. A worn brown recliner with splits in its upholstery sat in a corner facing a television that appeared to be at least twenty years old. A floor lamp was nearby, light filtering unevenly through the frayed, patched lampshade. Piles of old newspapers also adorned this room, stacked in the shadowy corners. An old metal T.V. tray, like the ones Julie remembered eating frozen dinners on as a child, sat next to the recliner. The single window was covered by a yellowed sheet used as a makeshift curtain. A Don Williams song filtered from the aging portable radio on the floor by the recliner. Clicking of sleet and snow flung against the window could be heard now and then.

She took all this in quickly, because her attention was immediately captured by the only other objects in the room, the only new things, which made them stand out in contrast even more. The corner opposite the recliner had been set up for Molly. A shiny red circular track on the floor held a little ball. The cat was darting around it, batting the ball. The small bell inside it jingled pleasantly. A small stuffed mouse and colorful toy fish lay nearby. A wicker cat bed with a clean towel folded inside it completed the ensemble. Julie forgot her previous shivering and the snow melting off her bangs. For someone who had very little in terms of material things, the man had made every effort to make this cat happy.

"Keeps me entertained, just watchin' her." The words cut into her thoughts and reminded her of where she was and how she got here. The man stood behind her, pale eyes on Molly, all wrinkles in evidence as he smiled at the cat's antics.

"Watch this," he said with a grin and a wink. He tossed the stuffed mouse across the room. The cat shot after it and returned a second later, proudly bearing its prey.

"She fetches. Pretty smart, eh?" His laugh was a dry cackle, almost a giggle. Something about it was infectious and Julie found herself smiling, then chuckling. Wincing now and then, the man kneeled down slowly to play with the cat. The cackling laugh broke out from time to time, as he teased and flicked its toys around. Ok, the cat darted here and there, paws a blur as it played. After a few minutes the man picked it up and stroked its head gently. He turned and faced Julie.

"She's a good little gal...almost out of food, though. We better take care of that." He pointed at the silvery bowls nearby on the floor, the cleanest dishes Julie had seen here yet.

Julie sat perched on the edge of the recliner gazing at the man and his pet. "You've made a big difference in her life."

"It's easy to get along with animals. People are another thing." A slight smile pulled at his mouth. All the while he kept stroking the cat, the bent fingers buried in her fur. Then, putting her down, he got up and went to refill the food dish.

"You've got a point there." Julie couldn't help smiling. She found herself kneeling over the toys and tantalizing Molly with one of them. The cat batted at it in delight, tail switching from side to side. For a moment, the storm and car were forgotten. Don Williams ended his song and Tammy Wynette started another.

"What's wrong with yer car?" the man called from the kitchen. The words brought her back to the situation at hand. Looking up from the cat, Julie described what had happened the best she could, given her limited knowledge of cars. A mechanic, she was not.

"Sounds like the alternator." The man set the food dish down and, lifting up a corner of the sheet, peered outside. A low whistle came from him as he looked at the raging elements rattling his windowpanes. Then he turned toward Julie again.

"I can probably give you a ride. Negaunee, is that where yer goin'?"

Julie nodded.

"My truck's gettin a bit long in the tooth...like me." The pale blue eyes narrowed to raisin shapes as he smiled. "I haven't driven it this week, but it should start okay." He walked stiffly to a closet door that opened with a creak and took out a grimy jacket.

Surprised by the offer, Julie was partly relieved and partly leery of riding with this man in a vehicle whose condition was probably questionable at best. However, her limited options left her no choice. Tucking a strand of wet hair behind her ear, she said, "That would be great. I'd appreciate it."

"From Negaunee, eh? Got relatives there?" The man was zipping up his battered jacket.

"No. I just moved to Negaunee last year. The rent's cheaper than Marquette, where I work."

"What's yer name?"

"I'm Julie, Julie Miller."

The man's head was buried in the closet again, finally emerging with a knitted hat on it. She wasn't sure if he'd heard her.

"We'll leave Molly to her gadgets here. Wait a few while I clear off my truck. Probably covered in a few feet of snow by now."

Julie sat on the floor by the cat, teasing it with a toy mouse. Such a thin cat, but it was clean and its fur shiny. It batted the toy around like a hockey player with a puck. After a few minutes it sidled up to Julie, laid down on its back and began to purr while she petted it. What a strange evening, she thought idly, letting her mind wander. The radio continued its recital of country–western tunes.

The groan of the door opening broke her reverie. The newspapers crackled in the sudden rush of cold air, and her host entered. Face reddened and clumps of snow sticking to his beard, he announced, "Truck's started. We're all set." Julie laid the cat in its wicker basket and stood up. Pulling her collar up and gloves on she followed him out into the night.

They waded through drifts a couple of feet deep to a battered Chevy truck. The noise of its engine nearly drowned out the sounds of the storm.

"Your door lock's broke, so I'll have to open it from inside," he called out as he rounded the truck to get in the driver's seat. She waited while he pushed at the door until it finally burst open. As she climbed in, her feet brushed against some objects on the floor of the truck. She decided it was better not to know what they were. A blanket covered part of the torn seat cover. Julie tried to fasten her seat belt, but it didn't work.

"Heater's broke. Sorry. Sometimes I get a little heat if I turn it up full bore." A slight wafting of warmth touched her face as he did so. He backed out of the driveway and they headed on their way.

"Shit, it's a real blizzard out here." He hunched over the steering wheel peering out into the swirling snow. "I'm Bill...by the way. Hutchens is the last name. Well, we'll get ya home safe and sound. You'll hafta call a tow truck for yer car." He turned on the windshield wipers to clear the snow from his view. The blade on her side trailed a torn piece of rubber across the windshield. The smell of cigarette smoke permeated the truck.

"So where do ya work in Marquette?"

"I'm a nurse at the hospital." Her teeth were chattering so much that she could barely get the words out. Her jaw muscles felt wired shut by the cold.

"A nurse, eh? A good profession. Yessir, I knew a gal once whose dream it was to be a nurse. I think she did it, too. I had my own dreams...wanted to have my own woodworking business...loved to build things."

"Did you end up doing it?" Julie was curious how this man came to end up this way. Besides, the conversation made her forget the numbness creeping through her toes.

"Nah. I made a lotta mistakes in my life. Let the bottle get hold of me for a long time. Really messed up."

A silence fell over him and Julie picked over her words carefully. The sound of the tires plowing through the snow and the wind pushing against the truck filled her ears.

"Do you have a family?"

He was surprisingly talkative. The words were like water that had been held back by a dam for many years. "Had me a wonderful woman once and lost her. I chose the bottle over her and the baby, so that was the end of that. Never had the nerve to show up in her life again, even after I got sober." His sigh could be heard over the sound of the wind and the engine. "By that time, too many years'd gone by. Louise'd moved away. Do you know, I never even knew if our baby was a boy or a girl! But Louise, she was a smart gal, wanted to go onto nurse's training, and I'll bet she did too. Yessir, she was one smart gal...and pretty, too."

The shivering and teeth chattering faded away as his words registered in her brain. For a second she felt breathless, like all the air had left her lungs. She must have heard wrong.

"Did you say her name was Louise?" she asked slowly. The crevices in his face looked even deeper in the dim dashboard light. His eyes were on the road, looking but not seeing snow. Seeing something very different from snow.

"Louise Miller. Pretty little gal with curly dark hair. You probably can't believe a woman'd be interested in me, eh?" His smile was grim. "Well, I was a different man then. Not bad lookin' and the bottle hadn't ruined me yet."

His words seemed to come from far away...the way long distance phone calls sounded when she was young. Unbelievable, what he was saying. This worn old man, living with such overwhelming poverty and crushing loneliness. He couldn't be!

"So...when would that have been...that Louise...had the baby, I mean?" The words stumbled out awkwardly, but with near desperation. Please let her be wrong...Please!

He looked over at her a little curiously, then went back to peering over the wheel. "Well...let me see. It was about the time that Nixon resigned I think, must've been about '73 or '74. I remember watching those Watergate hearings day after day, after she left me...drunk as a skunk. I'd lost my job and broken a lotta promises. She did the right thing, to leave me." She strained to hear him as his words grew quieter. "But I always remember those hearings on T.V., day after day...sittin' in the dark, drinkin' my sorrows away." His voice trailed away for a moment. "Sorry, I'm probably boring you."

"No." The word blurted out. Her voice was shaking, but not with cold this time. How to even go on and get these words out...but she had to know. "I just ask, because...my mother's name was Louise Miller. She was a nurse. I was born in 1973. I never knew who my father was. My mom never really talked about him...." Her voice trailed off with a sob.

The sound of the wind and snow and laboring truck engine could not fill the silence that followed.

The Lilac Paintings

Sandra Jo Jackson

She had to work quickly, for dawn was beginning to peep over the calm lake. As her porcelain hands colored the design on the white canvas, she knew that someone had to help O'Lot, who was slowly drowning in debt. O'Lot often asked Lacy why people no longer shopped in his store.

There—it was finished. She placed the lilac flower painting in the large front window as the sky showed the glowing brilliance of an early morning.

Tim O'Lot awoke early that day. He slowly dressed in his green jogging suit. Although his physical age was 70, his internal organs were like a man of 65. He went out the back door and headed for the eight–mile road that wrapped around Mackinac Island. Every morning like a wind–up clock, he biked once around the timeless island. Years ago his wife went with him, but cancer had robbed her of these golden years. The cool wind blew in O'Lot's aged face. The scenery enlightened his soul as he faced another workday.

Sandra Jo Jackson is a retired teacher now living in West Virginia with her husband, Bill and her son, Kenney. One of her poems won honorable mention from the *World of Poetry*, and she has had a short story published in a Bay Side, NY magazine, *Blood Moon Rising*.

Returning home, Tim quickly showered and ate breakfast. After feeding Chessa, the alley cat he found roaming in the garbage one evening, he hurried into his shop to open for yet another day. Approaching the door, he saw a middle–aged lady already standing there. She seemed to be pointing to something in the window. As he unlocked the door, she rushed in, dropping her straw hat on the floor. Picking up the hat, Tim handed it to the agitated woman.

"I must have it!" she stated, "I must."

"Can I help you?" Tim politely asked.

101

"Yes, I want the painting in the window. The one by the doll with the blue hat and long white veil." She quickly answered.

"You would like to buy my doll. Lacy. She is beautiful with her long white dress with lilacs around the hem," he smiled.

"No!" the exasperated lady said. "The painting, I want the painting."

Confused, Tim walked to the window and there it stood. His surprised eyes took in the scene. As his wrinkled hands picked up the painting, he handed it to the woman. When she left with her prize, people entered the shop all day, buying. Finally the day over, he looked up at the clock to see the time. The worn out timepiece showed ten after ten. Tim turned to Chessa, relief on his worn face.

"What happened today, Chessa? I made a lot of money, but where did that painting come from?"

He picked the scruffy cat up and stroked her back.

"Maybe tomorrow I will find the answer," he mumbled to himself. Completely exhausted, he decided to go to bed.

All of the shops on Market Street were closed for the night. A few people were milling around on the street, but no one seemed to be walking by the Scrimschanders's Shop. Then the moon spread its warming light across the water and looked into the wide windows.

***

Lacy's blond curls cascaded down on her gentle shoulders, surrounding her petite face with the small, permanent smile etched for eternity. Opening her light brown eyes, Lacy knew there was only so much time to make another painting. Quickly, she gathered the oil paints and pencils and began to draw a Victorian house.

"I will use a lot of lilac flowers on the porch and round the windows," she whispered.

Again, the night was chased away as dawn spread her light, decorating the sky with gossamer wisps of clouds.

Tim awoke a little later that day to the horses' hooves stamping on the lonely street. He still had enough time to take his early bike ride and be able to open the shop at the correct moment. The cool air tickled Tim's face, and he took long gasps of breath as he peddled the gray ten–speed bike close to the water. The lake's waves hit and smoothed the rocks while sea gulls rested on the little stretches of land that lay open on the lake. Tim swiftly passed the daisies and buttercups on the side of the road thinking how yesterday had been so rewarding.

Returning to town, Tim hurried to shower, have a quick breakfast and open the shop. As he walked to the door, a young couple stood there, patiently waiting.

"Good morning!" the couple chimed together.

Tim let them in.

"We would like to purchase the painting in the window," the cheerful young man spoke first.

Tim laughed nervously.

"You mean Lacy? The doll?"

"No." It was the demure wife who talked now. "The Victorian house painting with the lilacs."

Slowly, Tim walked to the window and there, next to Lacy's white–gloved hand, stood a painting—a Victorian house with lilacs! After Tim finished with the young people, the day was a repetition of the previous. Again he sold many objects. He closed early and went into the back of his shop where his small apartment was. He sat at his old pine table, his head in his tired hands; he couldn't understand what was happening. Chessa rubbed against his leg and purred.

"You are hungry, my pet?" he looked down. "Let's make supper."

Silence danced in the house as Lacy started on her next picture. This one is to be my last, she thought. Later, putting down her paints, Lacy stared at the picture, a satisfied look on her face, then she took a step toward the finished canvas.

The sun touched a window, and sent rays into the house. The rays went through the white blinds and attached to the coffee–colored walls announcing their entrance. Tim awoke, and this time he ran into the little shop, straight to the window. A gasp fell from his lips. As his sleepy eyes brought the painting into focus, his mind would not accept what he saw. A beautiful gazebo surrounded by lovely lilacs held a woman sitting inside on a white flowered swing. Lacy smiled back at him, her eyes glittering. He retired to his bedroom, his mind reeling, when he heard a light knock at the shop door. An elegantly dressed gentleman with a young school–aged girl stood at the entrance.

"I'm not open, yet." Tim spoke in a loud voice.

"Please, sir," the fragile looking girl spoke rather softly. "Could we buy the painting in the window?"

Tim reconsidered and let them both in noticing that, although she wore a long cape, she walked with a slight limp.

"I will give you any amount of money for the painting," the gray–haired man said, taking a black wallet out of his pocket. "My granddaughter just loves that picture."

Still in his blue and white striped pajamas, Tim hurried to the backroom to put on his gray cotton bathrobe. Coming back, he noticed a sadness in the little girl's eyes, as if she yearned for the painting. He sold them the canvas, watching them place their treasure in a carriage and lead the handsome horses away. Tim looked at Chessa.

"I'll never understand what has happened," he said. Surely, something special has touched us. Yes, something special."

***

On top of a high hill, sits a huge brown and pink Victorian house with round turrets on every corner. Inside is a child's yellow room decorated with red and blue roses. On one wall hangs a picture of a gazebo with a lovely lady in a white dress trimmed with lilacs who is sitting on a flowered swing decorated with petunias and zinnias. Below the picture sits an eight–year–old girl, dressed in an ivory silk dress, small primroses placed throughout her curly

104

hair. Her face is lying on a blue and white tiled table while her arms encircle her head. She cries ever so silently. Lacy hears her sobs, not knowing what to do yet, but sure that soon, she will be able to help. For Lacy, time is forever.

Hunt of a Lifetime

Mark Scott

The near–freezing water was starting to take its toll on the duck hunter. He had been in the water for twenty minutes or so, only being kept afloat by his life jacket. In late November, this was almost a death sentence. The ferryboats that had taken tourists to Mackinac Island all summer had since been dry–docked for the upcoming winter. The giant freighters that use the Great Lakes and frequent the Straits of Mackinac had all but stopped their runs due to the impending grip of winter. The hunter knew he was going to die and that he was powerless to prevent it.

***Mark Scott** has been a police officer for twenty years. He lives in Galesburg, MI. with his wife, Mary, and two sons, Paul and John. In Mark's spare time, he enjoys coaching his kids' sport teams, training his Labrador retrievers and hunting ducks.*

***

"Dad, why do they call them diving ducks?" Eric asked with a puzzled look.

"Yeah, Dad. Do they really dive?" Grant chimed in.

Patiently, Dale told his young sons that certain ducks dive down into the water for their food.

"But Dad, I always see the duck's butt sticking out of the water when they eat," said Eric. Dale did his best to tell his five and seven–year–old sons that some ducks, such as mallards, are dabblers. They can only feed in water that is about half their body length. He explained, "Diving ducks, though, prefer large lakes or even oceans and usually never touch land their whole lives." The boys were interested that some diving ducks can go to depths of forty or fifty feet in search of food.

"How can they hold their breath that long?" Grant wanted to know.

"I can only hold mine until 'thirteen Mississippi' in the bathtub," said Eric.

Dale told them how a diving duck's wings are shorter and further back on their bodies, allowing them to glide through the water propelled by their feet. "That doesn't sound as funny as a duck butt," Eric said, and the boys broke into simultaneous laughter.

Dale realized that the boys couldn't understand how a duck could captivate him. Maybe it was the way the ducks made their appearance in a two or three–week stopover in Michigan. It could have been their beautiful plumage, or the way their wings sounded as they buzzed a decoy spread at sixty or seventy miles per hour. Maybe it was the way the ducks had to be hunted on their terms, usually miles from shore in open water. Anyway, they symbolized everything that was wild and free to him. In the twenty years of hunting them, Dale never tired of the magic.

"Boys, get in the tub and let Dad finish packing for his trip," Jan said firmly, and Eric and Grant ran toward the bathroom, shedding clothes all the way.

"How long is the drive, honey?" asked Jan.

"About five or six hours," Dale said excitedly, knowing that Jan could still see the boy inside his aging body and receding hairline.

Jan smiled tolerantly. "Why do you want to drive all that way just to hunt ducks? Aren't there any around here?"

She knew the answer before she asked. After all, she'd been married to the duck hunter for ten years. She had heard Dale talk about how "someday" he wanted to hunt the Straits of Mackinac. She had heard many times before that this area, where Lake Michigan meets Lake Huron, was a major stopping point for weary waterfowl on their southern migration.

Dale remembered that anytime they crossed the Mackinac Bridge in the fall, Jan would drive so that he could look for ducks bobbing in the water beneath the massive bridge.

His thoughts were disturbed by the boys' argument coming from the tub. "I want to be the diving duck this time, Eric. You have to be the dabbler," Grant was screaming to Eric's howls of disapproval.

Jan quickly settled the argument with a compromise. "There will be two diving ducks in the tub tonight," she declared, a solution both boys respected and of which neither had thought. Dale chuckled.

Dale finished packing as his two junior diving ducks in their pajamas were climbing into their bunk beds. He and Jan kissed them and headed downstairs. While he felt slightly guilty to be leaving his family, Dale grew more excited each moment. This would be the culmination—the hunt of his lifetime.

***

Dale woke up and got dressed well before the alarm was set to go off. He rarely slept the night before a duck hunt. Jan always said, "Honey, you are worse than a kid on Christmas Eve." He didn't disagree.

He went to his backyard to let Suzy out. She was an energetic black Labrador who could sense when a hunt was near. Possibly it was the camo clothing that Dale seemed to live in during the fall, or just that extra sense that dogs seemed to have.

"Calm down, girl," he said to the two–year–old retriever. After his usual greeting and petting, she ran toward the backyard to play. Dale hooked up his duck boat and loaded his gear, which was piled up by the back door. He looked up to see his sons standing in the doorway.

"Close that door, guys. It's forty degrees and we don't want to heat the outdoors." Dale smirked as the door shut. That was one of those many phrases he'd heard from his own parents when he was a boy and found himself using now. He went inside for breakfast and the four of them sat down to Captain Crunch and Life cereal.

"How many days are you going to be gone?" asked Grant. At the same time Eric said, "Does Suzy have to go?"

109

"Sunday, Monday, and Tuesday, and yes," Dale answered them. "I would never miss your mother's birthday on Wednesday." He was proud of himself for remembering.

"Well, in that case, you'd better stay an extra day. My birthday is Thursday," Jan said dryly. The boys missed the dirty look she shot Dale across the table.

"I got it confused, honey," Dale said quickly, backpedaling. "I knew it was November twenty or twenty one." He knew a big celebration would be needed when he returned, to erase the errant birthday guess. He began planning what to buy her, where he could pick up something nice on his trip. She loved jewelry, and flowers helped any situation, he'd found. She wouldn't stay mad long. After all, Dale was constantly doing little things to spoil her, even if he did sometimes forget her actual birth date.

"Dad, get us lots of diving ducks," Eric said as he got ready to leave.

"See you in three days," Grant said. He fought back tears, trying to be a big boy.

"Love you," Dale said, hugging them both as he got into the truck. He rarely left the family, except for the occasional business trip, so the goodbyes were hard for everyone. Men didn't talk about the ambivalence they felt when they left their families, Dale thought, but it was there, hidden in their conscience.

"Drive carefully," Jan said just before the long goodbye kiss.

"I'll call you tonight," Dale told them as they waved at him and heated the outdoors.

***

Late November in Michigan has many faces. Some years, Mother Nature covers the landscape with white. Others, she is content to wait a bit. Regardless of her wishes, late November is usually a cold, windy time with unpredictable weather. It's a time that sends most people into their houses to start their hibernation. The lure of nasty weather, northwest winds, and ducks made Dale push harder on the truck's accelerator as he headed north, full of anticipation.

110

As Dale got within fifty miles of the straits, the rain started. When he got close to Mackinaw City, he saw the two suspensions that support the five–mile long bridge. Even after all the times Dale had crossed the bridge, the Mighty Mac was still breathtaking. He wished that Jan were driving so he could look down more. Halfway across, Dale saw them. Thousands of little black dots rafted up under the bridge, bobbing with the waves. Though it was forbidden, Dale had to stop and look down to admire the sight.

"Divers," he said, to no one in particular. He stayed, mesmerized for a moment, until the honk of an impatient motorist brought him back to reality. He shifted the car back into drive and finishing the crossing.

Dale arrived at his in–laws' cabin in the Upper Peninsula. It had been vacant since Labor Day, and was certainly quiet compared to when most of the family assembled there during the summer. Suzy bolted out of the truck, happy to stretch her legs. Once inside, she gave the cabin her smell of approval and lay down.

Time was put to good use in preparation for the next morning's hunt. There was something very primal about a lone hunter and his faithful companion taking on the elements that stirred Dale's soul. He often hunted with other guys around home, but none had been available for his hunt of a lifetime. After a supper of canned chili and saltine crackers, Dale called home.

"Hi, Eric," Dale said at the sound of his son's voice.

"Daddy! Mom! Dad's on the phone. How's Suzy?" came in a rush. Dale had to laugh at his question. No "How was the drive, Dad?"—Eric had really attached himself to Suzy last summer, since she got over the habit of knocking him over.

Dale talked with his wife and sons, checked his decoys again, and a short time later fell asleep to the sound of the wind blowing and the light patter of rain on the shingles. He heard Suzy's rhythmic breathing on the rug beside the bed. He was glad for her company; the cabin would have been very lonely without her.

He awoke to the sound of something hitting the bedroom window; it sounded like a container of BB's falling onto linoleum. No doubt about it; it was freezing rain. The early morning radio station verified that a fast moving cold front was coming in. It was perfect, Dale thought, as he headed into the blackness with Suzy.

At the access site, Dale was happy to see no other hunters. He would have the ducks all to himself. The freezing rain was changing over to snow as Dale launched the boat. Suzy went to her usual spot at the front of the boat and shook with excitement as Dale strapped on his life vest. He had gotten safety conscious since Grant's birth. Dale and the guys joked that wearing a life jacket during the bitterly cold duck season only prolonged life briefly and made body recovery easier. The trick was not to fall into the water in the first place.

The outboard motor hummed as Dale headed the boat out of the protected St. Ignace harbor. The wind took them full force as soon as he got away from land. A small wave of fear sent a shiver into the duck hunter. Had he misjudged the weather? Tombstone courage or macho pride prevailed. He hadn't driven all this way, taken a vacation from work, and left his family for nothing. The lure of fantastic duck shooting kept him bow first in the waves.

Dale motored several miles toward the area where he'd seen the rafts of ducks the day before. The snow had become so heavy that Dale could hardly make out the heavily illuminated bridge. He knew that somewhere overhead the early morning traffic was crossing. Sunrise was still an hour away, so Dale knew he would have enough time to set the decoys before first light.

Wet snow stuck to Suzy and the black dog looked more like a Dalmatian as she sniffed the air. This was her second hunting season and things had come together nicely, Dale thought. All their work had turned Suzy into a fine retriever. Dale had a special place in his heart for her, as she was the first dog he had ever trained by himself. For almost twenty years, Dale had hunted ducks with no dog to retrieve the downed birds. Maybe it was lack of confidence or time, but he never thought he could properly train one. Then came Suzy. They had learned together and had formed a bond that only hunters and their dogs can truly understand.

Dale motored on in the chop and was coming down from a wave when he heard a metal on metal sound, and felt a sudden jolt. A loud cry from Suzy filled the cold air; Dale knew he had hit something. Life became slow motion as he was thrown out of the duck boat at full force. Just before hitting the water, he saw the outline of an anchored metal buoy which was used to mark the shipping lane. Then everything went dark.

The duck hunter awoke to find himself in the icy water. Immediately he looked around for Suzy or the boat, but could see nothing. Dale felt groggy in the way that a head injury makes a person feel. Panic overcame him as he realized his predicament. He felt the squeezing of the water pressure on his hunting clothes and the bone–chilling cold of Lake Huron. With the darkness and snow, visibility was near zero. Through the wind and waves, he thought he heard a whining sound. He whistled loudly in hopes of finding Suzy. He whistled until shivering wouldn't allow him to continue.

Suddenly she was there. Suzy had found him. Dale grabbed her with both hands and hugged her tightly. When he looked closely, he saw that she had a large amount of blood on the top of her head. The waves slapped the two friends; they were at the mercy of the elements, but they had found each other.

He could tell by her cries that she was badly hurt. He realized that she must have hit the buoy when the boat did. He hadn't seen a light or heard any horn or bell before the collision. Dale held his dying dog and they stayed afloat by the life vest. Dale was quickly losing feeling in his arms and legs and, though she was light in the water, soon he could no longer hold onto her. He looked into Suzy's eyes, trying to reassure her. Dale cried as she drifted out of his arms, trying frantically to swim. A few more waves, and then Suzy was gone.

Dale thought of his young sons who just the day before had waved goodbye from the doorway of their home. They'd seemed so warm and cozy as he had pulled away for the great duck hunt. A calm feeling came over the hunter. No more flailing around or attempting to swim; he felt sleepy and numb.

Dale wasn't seeing his life flash before his eyes, the way people said. His mind was filled with a burning desire to see Jan and the boys again. Though he was miles from shore and no one was near, he heard his voice calling out their names.

He was hit by an over whelming guilt for having misjudged the elements. He thought of the sharp look Jan had given him at breakfast the previous morning when he'd forgotten her birthday. He knew she'd always remember this on her birthday, and for that he felt badly.

By now Dale was shivering uncontrollably and was in and out of consciousness. There would be no rescue; only the labored breathing of a dying man bobbing with the waves, like the diving ducks he loved.

Surrender

Marti Towne

They came for him in the gray light of dawn, the same two as usual. The man had deceptively mild blue eyes, a bristly red beard, and beefy shoulders. The woman was fat but strong. Even with his damaged eyes he could see she jiggled when she walked. It was the woman who pulled him up. Together they dragged him to the bathroom, then stood watching. God, what did they think he was going to do? Four solid walls, a toilet and a sink. No escape here. They led him back to the room's single chair, tied him, and left.

Through the small window the skeletal trees were just visible in the dull light, and the fence beyond stood tall and solid and black. A dirty crust of snow covered the ground, but to

> Mackinac Island is a favorite vacation spot for **Marti Towne's** family from southwestern Michigan where she has lived for twenty-five years. She works in a family business though her three sons are recently out of college and on their own. Marti writes simply because she enjoys it.

him it might have been the Garden of Eden. If he could just get that far!

Once, before things got so bad and they stopped taking him out for exercise, he saw the fat woman leave through the door at the side of the building. He had watched her surreptitiously and saw she had no key. The realization that the door was sometimes left unlocked gave him hope, kept him alive.

His icy fingers automatically gripped the rough strap, pulling it forward, back, to the side. He had done it so many times before. But this time it was different: suddenly it gave way. Hope shot through his pain like a sunbeam through the clouds before the shadow of despair descended again. He had no plan, and in his condition how could he possibly get out without being seen?

115

With a speed and certainty that took him by surprise, his soldier's instincts kicked in. Thought and action became one. Carefully, slowly, quietly, he maneuvered himself into a standing position. He held on to the iron bed frame, willing his legs to work. If only Anna were here to help him. But she was dead like all the rest.

Inch by inch he turned, holding tight to the back of the chair with his good hand. Finally, he stood behind it, gripping the back of it for support. He began the laborious journey to the cupboard on the back wall to collect the few clothes they had left him. He would need what little warmth they could provide. Using every bit of strength he could muster, he pushed the chair forward and shuffled his feet after it. The chair screeched alarmingly and he held his breath, but there were no approaching footsteps and no voices. He repeated the action, taking care to slide the chair over the hard floor. The effort almost caused him to topple over backward.

Finally, he reached the cupboard and stood for a moment fighting for breath. He wouldn't last much longer now. He knew if he were to make his escape, it would have to be soon.

Suddenly, he heard voices outside his door. Without thinking, he pulled open the cupboard door and thrust the chair inside. He pushed the few things that hung there out of the way and pressed his emaciated body against the chair back. Just enough room. Slowly, with a great shaking, tremulous effort, he reached back and pulled the door shut behind him.

The footsteps gradually receded. He strained to hear the sounds of voices. He mustn't wait too long, for he would need every minute. The voices were distant now and becoming more faint.

Finally, silence.

Slowly, gently, he pushed the door open. He took one cautious step backward and began to turn.

He hadn't heard her come into the room. The fat woman's eyes bore into his, flashing anger.

"Mr. Armstrong! Bless my soul, what *are* you doing? You're going to fall one of these days and break a hip, and *then* you'll be in a pickle!"

She wrapped one strong arm around his waist and held his arm firmly with her free hand. He let himself be drawn from the cupboard.

"I brought you a tray in case you didn't feel like going to the dining room. I thought you were looking a little peaked this morning. There we are." She lowered him onto the side of the bed. "Now. Two bowls of oatmeal, just the way you always like. And I brought you a little scrambled egg in case you feel like trying that. *And* apple butter for your toast. I know you like apple butter, so I got some from the cook specially...."

She swung the tray around in front of him, the white carnation bobbing gently in the silver vase like a little white flag of surrender.

The Message of Manitou

Jennifer Niemur

Breakfast at the Early Bird never disappointed. Erin savored every bit of her hot scrambled eggs and cinnamon french toast, knowing this would be her last meal of the weekend to come from a kitchen, as opposed to a propane stove.

Breakfast at Leland's Early Bird diner had become an annual ritual for Erin Girard and her friends, the eye-opening start to a weekend of backpacking on either South or North Manitou Island. Erin twirled her fork as she considered both islands. South was rich with history, but North held more freedom—she could camp wherever the spirit moved her.

"Penny for your thoughts?" A voice from across the table snapped her back to reality.

After graduation from Kalamazoo College, **Jennifer Niemur** worked at the National Endowment for the Arts in Washington, D.C. After four years, the collective pull of friends, family and Lake Michigan inspired her to move back to Michigan where she lives in Grand Rapids with her husband, Adam, and their son, Elliott.

She looked up. "Just thinking about the differences between North and South Manitou."

Murphy, Erin's husband of five years, smiled. "Are you sure about going to South this year? It's not too late to change your mind."

"We can go to North if you'd rather—I'm just ready for a change, that's all."

"My lady, your wish is my command," said Murphy, bowing his head with dramatic flair.

There he goes again, thought Erin. *Trying to cheer me up. I love him, but I wish he'd stop it.* She wondered if getting away like this would really do any good. Murphy had insisted that they get away, just the two of them. These days she barely had enough energy to leave the house, let alone go on a backpacking trip. But she had had even less energy to argue with him, and so she went along with his plan.

Her mind began to wander again, back to the last group outing about two months ago. The last time she had eaten here at the Early Bird she was about four months pregnant, and the whole gang had shared in their excitement. Only one week later she was in the emergency room, facing a miscarriage and wondering what she could have done wrong.

And so here we are again at the Early Bird, she thought. *Just the two of us.*

A young waitress snapped her gum as she laid down their check. "You two better get a move on if you're heading for the ferry."

"Right–o!" Murphy hollered. He gave the waitress the total plus tip, and sprang up. "Ready, babe?"

Once more Erin was jolted from her thoughts. "Ready as I'll ever be!" she responded, trying to make her voice match her husband's enthusiasm. Together they trotted down to the ferry dock to register and load their packs onto the boat. As they neared the dock, Erin slowed her pace and turned her face to the bright July sun, letting its rays warm her up. Even in July northern Michigan could be cool, and this morning was no exception. Luckily, the forecast had promised perfect camping weather: partly sunny and highs in the lower seventies.

After about twenty minutes, the South Island ferry was ready to depart. Erin and Murphy climbed up to the top deck and grabbed two seats in front. As the ferry left the harbor, Erin slowed her pace once more. She closed her eyes and allowed the cool lake breeze to penetrate her skin and lungs. The soft back and forth motion of the boat was soothing her senses, and she reminded herself to be thankful for simple moments like this.

They shared a quiet ride, breaking the silence only once to go over their itinerary. With two nights at their disposal, they decided to head straight for Popple Campground, then spend Saturday night at Bay Campground, which was closest to the ferry dock. Too many mornings of sleeping late had taught them to camp close to the dock on the last night of their vacation.

The ferry pulled up to the South Island dock, and a long–standing tradition began as campers quietly lined up single–file along the dock, and packs were unloaded by passing them down the line. After finding their packs, Erin and Murphy listened patiently as the ranger gave a mandatory talk on the importance of steering clear of the endangered Pitcher's Thistle and nesting pairs of piping plover.

Soon they were off at a good trot to Popple. "Always out in front," Murphy teased Erin. "Why don't you ever just slow down and smell the, ah, Pitcher's Thistle?"

Always the comedian, she wanted to say, but instead managed a polite laugh in response.

They hiked a trail which cut through the middle of the island, promising each other they'd come back to Bay Campground by way of Weather Station, their usual camping spot. After hiking for about half an hour, Erin could feel her soul being soothed by the cool lake breeze and the repetitive sound of the gravel crunching underneath her boots. *Perhaps this wasn't the worst idea*, she thought. *I can get by for two nights up here.*

They arrived at Popple in record time and decided to have lunch on the nearby pebble beach after setting up camp. After the tent and sleeping bags were set up, they walked down to the shore with water bottles, sandwiches, gorp and cheese.

"How are you doing, babe?" Murphy asked, as he laid a blanket down on the pebble shore.

"I'm doing alright." She paused. "I'm glad we came."

After lunch, Erin decided to take Murphy up on his offer to take the dirty dishes back to camp. She stayed behind to wade in the water and look for Petoskey stones. She was so engrossed in

121

her search that she almost walked right into another man wading in the shallows.

"I'm so sorry—I was looking for Petoskey stones. Are you, ah, here for the weekend?" asked Erin sheepishly.

"Oh no, I live here—I just came to enjoy the shore for a while," the stranger replied. "I like to get away from the farm and watch the horizon. It's very calming. Are you visiting family?"

Erin cocked her head. *Why would he ask that?* "Um, no..." she said. Changing the subject, she asked him what farm life was like these days.

"It is difficult, but this year is better than the last. You see, about this time last year we lost our son, John. It nearly destroyed us—but the other families came to our aid and kept the farm going for us when we couldn't go on. Some even took losses on their own farms to help out. My wife, Frances, still says those farmers were angels sent to ease our struggles and grant us peace. I suppose only God knows." The man shrugged and regarded Erin with a kind smile. "Well, then. In that spirit, peace I leave with *you*." With that, he turned and walked away from her, following the shoreline.

Erin stood in the water, dumbstruck. She wanted to say something in response, but no words came to her. When she finally called out to him, he had already rounded a curve in the shoreline and was no longer visible. She felt hot tears streaming down her face.

That evening, as she prepared a dinner of vegetarian curry with pita bread, Erin decided not to tell Murphy of her dramatic encounter. She wanted to keep this weekend *simple*. She would try on her own to figure out what it had all meant—maybe it had meant nothing, and she had wanted to read something into it, something that would give her closure on her own grief. That was it. *Simplify, Erin,* she told herself. *He's a farmer from Leland; he doesn't know you. Don't read anything into it—just let it go. Let it all go.*

After dinner they sat by the fire, eating s'mores and chatting with other campers about past hiking adventures. Erin listened politely to Murphy's banter, but her thoughts were of the stranger on the beach.

The next morning brought another warm, sunny day. Erin and Murphy packed up their belongings and hiked out of Popple, thanking it for a good night's sleep. They set out at a leisurely pace, their only goal to reach Weather Station Campground by lunchtime. Usually they hiked along the coastline, but this was done at the cost of missing Manitou's history. Old farms, a cemetery and even an old school building could be seen between Popple and Weather Station Campgrounds, and this was their opportunity to check it out.

Around mid–morning, they reached the cemetery. "Whattya say to a little snack?" asked Murphy. "Let's take a break and check out some of these headstones."

Erin nodded in agreement. The idea of munching a granola bar among the dead seemed a little irreverent, but curiosity got the better of her and she started inspecting some of the older headstones. Most of them were family plots: husbands and wives, sometimes with children. The names sounded like pages from a history book: Elmer and Anna, Henry and Ruth, Jameson and Frances…*Frances. Wasn't that the name of that man's wife?* Erin tried to remember. *Yes, it was. Hmm. Small world,* she thought, and continued to wander through the cemetery grounds, reading more names.

"Well that's enough for me, babe—ready to head out?" Murphy asked as he collected his bags of gorp and dried fruit.

"Sure–do you still want to wander through those farm buildings?" asked Erin.

"Yeah, let's head over that way—that should put us in Weather Station just in time for lunch."

They took their time along the trail, meandering through old barns, storage sheds and stone fences. The wilderness was aptly doing its job of taking over these abandoned structures, and soon only scattered pieces of wood, stone and metal would remain. Erin was grateful for the opportunity to see it while it was still here.

They arrived at Weather Station around noon, and sat on the beach for a lunch of cucumber and hummus, with apples and sesame sticks. Erin stared out across the water. She took off her boots and socks to enjoy the small luxury of sinking her bare toes into the warm sand.

"Honey, I know you think I'm an optimist to a fault, but I really believe things will work out for us. This baby is gonna happen, I know it." Murphy smiled and rubbed her back.

This peaceful moment interrupted for you by Murphy A. Girard, ladies and gentlemen, she wanted to say. She chose a more diplomatic tone. "I want to be as positive as you, honey, but it's hard." She looked out again at the horizon and mustered a smile. "I'll try."

They finished their lunch, packed up and started hiking slowly to Bay Campground. After a couple of hours, the Manitou lighthouse came into view as they emerged from the woods.

"Let's get our stuff set up at Bay and come back here," suggested Murphy. "I've always wanted to check out the museum and lighthouse."

"Sounds good," Erin replied. They were now back where they had started on Friday, near the dock. On either side of the trail, now more of a road, stood cottages of former residents now used as Park Service buildings—a small museum, a ranger station, and Park Service employee housing.

She looked ahead, aiming for the spot where the Bay Campground Trail diverged from the Park Service road. They were soon ambling through the campground, looking for an empty site.

"Here Murphy—let's take this one," said Erin, pointing to a site that was near the beach but still sheltered by some trees and shrubs.

"Good eye, babe." Murphy got to work setting up the tent and organizing their equipment. Erin filled her fanny pack with a water bottle, some gorp, fruit leather, and a packet of instant lemonade. When they had completed their tasks, they stretched and headed back to the lighthouse.

They took in a tour of the lighthouse and then watched two divers prepare to dive a nearby wreck. It was getting close to dinner when Murphy suggested they hit the museum. "I'm not really up for it, Murph—tell you what. You check it out, and I'll get dinner started. Tonight Chez Erin is serving linguine with pesto and garlic toast points."

"Sounds good! I'll hurry back."

"Take your time," Erin replied.

That night after a satisfying meal, they shared a campfire with the rest of the Bay residents. Erin was feeling more at peace, allowing herself to get absorbed by the flames as they danced and jumped. She went to bed sleepy and full, feeling restored.

Morning brought gray clouds accompanied by a cool breeze. It was the kind of sky that promised a cloudy day, but hopefully no rain. Erin and Murphy took their time over a breakfast of dehydrated scrambled eggs brought to life with salsa and potatoes. After breakfast, Murphy broke down the tent as Erin finished packing her backpack. Soon the campsite held no trace of their stay.

"Thank you campsite, thank you, Bay," Erin hollered as they headed down the trail.

"You know, we've got some time before the ferry comes," Murphy said. "Why don't you check out the museum when we get to the dock? I'll watch the packs if you want to poke around."

Erin mulled it over. "Sure, thanks." She had always been a little curious about what the museum looked like inside. They hiked to a grassy area between the ranger station and the shore, and dropped their packs.

"I won't be long," Erin said.

"Take your time. I'm going to catch up on some reading."

Erin walked to the small cottage now housing the modest Park Service museum. The screen door creaked as she pulled it open and walked in. She wandered around, browsing walls of photographs which depicted Manitou's former residents. Suddenly her heart stopped cold. Staring her in the face was a photograph of the man she had met at Popple. The caption read Jameson and Frances Dawson, 1847.

Erin stumbled out of the museum and slowly walked toward Murphy. He looked up from his tattered paperback novel.

"Hey babe, you look like you've just seen a ghost," Murphy said.

Erin was jolted for a moment by his comment, and then she smiled. "No," she said quietly, "more like an angel."

Lemonade and Paint

Cheryl Ann Clark

BIG YARD SALE > 1.4 MILES

The hand–painted sign pointed down a sandy dirt road. Ellie slammed on her brakes in time to make the turn off the highway. She was looking for distractions and was in no hurry to get where she was going. She wasn't exactly sure where that was, or what was there. Not anymore.

The dirt road curved through a dusty, suffering cornfield that looked like it was, well, dying for a drink. Like me, Ellie thought wryly. She was hot and thirsty and had been driving too long. Maybe later she would have a chilled Chablis to take the edge off. Before she faced them. Right now water would have to do. She took a swallow from her water bottle. The drink was warm and unsatisfying. She wanted something ice cold and numbing.

> **Cheryl Ann Clark** is the mother of three–year old Sean Charles. She works as a senior computer analyst. Cheryl is a former marathon runner and an aspiring writer who believes similar skills are required for the two activities including tenacity and willingness to endure pain.

The road curved past an old red barn and a sagging farmhouse that was settling comfortably into a scraggly, unkempt lawn where chickens were scratching. A few small ranch houses came after that, set back from the road on lawns that were mowed but burnt brown with the drought. Around the next curve, Ellie saw a dozen or so cars parked near another farmhouse—this one trim and white. On the mailbox was a second *BIG YARD SALE* sign. It was big, all right, a neighborhood sale or something, Ellie thought. There were several tables lined up in rows in the shade of a few old oak trees. The tables were piled high with miscellanea overflowing onto the lawn. Strewn about were farm implements, furniture, wooden trunks, plastic toys. The usual. What wasn't usual was the lemonade stand under a banner of painted lemons and yellow balloons. "Perfect!" thought Ellie. She scrambled out of her car and headed straight for the lemonade.

"You don't see these around much anymore," she said to the wrinkled man with yellow paint on his fingers who took her seventy five cents. "At least not in the city." He poured her a tall glass with shaved ice and a slice of real lemon floating on top.

"Nothing like an ice cold glass of fresh squeezed on a hot muggy day," he said with a smile. "Squeezed 'em myself. "

"It's very good," Ellie said, taking a big drink. The juice had a pleasant bite to it—not at all like the sickly sweet artificial stuff—and it was cold. Wonderfully cold.

"Enjoy. While you're looking around," said the man with a wave at the yard. "Before it rains. Got ten families here sellin'."

"Thanks very much, I will," said Ellie. She headed for the tables, looking up at the sky as she went. It did indeed look like rain. Funny that she hadn't noticed earlier but a lot of details escaped her now. The clouds were moving in from the west, already dark and ominous on the horizon. Ellie didn't know if a storm was expected—she was making it a habit to avoid weather forecasts lately. What's the point, was her thought. They really didn't know anything about the future, did they? Look how often they were wrong. The meteorologists. Her family. The doctors especially. So very wrong.

Ellie picked up a little glass figurine from the table. It had pale iridescent wings, one of them cracked. "Poor little angel," she whispered. She set it down and reached for an embossed crystal bowl with hand–painted cherries. Too easy to break, she thought and set that down, too. There was a green frog carved out of soapstone that she held for a moment before putting it back next to a blue glass fish. Ellie went down the rows of tables like this, picking things up and setting them back down. Nothing held her interest long enough to stick. When she got to the pile of baby clothes, she had to stop. She couldn't help herself. There was a tiny pink sleeper on top, practically new, with pale yellow stars embroidered on the front next to a crescent moon. She fingered the soft lace around the unbelievably small collar before finally pulling herself away and leaving it too behind. She was suddenly tired. Ellie walked to the end of the table, leaned against one of the oak trees and took another long, cooling drink of her lemonade. She rubbed her belly absentmindedly and then snatched her hand away angrily when she realized what she was doing.

"A little too hot, isn't it?" said a voice behind her. Ellie turned.

"Yes. Yes, it is," she said to a plump woman who was carrying a basket filled with dried flowers, a crocheted blanket of some sort and an amber crystal plate.

"I can't resist yard sales," the woman said. "You never know what you're going to find." She held up the plate to Ellie. "Only fifty cents and just one small chip," she said.

"That's a find," agreed Ellie.

"I think it's going to rain," said the woman looking up at the sky. "It's about time. The corn needs it bad. They better be getting all this stuff in soon, though."

"Yes, they better," said Ellie. The woman scurried off to rummage through more things, apparently anxious to find other deals before the storm. It didn't matter to Ellie. She was striking out—nothing interested her. She walked past a rusty farm plow and headed back toward her car. It was then, of course, that she saw it.

It was a painting, leaning against one of the trees.

Ellie didn't know why it caught her attention. It was just rocks, after all. A large oil painting of rocks.

"Who would paint only rocks?" she wondered, kneeling down for a closer look. But it wasn't just rocks, she saw. There was a piece of bleached driftwood branching from one corner and a shadowy crab claw caught between two stones and there, in another corner, a piece of pearly shell and a curious dab of yellow. But mostly it was rocks. It was a beach painting, Ellie realized. A rocky beach. The stones were pale pastels and grays, wave–rounded and resting on sand. They looked hot. They looked like the rocks that are pushed up past the high water mark and lie baking in the sun untouched for a long time, waiting for the next big storm and the cooling caress of waves again. They looked exactly like the rocks on the beaches of Ellie's childhood in northern Michigan.

She had been away a long time but Ellie remembered those northern beaches well. Her parents had a home on Lake Michigan, and Ellie and her sisters grew up there watching the water and the storms come and go. They walked the lakeshore in their wet tennis shoes, and searched for interesting stones and things. The water always made their stones prettier—the pale, dry pastels became vibrant reds, yellows and greens with a little cold kiss of a wave. The water was magical that way. Especially with the Petoskey stones.

The Petoskey stone is Michigan's state stone and Ellie and her sisters collected hundreds of them. The stones were dull gray when dry but a dip in the water revealed the hidden pattern of fossilized coral: clusters of hexagons with dark–eyed centers that radiated tiny white lines. "Like quiet fireworks," Ellie thought. The stones were lovely when wet and she always wondered about the power of the water that transformed them. It transformed other things.

Once, when Ellie was little she caught a tiny frog in the surf at the beach. She held it cupped in her hands and felt it squirm as she carried it carefully to show her father. When she reached him and opened her hands, there was only one wet rock.

"You didn't catch it," her father said. "You must have missed."

But Ellie knew better. The frog had turned to stone. She returned the rock to the surf so the waves could kiss it back but the transformation did not happen while she watched. The magic took place later, when she was gone, she was sure. Even as an adult, Ellie believed the water was enchanted and it could change things.

Ellie felt a drop on her forehead. It was starting to rain. People were running for their cars or scrambling to retrieve their things from the lawn or cover tables with plastic. Ellie stood up and headed for her car. At least the rain would cool things off, she thought. For the rest of the drive.

She was in her car and turning the key when the rain started to come down hard. Through the windshield, she could see that her rock painting was getting wet, forgotten. *Her* painting. As if it really were hers. As if she wanted it. Ellie realized, suddenly, that she did. She fished in her purse for money and jumped out of the car. She grabbed the painting and ran for the farmhouse porch where the wrinkled lemonade man and others were congregating with various things rescued from the yard.

"I'll take this painting please," Ellie said to the man. "It was next to that tree," she pointed. "The sticker says ten dollars."

"Geez, it got wet. We forgot it, didn't we! Hey, Martha," the old man called to a woman nearby. "Isn't this one of our paintings? Ten bucks, right?"

The woman named Martha came over. "Oh, yeah. I remember that one. Found it in the attic. The frame's fine even though the picture's not much to look at." Martha glanced at the old man and a look passed between them that Ellen could not interpret.

"Here," Martha said, taking Ellie's money and handing her a torn sheet from a stack of old linens. "Dry it with this. It'll be fine."

"And here's a big plastic bag so it doesn't get any more rain," said the old man.

"Thanks," said Ellie. He helped her ease the painting into the plastic.

"I always liked this painting, actually," the old man winked. "Enjoy."

"I will," said Ellie. "Thanks again." She picked it up and ran for her car, pushing the painting ahead of her into the passenger's seat. Once safely inside, she took the wrappings off to assess the damage and dry it thoroughly. The painting looked fine. But different...brighter somehow. Ellie leaned closer. It was as if

131

the colors of the rocks were bolder. As if...and then she saw it. In the middle of the painting, one of the rocks that had been a dull gray before had changed. There was a pattern on it now. A pattern clearly recognizable. A Petoskey stone.

Ellie caught her breath and stared for a few minutes without moving. And then she slowly wiped the drops of water off the painting, watching as the firework pattern on the stone and all the vibrant colors slowly faded. She smiled. It was the old magic, after all. Suddenly she knew where she was going—what this long drive north was all about. She needed to walk the old beach again and be touched by the cold lake water. Everything would be fine again, after awhile. She was going home.

Non–Fiction

Misha Dodge

Against the Pitch of Winter Sky

Roger Leslie

"Take your little brother to church with you."

I know my mother meant well, but she had no idea what she was asking. It wasn't having to go to church. I was glad to go on Saturday night—masses were shorter and I could sleep in Sunday morning. It wasn't the weather. I had boots and leggings, my new parka and gloves. Besides, it hadn't snowed in a day or two so I could even take my bike, a rarity in the middle of a Dearborn Heights December. It wasn't even the distance to the church less than a mile away.

It was the distance between my brother Ray and me that scrambled my emotions and spit them out as objections. "I don't think he'll be ready on time. You know I don't like to get to church late."

That was a lie. Though I wanted to meet my holy obligation of going to church every week, I only felt guilty about leaving church before the closing hymn. Arriving a little late couldn't hurt anything, I always thought.

"He's your brother," Mom pleaded, coils of frustration singeing my conscience.

She didn't understand. Ray and I didn't get along, especially when we were alone. The three years between us were as wide and frozen as Lake Huron in winter. Who knew how far one would have to dig to reach the water that stirred beneath it? So it was with Ray and me.

"Give me one good reason why you shouldn't take him."

> **Roger Leslie** is an author, editor, book reviewer, and motivational teacher. He writes inspirational and history books, biographies, and novels, including the 2002 publication, *Drowning in Secret*, which is set in Michigan. His essays appeared in Volumes II and III of the *Voices of Michigan* anthology.

I didn't have one reason, I had thousands. He brought out the worst in me. Though he was only 11 and I already fourteen and in high school, he was a constant reminder of my fears and insecurities. He was a bold daredevil who straddled fences and sneaked past the boundaries of our cul–de–sac because somehow he knew that what our parents told us not to do held a promise of excitement unattainable elsewhere.

I, on the other hand, still felt guilty for years ago running into the forbidden street one time to retrieve a superball I'd bounced too high.

"You don't want to go alone."

My mother was right. Only one emotion strummed harder against my chest than the frustration of trying to corral my younger brother when I was left in charge: loneliness. Insecure about starting high school, I had emotionally withdrawn that year and become exactly how Ray always saw me.

He'd tell me, "You're so shy that you're never any fun."

I understood what he meant, so I worked on being a nice guy.

"You're too nice," he scowled. "Yuck. Nobody likes that. When are you going to act like a normal person?"

I appreciated fully the spirit in which he shared his observations. I was nauseatingly polite. My peers may have respected me, but they had no interest in being my friend. Adults patted me on the shoulder proudly, then just as quickly forgot I was standing beside them. Unlike mine, their lives had substance.

"Okay, Mom, I'll take Ray with me."

I could only imagine the kind of trouble he would cause me this time. Every outing together was a disaster, and I was the only casualty.

I found Ray in our bedroom. "Come on, let's go to church."

"Gah! You're fourteen–years–old. What do you wanna go to church for?"

"You have to go to church every week. It's an obligation."

"Who else our age goes to church without their parents?"

It had been less than a year since my confirmation. I remembered what I'd committed to. "What's wrong with going?"

"For one, we might not end up havin' to go at all. Sometimes Mom and Dad sleep in on Sundays, you know."

I remembered. When we were little, we used to play quietly in our bedroom on Sundays watching the clock excitedly on those rare mornings our parents slept till it was too late to make it to the last mass.

"For another, it's the reason you don't have no friends. You're weird. Quit doin' stuff like this."

"Mom said we have to go."

He knew I was lying.

"Besides, we'll get it over with. We'll go to the 6 o'clock mass and be home before 7:30."

After a few more protests and some exaggerated sighs, Ray bundled up and we headed out the back door.

"Take care of your little brother." These words from my mother were always the last command whenever Ray and I left the house together. They echoed through my head most loudly whenever Ray gave me a hard time.

"Hey, let's skip church and go to Tri–Daly's. We'll buy some candy," Ray suggested as he hopped on my handlebars.

The mere thought of deceiving our parents flushed me with guilt. "We can't do that. It's the opposite direction. What if Mom's watching us leave?"

"All right, then Jack in the Box. It's down that way. We can get tacos and chocolate shakes."

"Don't have any money." That was true. "So we either ride around in the cold or sit in a warm church for an hour. I vote for church."

"You're drivin'," he relented, and I took us to St. Linus for the 6:00 mass.

I remember only one thing about that service. There was a guy, probably seventeen or eighteen , who came in and sat alone in front of us. How odd, I thought. What's a guy his age doing here alone on Saturday night? I didn't remember seeing anybody his age go to church, especially alone.

While staring at the back of his head, I imagined how homely and nerdy he must look. No date, no friends, nothing to do but go to church on a Saturday night.

"Oh, God," I uttered aloud. This must be what Ray thought of me. All the mean–spirited thoughts I was having about this guy, Ray had said to me not an hour earlier.

It was a shock. I always prided myself in being a good person. I never saw myself through Ray's eyes before.

When we got to the "Peace be with you" handshakes, I was afraid for the guy in front of us to turn around. I didn't want to see how I must look to my little brother.

Ray and I mumbled a "Peace be with you," then jabbed each other so we didn't feel so stupid.

The nerd in front of us turned. He looked normal—no chubby cheeks, no sagging glasses squeezing his nose so he talked like a mouse. Instead, he, a handsome, masculine guy, looked at us and beamed. "Hey, guys, peace be with you." He shook our hands, surprising me with his firm, enthusiastic grip. After he turned back around, Ray and I looked at each other and grinned.

I couldn't read Ray's expression. Maybe he was laughing at the guy the same way he laughed at me, but I don't think so. I sensed a mutual understanding between us.

In that moment, I wasn't ashamed of being me. I didn't feel alone and confused about why others weren't more impressed by my efforts to be a good person. If I could end up like him, I thought looking at the guy in front of me, that'd be all right. His was about the happiest expression I ever saw. And he was in church, alone, on Saturday night.

If I was all right just as I was, I wondered, why couldn't I believe the same of my own brother? So we were different. Until then, I always contrasted us. It was an easy habit; we had almost nothing in common. In every comparison, I found fault with one of us. When Ray didn't do his homework, I thought he was lazy.

When I saw Ray playing with his legion of friends as I roller skated around the court alone, I thought I was a loser.

Through my comparisons with Ray, I judged the world. Black/white, good/bad. I could always find fault when I noted how one of us was less than the other.

I looked at Ray beside me. Instead of reprimanding him for scratching a design into the wooden pew with the zipper of his coat, I studied his profile. First I noticed his small nose and felt self–conscious that mine was too big. But then I noted that his cheeks were full like mine. We had the same little curve above our earlobe. I listened to him breathe. He was wheezing softly. We had both inherited asthma from our mother.

My dad would always say, "You may fight now, but one day you'll be the most important people to each other. You two have the same blood. You match each other more than you'll ever match your mom or me."

When he said that, the thought repulsed us both. Now I had a glimpse of what Dad meant, and it didn't seem so bad.

Mass went on longer than either of us wanted. By the time we left the church, snow was falling. A slick layer of white covered the sidewalk, making the ride home treacherous.

"We better walk the bike home," I warned. I was the big brother. I had to be responsible.

"Don't be such a wuss," Ray demanded. "Just drive me home. Have a little fun for once."

He barely waited until I had the bike balanced before he hopped onto the handlebars. Normally I would have objected. But I realized I never tried anything Ray's way. I was too busy judging him. Maybe he was right. I could stand a little fun.

I was cautious at first, but pedaling so slowly made the ride more precarious. So I sped up. With Ray's weight on the front tire, the bike gripped the snow just fine.

I went even faster. He giggled, "Go, go!"

And I raced. The wind was cold. My thighs strained. But I raced. Snowflakes clung to my glasses, then streamed down as water. Even with my obstructed vision, I was unafraid. I stood on the pedals and soared faster, all the way down Hass Road, around the empty intersection, and then along Beech Daly toward home.

"Let's not go home," said Ray. "Turn here, turn here."

Warrington was a long residential street that continued for several blocks. There wasn't a car in sight. So I raced. The back tire flicked snow high into the air. The faster I went, the farther it flung, and the more joyful was Ray's laughter. I never inspired such a response from him before. I was showing my little brother a good time. I pedaled and pedaled. Ray laughed and shouted, "On Dasher, on Dancer . . ." It was like riding through the winter sky.

Then we hit a patch of ice. We didn't see it under the layer of snow, and we hit it full on. The tires slid out from under us. "Ahh," Ray's cry was simultaneously scared and excited. We both landed on the ice about the same time and slid all the way to the curb. The bike skated several yards farther away.

When everything stopped moving, Ray and I were lying side–by–side in the snow, looking up.

"You okay?" I asked.

"Cool. That was so cool!"

We lay there, bundled in the padded winter gear that protected us in our fall. Above us, surrounded by the pitch black winter night, was a street lamp. Moisture on my glasses created a kaleidoscope effect that mesmerized me. I could see flurries of snow passing in front of the light. Caught by different gusts, they swirled around in all directions, yet they all looked the same.

I knew from science class that every snowflake is unique. But that night, lying beside my brother on that empty, snow–covered street, I saw that, from a distance, every flake was like every other. When they landed, they blended together to form one sheet of snow that invited all kinds of adventure.

Ray sat up. "You're not hurt, are you?"

"Not a bit," I smiled.

"See," he told me. "You can have fun. We didn't hurt anybody."

I got up and retrieved my bike. "Look, it bent the rim."

"Just a little. I can help you unbend it."

Together, we gripped the wheel with our gloved hands and pressed at the bend with our boots. It worked. We straightened the tire enough to walk the bike home.

I don't remember what we shared during the rest of the journey, but I recall unquestionably sensing that he was as happy with me as I with him. We talked, not nagging or snapping, just talked.

Until that night, my black and white perspective of the world kept me from understanding what Dad meant when he said Ray's and my blood were the same. Yet it was that very contrast in color that forever united us from the moment we fell in the street and I looked up to see a flurry of white against the pitch of winter sky.

One Desert Night

Mike VanBuren

It's a cool September evening and I'm traveling across the northern Arizona desert with two friends in a black and white Rambler Rebel. We're somewhere near Tuba City on Highway 160 in Navajo Country, hoping to make it to Gunnison, Colorado, by dawn.

The sky is solid black and the high–beam headlamps have trouble slicing through the thick darkness. We've been driving for several days in a giant sweep through the West. We're anxious now to get back to the Rocky Mountains and rest a few days before returning to Michigan. Nothing short of flat tires and police roadblocks will impede our progress as we zoom through the rural countryside toward the Four Corners region. Nothing, that is, except pretty young maidens in need of rescue by three college–age drifters in wrinkled T–shirts and faded jeans.

> **Mike VanBuren** has long enjoyed exploring America's highways and back roads— especially when he discovers new people and places to write about. He is working on a collection of such stories based on more than 30 years of travel. Mike lives with his family in Kalamazoo County's rural Richland Township.

The two women look nervous and forlorn standing against the sandy landscape as we whiz by at sixty miles per hour. We barely see them in the blackness. We screech to the side of the road for a U–turn and race back to see if our eyes are playing tricks on us. No tricks. They're here, leaning against a light blue Chevy Impala, buried to its axles in the loose, granular soil of the Indian reservation.

At first, the young women seem suspicious of our motives, but look us over carefully and decide that we're probably harmless. "I swerved to miss a jackrabbit," one of the women says sheepishly, climbing back into the driver's seat. She spins the sunken tires while the rest of us push and shove with all our might, trying to rock the vehicle into motion and return it to the hard pavement a few feet away. But the wheels just drop deeper into the sand and we fall exhausted to the ground.

We learn that the women are returning home to Denver after a vacation in California and that they've been stranded beside this rural road for the past two hours. They welcome our company, they say, but they'd like it better if we could get their car back onto the two–lane blacktop. We try several more times, but fail to move the car more than a few laborious inches. Occasionally another vehicle passes by, but few even slow down to acknowledge our predicament.

A drunken man with taut, leathery skin eventually arrives in a dull and battered pickup truck to survey the situation. He doesn't offer any help, but mumbles that he'll send someone from town and drives off in a cloud of dust. We wait for another hour before deciding that the man didn't keep his promise.

"It's nice of you to wait with us," the women say. "It was kind of scary out here by ourselves."

We raise our eyebrows and smile at the heroic service we're providing, then try a few more times to push the car from the sand. We're about to give up and go in search of a tow truck when an antique Oldsmobile approaches from the distance. It swerves off the road and shines its bright lights into our eyes. Three dark shadows emerge from the car—two Navajo men and a large elderly woman who is dressed in a colorful skirt, and adorned with silver and turquoise jewelry. They confer for a moment in their own language, then go about their work. We watch as they wade into the desert sand and uproot dry sagebrush from the parched ground. The old woman seems to be in charge of the operation, yanking out brown plants and carrying them by the armload to the immobile car. She drops to her knees and packs the sagebrush as tightly as she can under the drive wheels, and lays it along an imaginary track where the car will need to travel. Then one of the men climbs behind the wheel, starts the car and drives it easily onto the roadway. They've done in minutes what we couldn't do in hours.

The old woman offers a satisfied nod and brushes her hands together to remove the sand that clings to her rough skin. The mysterious rescuers still haven't spoken directly to us, but we thank them profusely and offer to pay them for their trouble. All three just shake their heads from side–to–side and wave us away. They climb back into the Oldsmobile and disappear into the dark night as quickly as they arrived. We stand staring at each other for a few moments, uncertain about what we have witnessed and clearly ignorant about the ways of the desert.

There's not much to do now, except bid the young ladies farewell and continue on to Colorado. They thank us for what little help we provided and we tell them that we might look them up in Denver.

"That would be nice," they say, waving and driving off to the northeast.

Later, my traveling companions have fallen asleep and I'm behind the wheel, listening to a distant country music station on the radio. The world seems empty and I see no other cars for miles in either direction. A lone coyote crosses the highway at the far edge of the headlight beams and I press lightly on the brakes. Millions of bright stars have emerged and are suspended high in the heavens, so I lean closer to the windshield to gaze at the sparkling sky.

I think about the anonymous Indian woman and the two weathered men who reached into the lives of five young travelers with unheralded kindness and generosity. They came and went like humble apparitions, speaking only to each other and not revealing their identities. I'm beginning to wonder if they were truly flesh and blood.

The thought brings a cool chill to my spine, but the shiver is quickly replaced by a peaceful calm that floods my soul. I breathe deeply and tap my fingers on the plastic–coated steering wheel. Life can be good. Especially when you meet unexpected angels in the dark Navajo night.

Onus

Addison Thomas

A patriotic mood had swept the nation as we headed into the second year of World War II. Victory gardens and the conservation of items critical to the war effort were expected of everyone. Rationing went into effect and many foodstuffs were scarce.

We lived on a small farm twenty miles west of Detroit. My parents had always raised a vegetable garden and cared for a dozen fruit trees. A large portion of this bounty found its way into Ball and Mason jars. The excess was given to those families still suffering from the debilitating effects of the depression.

With the advent of the war, Dad decided to increase the size of the garden, add a couple dozen chickens and buy a cow. Diamond, the cow, was a good producer, so good that a cream separator and hand butter churn were purchased. Now we could provide ourselves with all the butter we needed and gallons of buttermilk. It soon became apparent we had too much milk for one family and would have a surplus of butter, not to mention the gallons of whey that we didn't consume. The dilemma was solved with the purchase of a piglet. Mixing the whey with dry feed and table scraps in a fifty–five gallon drum and letting it ferment provided gourmet slop for our hog.

As the youngest, I was always afraid of not being included. Whenever our family discussed an adventure, a trip, or a picnic, I

Addison Thomas has lived in Michigan, Georgia, Colorado, Florida and currently lives in Chattanooga, TN. He is a graduate of Albion College and did graduate work at the University of Michigan. He has had numerous articles, letters and several short stories published, and has completed three novels, *Confluence, Implosion* and *Presage*.

would ask as the conversation drew to a close, "Me too?" worried that I would be left out.

Dad decided the care of our animals should be shouldered and divided among his children. He assigned my brother, Mel, the care and milking of the cow and slopping of the hog. My sister Rosemary assumed the responsibility of the chickens. I waited for Mom or Dad to add a specific chore for me. It didn't happen. So when "Me Too" asked his parents what his chore was, I was instructed to "help your brother and sister."

Because my sister was the oldest, she had first call on me. I didn't like helping my sister. I didn't like taking orders from a girl. Even though the daily routine was the same, Rosemary delighted in barking out orders each day. First, she would send me to the barn to get a bucket of laying mash to refill the feeder while she collected the eggs. Taking her time inspecting each egg, she would string her chore out until I returned. "Tom, have you given fresh water to the chickens?" she would question.

Scurrying off, I would work the pitcher pump lever until my bucket was full. Returning to the chicken coop, sloshing a good portion of the water on the ground, I would fill the galvanized waterer.

Rosemary had it timed perfectly; she would pluck the last egg from the nest as I finished. Then she would announce, "Well, we're all done; it doesn't take long when we work together."

I wondered about my sister. I wondered what she meant by "working together." Rosemary realized I was leery of both her words and motive, trying to assuage my feelings with, "Tom, you know you're too short to reach into the nests. When you get tall enough, I'll trade with you. I'll feed and water and you can gather the eggs."

I listened without replying.

She continued, "You know these chickens get angry and peck your hands when they're on the nest. Sometimes they fly out of the nest into your face."

I wasn't sure what she was driving at, but I knew how frightened I had been when our Plymouth Rock rooster flared his feathers, extended his wings and charged, attacking me with spurs and beak. It was a horrifying experience. I had heard the older kids at school talk about having the chicken pox, how sick they were, being driven to madness wanting to scratch the blisters. Another youngster had told that he knew a kid who had died from the disease. Was this how you caught chicken pox, from pecking chickens? If it was, I didn't want anything to do with gathering the eggs.

"Rosemary, I'll just keep on getting the feed and water. You can collect the eggs."

"Okay," she replied.

My helping Rosemary first worked out fine for Mel. He would stay busy slopping the hog, then priming the well pump and filling the eight–foot watering trough for Diamond, the Jersey cow. Completing these chores, he would add grain to the feeding trough. Last, he would lead Diamond into the barn, attaching a rope to her halter to hold her in the stall. He was ready to milk. I was supposed to be at the barn to hold the cow's tail.

Holding the tail became more complicated in April and May as the number of flies multiplied. Deprived of her primary weapon against fly bites, Diamond would reach back and kick her hind leg, landing straw and bedding in the milk or occasionally landing a direct hit with her hoof in the milk bucket. Mel would send me with the soiled milk to the fifty–five gallon drum. The pig would enjoy it. I'd rinse the bucket out and he would finish milking.

Restricting the use of Diamond's tail was no longer enough. We decided to tie her leg. Now I would hold two ropes. The first few days I was frightened, knowing that I could get kicked. But I grew into the job and overcame my fear.

The summer was ending and I was really tired of my sister getting all the credit for taking care of the chickens. Having had enough of Rosemary's bossiness, I begged my parents for a rabbit as a birthday present. That was all I wanted for my eighth birthday.

"Your father and I aren't sure you're old enough to care for a rabbit each day," Mom answered.

"I promise I'll take good care of it, rain or shine."

Mother convinced Dad it would be good training for me. On my birthday near the end of August, I received Snowball. I was thrilled.

Everett Smith, our neighbor, had been mowing a berry thicket when he cut into a rabbit warren. Jumping from the mowing machine, he chased down and caught a young rabbit. Late that afternoon he walked to our house and gave it to me. I now had a pair of rabbits, Snowball and Buck.

Every day I tended to my rabbits, feeding them grass clippings in the summer, alfalfa hay in the fall and winter, plus all the kitchen vegetable scraps. I loved my rabbits and I loved taking care of them.

One day Mom remarked, "Thomas, your Dad and I are so proud of you and the way you take care of your rabbits."

I beamed with pride, confident I wouldn't betray my parent's trust in me.

The Wednesday after Labor Day we returned to school. Dad hired a neighbor to milk in the mornings.

Our grade school, located on the same dirt road as our home, was a mile away. It was a two–room school. The first four grades were in one room and the fifth through eighth in the other room. We had two teachers, twins, the Butcher sisters.

Dad would drop us off at school each morning on his way to work. After school we walked the mile home with the eight or ten other kids who lived on the same road. Arriving home, we would change into old clothes and do our chores, finishing early enough to listen to the fifteen–minute serial shows on the radio.

The barn and out buildings were all located in the same area, a good distance from our home. This never was a problem except in stormy weather or if we played too long and darkness caught us before doing our chores.

Before Halloween, I became the owner of five baby rabbits. My rabbit chores soon quadrupled.

Christmas passed and the moderate temperatures of the annual mid–January thaw vanished. Cold nights left our dirt road with deep frozen mud ruts. A howling blizzard blew in from the northwest, dumping two feet of snow overnight. The temperature plunged and the bone chilling winds increased. Our home creaked and popped that night.

Dad was up early the morning after the storm, getting his Nash out of the garage, leaving the engine running, allowing it to warm up while he shoveled snow from the walk. Mother had our breakfast of oatmeal and hot chocolate ready and our lunches packed by the time we came downstairs, warning us to keep bundled up in the wind and cold.

"Mom, will you pick us up after school?" I asked.

Before Mother could answer, Dad chimed in, "If the drifts are deep, I don't think your mother will be able to get down the road."

Mom added, "If it is pretty and sunny this afternoon and if the wind lays, you children can walk home. It will be good for you to get the exercise and fresh air. If not, I'll call the Feagans; maybe they can pick you up with their truck. Just remember to stay bundled up."

"Come on, gang, let's go," Dad shouted, heading out the kitchen door.

The frigid air hit hard as I started down the walk. The moisture in my breath froze into white crystals. Dad yelled, "Get behind the car and push. When we get rolling, jump in!"

The exhaust mixed with the fresh air smelled sweet. Straining with all of our might, the tires spinning, the car began rolling forward. "Come on, jump in! I don't want to stop," Dad called.

151

We piled in, Dad gunned the engine. The car bolted onto the county road, falling into the deep ruts with a thud, jostling Rosemary and me to one side of the back seat. The spinning tires whined, spraying snow, dirt and gravel behind us. We reached the top of Porter's Hill and headed down toward the bridge, crossing the creek. We were rolling along, the Nash blasting through the many drifts and spraying the snow. All too soon, Dad stopped in front of school. "A kiss for luck," he demanded. Mel and I reluctantly obliged, pecking him on the cheek, hoping none of the other boys would see us kissing a man.

School was a bust that day. One half of the kids never made it. The furnace blower, which forced hot air into the registers, was on the fritz. The classrooms were bone chilling cold. To conserve heat, Miss Butcher closed all the vents except in one room, then she moved all the students into that room. We spent the morning studying geography, then reading from our primers aloud. The balance of the morning Miss Butcher spent reading from a biography of Abraham Lincoln.

At lunchtime, we were allowed to go outdoors. Soon a game of fox and geese got underway, followed by the usual snowball fights and face washings. Some of the girls made snow angels in the untracked snow. The lack of wind and the sun's reflection off the snow made the day feel warm.

At three o'clock, Miss Butcher dismissed us, a half–hour early. No one was there to pick us up. Seven of us began the hike home. The sun was much lower in the west, the temperature had dropped, and the wind had gained strength. The first half–mile took twice as long as it would on a clear road. My sister and her friend were out in front. Mel and his two buddies were five minutes ahead of Richie Porter and me. By the time we reached the top of Porter's Hill, Rosemary was heading up the driveway to our house with my brother close behind. I had a quarter of a mile to go when Richie dropped off at his house.

The last stretch would be over or through the deep drifts along an open field. I hoped between the wind and the warm sun of the early afternoon the drifts had crusted enough to hold up my forty–five pounds. I trudged on, but every hundred steps or so I ended up floundering in the deep drifts or sinking into the snow. Snow seeped into my gloves and over the top of my boots. They became wet, my hands and feet were freezing. Struggling out, I tried following my brother's steps, but with little success. The sun fell hidden behind a cloudbank in the west. The temperature dropped ten degrees in minutes. I tried following the car track but the frozen ruts, full of ice and packed snow, proved to be even more difficult. Returning to the crusted snow, I eased along, managing to get home a half an hour after my brother and sister. My hands were freezing cold, my feet wet, I was shivering and exhausted.

Rosemary and Mel had already left for the barn. I was upset that they hadn't waited.

Mother called from the basement, "Thomas, is that you?"

"Yes, Mom,"

"I'm glad you're home."

I found some dry mittens. Pulling my old winter jacket on, I opened the kitchen door to leave. There, halfway back to the house, were my brother and sister. I didn't want to go to the barn alone with darkness falling. Floundering in the snowdrifts on the way home from school had been enough for one day. My rabbits would be okay till tomorrow, I had given them plenty of food the night before.

I wrenched my galoshes off and slipped out of my coat and shoes. I hoped Mom had heard me open the door and thought that I had gone to the barn to do my chores. Upstairs in my bedroom I played with my carom board while I listened to *The Shadow* and then *Jack Armstrong*. I heard Dad's car turning into the driveway. Twenty minutes later, Mom called us to dinner.

I scooted past the others to my place at the table. Mother returned thanks and we sat down. There was something missing. I had neither plate nor silverware. Was Rosemary playing games with me or had she failed to set the table correctly? My family began passing the food and helping themselves. It was one of my favorite dinners, potato pancakes and a ring of bologna. I slid my chair back from the table to get a plate when my mother asked, "Thomas, where are you going?"

"To get a plate and some silverware."

"First, young man, answer one question."

"Sure, Mom."

"Did you feed your rabbits this afternoon?"

I stuttered and stammered, finally allowing a barely audible "no" to escape from the lips of my hung head.

"Thomas, if the rabbits don't get to eat today, then you, too, can go without supper."

I sat down, hurt, biting my lip to keep from crying. I dropped my head lower, and then glanced up to see my father's eyes fixed on me.

A silence engulfed the dinner for what seemed an eternity. My brother and sister wolfed down their potato pancakes.

After five minutes my mother spoke. "Now, if you go and feed the rabbits, I'll fix you some hot potato pancakes."

I quickly dressed, finding a flashlight and drawing half a bucket of hot water, dreading the trip to the rabbit hutch in the dark. Leaving the house without any encouragement, I plodded the path beaten down by my brother and sister. I choked back my tears, I felt like an outsider in my own family. Maybe it was true that I was adopted like Rosemary said. Maybe I didn't count. I thought about staying in the barn all night. Let them worry about me and how they had treated me.

The wind had settled, the light from a quarter moon reflected off the snow, illuminating the night, and the cold, crisp air felt good after the embarrassment I had suffered at the dinner table. Even the walk was easy, following Mel and Rosemary's footsteps.

I reached the rabbit hutch. Snowball, Buck and their offspring were delighted to see me. They were famished and devoured the potato peelings. I knocked the ice from their frozen water dishes, filling them with luke warm water. They had needed food and water, I had been wrong to shirk my daily chore. Twenty minutes later I returned to the house, flashlight in one hand and empty bucket in the other.

Dad, Rosemary and Mel had left the kitchen. By the time I pulled off my winter garments, Mother had the potato pancakes ready. She plucked some bologna from the pot of boiling water and served me a heaping plate. Reaching for the catsup bottle, I poured a sizable portion on my pancakes. I ate alone while mother fussed at the kitchen sink. Halfway through my dinner, she sat down next to me.

"Thomas, you've grown today, you've learned that responsibility is more than a promise. It is carrying out your pledge, fulfilling your promise, performing the task."

"Yes, Mother," I choked back the urge to break down and cry. I looked up at her. "I feel better knowing my rabbits have food and water."

"And I feel better knowing you had a plate of hot potato pancakes," Mom threw her arms around me and kissed me on the cheek. "I'm proud of you, Thomas."

I knew all was right and that I wasn't adopted. I looked up at Mom; she wore a warm, loving smile.

Like the rabbits, I was famished and ravaged the pancakes and bologna, smothering them in even more catsup. As I finished eating, Dad came into the kitchen and placed his hand on my shoulder. "Son, your mother has taught you a lesson tonight, a lesson you will remember the rest of your life."

Traverse City Two Step

Imogene A. Callander

"You!" It was a full–blown lunatic shriek.

"Stop right there!" The elderly male voice echoed thin and ringing. I stopped and turned. The shouter, in full voice, strode stiff–legged around the back of a sleek little gray Peugeot. He was screaming at me across seventy–five feet of sun–baked and littered cement.

Less than one hour ago I had driven this huge truck into this parking lot and finally found an empty parking place. Then, braced by the steering wheel, I lifted my bony bottom up off the driver's seat straining to see over the dashboard. Brushing aside a strand of white hair, I peered through my bifocals down the vast gray expanse of bug–spattered hood. Oh so gently I touched the accelerator. The truck crept forward. I pressed the brake pedal and shifted into reverse. Maneuvering forward and back, inch by inch, I finally wrestled the ¾ ton Ford Pickup exactly between the yellow lines and turned the motor off.

Imogene A. Callander has been writing since the 1960's including ten years as creative director of a small Michigan Advertising agency. She established Straw Hat Publishing in 1996 and published a biography of her family, a Trade Paperback, and her feature–length film script, *Blindfold,* is in the hands of film companies and producers.

I have borrowed this wonderful truck several times this summer from my neighbor and handyman, George. At the moment, my Lincoln is in the shop for servicing.

A widow these past four years, seventy years old, I still grieve for my Alvin. The year after he died, I started a little investment firm on my dining room table. In addition, I have a small office here in my summer cottage on Lake Michigan. My four grandchildren love the water and the Bay almost as much as I do. Every summer the kids trickle "Up North," tooling up I–75 or 31 South with sleeping bags and swimsuits, dragging a little sailboat. We climb the sand dunes, ride our bikes out Old Mission to picnic at the Lighthouse, and sail in the bay.

"Don't try to leave! I've got your License Number!" Less than an hour ago, before turning off the motor, I had carefully pressed the brake pedal one last time. I was sure that the enormous front bumper was not touching the dainty bumper of the car facing me. It was a tiny, gray, two–seater Peugeot with delicate red striping along the edges of the windows and fenders. The car was so new the factory paper was still glued to the side window. Congratulating myself on my parking expertise, gathering my brown Spanish Leather purse and my wallet, I hurried into the bank hugging a bulging file folder of customer accounts and jangling the ring of brass truck keys.

George and his wife Mary vacation with this truck, pulling a big trailer. Perhaps you've seen the two of them traveling up and down I–75, their bicycles secured on a double bike rack bolted to the front bumper. In fact, just yesterday George had repaired that rack and replaced the two long steel bolts.

Walking out of the bank building forty–five minutes later, buoyantly happy after a very successful transaction, I noticed that even though the parking lot was now almost empty the Peugeot remained snuggled up to the big truck's grill. It was like a newborn piglet suckling at its massive mother's breast. Smiling at the cleverness of my metaphor, fumbling in my purse for the ring of keys, I had not noticed the small elderly man striding away from the little car. He stormed across the lot in my direction, his leather heels striking the blacktop smartly. Neatly dressed, about seventy, with carefully combed white hair and rimless glasses, he was enraged and SHOUTING.

"So!" He yelled. "You're the one!"

Not sure to whom he was shouting, and not wanting to embarrass whomever he was shouting at, I blithely slid the key in the driver's side door and turned the lock.

"Oh, no, you don't!"

Stomping with outrage, the man marched directly at me, stopping only about five feet away.

"Good afternoon," I chirped, secure in the knowledge that he couldn't possibly be angry at my lovely self.

"Never mind good afternoon. You just come and look at what you've done to my car!"

Taken aback by the ferocity of his attack, not sure what he was talking about, I stood with both feet flat on the blacktop, thumb and finger still on the key in the lock.

"That's a brand new car," he bellowed. "Waited three months for delivery. It's the first new one I've had in ten years. Drove all over the damn state looking at cars. Had to do it all by myself. Wife died last year. Not that she was much help with cars anyway. Never took care of her own...."

Tolerance of criticism is not one of my virtues. Controlling my resentment of his abusive tone of voice, I tried to interrupt to ask what was the matter with his car? Obviously delighting in his tantrum, he was in no mood to listen to sweet reason. He was blocking my view of the gray coupe, and I was not about to brush past to look. I tucked my hands into my pockets, propped one shoulder against the truck door and willed myself to drift into calm speculation.

"...do you know how much..." he sputtered.

How long had he been working up this head of steam waiting for the truck's driver to return? My business in the bank has taken more than half an hour, so he'd had at least twenty minutes to seethe.

"....what's the matter with people these days? They get a big truck...."

Watching his livid face and listening to his words, I knew that he had been rehearsing this speech for months, long before

159

this interlude in a parking lot. Whatever had been done to his car he considered to be the last straw of repeated insulting attacks on his very person. This dapper little man reminded me of our old French poodle. Peppie employed the enormity of his anger, and the volume of his bluster to compensate for his small size.

"...there's no respect for property..."

Bored, glancing around, I half expected a crowd to have gathered by now. But we, this French–poodle–of–a–man and I, were still alone in the almost empty lot. Opening my mouth and inhaling about to say something like, "If you'll kindly..." drove Peppie deeper into his temper tantrum. His tone of voice became, if possible, more shrill, his face even redder. I wondered if he might have a heart attack right there beside his new Peugeot.

"...doesn't anyone...?"

Still clutching the file folder under my arm, I reached down into my purse to find a Kleenex. Alarmed, Peppie stopped in mid–syllable.

"...wh!!?..." his eyes widened with terror as he watched my hand disappear inside my purse.

"What have you got there?" He obviously thought I was reaching for a weapon! Dear God! In what kind of a dreadful world did this pitiful man live? Did all the old gals carry guns in their Guccis?"

Cheered by my own irreverence and flinging a withering glance in his direction, I attended to my nose and stuffed the Kleenex in my pocket. His eyes now shifting nervously from my purse to my face, the man took a deep breath and resumed his tirade...

"All my life..."

Three young boys from the nearby campground, riding skateboards, drifted across the parking lot, their ten–year–old chatter silenced by the tension between the old man and me. Their baseball caps were worn backward, the peaks shading the backs of their necks. The three wore T–shirts and enormous cotton shorts billowing below their knees. Sporting Michael Jordan

high–top Nikes, shoelaces dangling, they decided to hang out and watch the action. The boys began rolling back and forth on the pebble–strewn blacktop behind the Peugeot. Making little
pivots on the rear two wheels then flipping the skateboard—wheels still spinning, up into the air and catching them, they listened. Peppie scornfully chose to ignore the lads.

Somehow mesmerized by this poor old soul, I tried to remember the sequence of expressions on his face and his body language from the moment when he first saw me. Astounded, I realized that the instant he discovered that the driver of the truck was a woman propelled some grateful impetus to his wrath. He would not have had the courage to address a man in these tones. He felt safe, yes, entitled to verbally attack a woman. My anger gave me courage to brush past him and demand to see what had happened to his car.

There it was! The truck's bug encrusted grill loomed above the glistening hood of the tiny car. The bottom edge of the huge bumper just met the upper edge of Peppie's dainty little bumper. The bottom two of the four shiny new bolts George had installed yesterday to secure the bike rack had slid over the sports coupe's bumper, each bolt displaced an inch of black plastic trim.

"Look what you've done! The poor old man shouted in my left ear. "Just Look!"

What in the hell was all the fuss about?

"I'm sorry." My murmured apology was not as fervent as I hoped. It was diluted by relief that there was so little damage.

Peppie, hot on my heels, shouted, "out of the way, " as he rushed past me, trotted around the back of his car and climbed in.

"You! Stay right there!" he ordered through the open door as he started the engine and put the gearshift in reverse. The old man's foot touched the accelerator with the same timid tenderness as one would use to withdraw a splinter from a baby's wee toe. The bumpers separated. Peppie stopped the Peugeot's engine. Hopping with anxiety he raced to look.

My intense relief to see only some scratches on the plastic and a minute crease in the chrome almost matched his shocked disappointment. However, if he felt even an instant of chagrin, Peppie suppressed it immediately with another surge of bluster.

"So! What are you gonna do?" Shrill. Demanding.

"What do you want?" I asked happy to at last take the initiative.

"What are you gonna do?" He squawked.

"Do you want me to call the police?" I kind of liked that idea. But then the policeman might be annoyed with me for bothering them on such a trivial matter, and I had endured about as much abuse as I could for one day.

"No police!" snarled Peppie. The three skateboarders had drifted some distance away. At the suggestion of police, they swooped back and made little lateral patterns parallel to our two vehicles. None of the three had acknowledged the presence of either the old man or me, only exchanging quiet, one–word signals and triangular secret glances form time to time.

"As a matter of fact..." Peppie resumed the tempo and meter of his castigation as if there had been no pause.

"...you..."

"Money? Do you want money?" I snarled.

"What?" he yelped, feigning bewilderment, touching with his forefinger the control of the tiny pink hearing aid in his right ear.

Ah Ha! Finally! I had struck a chord.

"How much money do you want?"

The smallest of the skate–boarders lost his balance and pitched forward onto the blacktop scraping hunks of skin from elbows and knees. Without a sound he leapt up, retrieved the still moving board and stepped back onto it, examining his wound as he rolled past. Peppie's eyes followed the lad unseeing. He seemed to have been struck speechless by my seizing the moment with those magic words.

"How about..." trying to remember how much cash I had..." twenty–five dollars?

Loath to yield the battleground, still feverish to punish me and the world, he had no idea what to answer. To give him time to think I fished around in the depths of my purse (Peppie watched rolling his eyes in apprehension) and found my ring of keys. I unlocked and swung the driver's door open. Then, with measured dignity and drama, I dug back into my purse and withdrew my wallet. Reaching inside the truck with deliberation, I carefully placed on the driver's seat: my purse, the bulging file folder and the truck's ring of keys.

Wallet in hand, positive that I had almost a hundred dollars when I left home; I found only three twenties. Had I lost forty dollars? Although Peppie's hot eyes were on me expectantly, and the three young skate boarders had moved closer, curiosity conquering caution, my Scottish inclination was, before anything else, to account for those dollars. Gasoline! Of course. And the Birthday gift book. OK. I fingered the three twenties in consternation. I'd offered twenty–five dollars and he seemed receptive. The planned "out to dinner with the birthday girl" would cost close to forty dollars.

Raising my calculating eyes, I challenged Peppie.

"I'll give you twenty."

"You said twenty–five!" he whined, his eyes hot on my wallet.

"I need the rest of this money to take my daughter–in–law..." I heard myself explaining, reasoning, with this wretched little twerp. Guilty of scratching his bumper? Yes. I had suffered enough for that already this afternoon. Twenty dollars was enough money to bribe him out of my life. I pulled the twenty out of my wallet. Folding the fairly stiff bill lengthwise, then placing it between the tips of my index and middle finger, I extended my arm. I stalked toward him, arm outstretched, the twenty–dollar bill projecting like a knife blade from my fist.

"Take it or leave it."

Reluctant to give up the battlefield, uncertain if his victory was resounding enough, the old man watched the smallest of the boys mop at his bleeding knees with the hem of his huge T–shirt. I shuffled my feet and feigned turning away but left my fist with the bill between my fingers still extended toward him. "I'm waiting…"

In one swift spider–like movement he scuttled forward and snatched the twenty. Turning back to the open door of the Peugeot, he jumped in, started the motor and backed away. The little car's contoured door swung wide open then slammed shut, as he jerked the sleek little car around sprinting out of the parking lot toward the street. He pulled out onto Munson Avenue and disappeared in the traffic headed west. Our audience of three impassively watched him go, then turned their respective eyes to me to see my reaction.

My ego demanded that I make some last defiant gesture toward this whole humiliating episode. Probably I wanted to show the watching boys that I was entitled to the last word. I strode back to the truck's open door. My outrage was blemished by twinges of conscience. Still! I flung the wallet, symbol of my guilt, inside. Then with a grimace of sweet revenge, I mashed down the lock switch and with a mighty heave slammed the door shut.

There in the last moment just before the huge gray door swung completely closed, in that micro–second just before the final click of the mighty door lock, there, in the midst of my spiteful moment of triumph, I caught sight of something. Innocently laying on the gray upholstery of the driver's seat was my wallet, my purse, the bulging file folder, and the undeniable brass glitter of the truck's ring of keys.

Ships in the Night

Theodore J. Gostomski

August 1993: Tobin Harbor, Isle Royale

We sit quietly in the darkness; all of us bundled lightly against the cold aluminum of the fifteen–foot open boat and the even cooler air over Lake Superior. The water is flat, calm; everything is still, and a panorama of stars is spread above our heads. We listen and wait.

Theodore J. Gostomski is an aspiring writer whose work has appeared in *Natural Superior, YourLife in the North Country,* and *Wisconsin Academy Review.* He is also a contributing author to the *Wisconsin Breeding Bird Atlas* (to be published in 2005) and a member of the Lake Superior Writers. He lives in Mt. Pleasant, MI.

There are four of us in this boat. Joe and Ken, members of the banding team who came out two days ago from Houghton; Cory, a Resource Management Ranger for the park and one of three park staff who have come out to help us; and me. I have been here since May watching the loons that are already banded and recording their behaviors through the breeding season for use in a Master's thesis.

We are looking for loons here tonight; hoping to capture and band families so we can test them for toxins and watch them later on to record the behavior of paired males and females. Because there are no readily apparent differences between the sexes in these birds, the bands allow us to watch them tomorrow, even next summer, and know who they are and where they came from. Recapturing them in subsequent years will provide long–term blood and feather samples from known birds. This work began on Isle Royale in 1991, and we are now looking to recapture some birds and even recruit a few more into the sample group.

"Try the tape again," Joe says from the stern of the boat. Ken, who's sitting next to me, lifts a hand–held tape recorder into the air and presses the button. The disembodied wail of a loon pours out of the speaker and into the darkness, echoing off the shore of the nearest island. The call is repeated once before Ken turns it off. Instantly, a loon responds from somewhere off to our left. Cory switches on the light and turns it in the direction of the responding voice. The powerful, hand–held spot light has a coffee can (with both ends removed) taped to it, so the beam is a focused blade slicing through the night. She pans to the left first and then to the right a short distance before the bird appears. It is near the far shore about two–hundred yards away, a small black and white speck in a tunnel of light, its mate a short distance behind it.

I turn the key and the boat motor comes to life. Turning in the direction of the loons, I maneuver us slowly toward them, watching for submerged rocks in the periphery of the light. Cory holds the beam on the loon pair, while Ken, picking up a large salmon net made of black nylon strung to a telescoping aluminum pole, moves past her into the very tip of the boat's bow. Behind me, Joe clears a small space for Ken to set the net down and readies a towel that we will use to cover the loon's head when it comes into the boat; the darkness beneath the towel will calm the bird and protect *us* from its large spear–like bill.

As we draw closer, we can see a pair of chicks just behind the rear loon. The adult nearest to us swims back and forth in front of this trio, covering their escape to the weeds along the shoreline where the chicks take cover while the adult stands guard. Once they are secure, the closest adult turns and swims toward the light. Ken begins to make low hoots as a loon would when saying hello to another, a sign of social intentions and not aggression. With no moon to reveal us, the approaching loon cannot see the boat. It only sees a bright light and hears another loon on its territory, and it is swimming toward this intruder to investigate. With the loon coming in closer, I throttle back to neutral. We are drifting now, the motor still running in case the bird dives and we need to change course and go after it.

Some people have the privilege of observing a loon as it swims in close to their boat or dock, but many see them from shore and usually through binoculars. That perspective, while satisfying, does not give the observer a good sense of the size of this bird. It isn't until a loon is swimming right up alongside you that you realize just how large they are; at almost three feet in length, they are between a Canada Goose and a Mallard in size. If you stretch out your hand and then bend your fingers down into your palm while keeping the palm open, you have the size of a loon's foot. This is a large, beautiful, prehistoric, mythical animal, and at the moment, one is coming right at us, quickly closing the distance between curiosity and surprise. Ken leans over the side, dipping the net in front of the approaching bird, and as the loon enters the circle of aluminum, he scoops it up.

Once a loon is captured, things move quickly for a few moments. In loons, as with humans, moments of "fight or flight" elicit amazing acts of strength and endurance. During one capture session last year, we watched a loon leap from the net as it was being drawn up from the water. It rocketed straight up and over the aluminum boat and then ran over the lake's surface, sounding an alarm to any other loons that might be listening. We were left sitting there, astonished at such an evasive maneuver from a bird that needs a quarter-mile running start to become airborne. Those things don't happen often, though, so once a loon is caught, it is usually flailing wildly in the net, just as this one is now.

Ken lifts the eight-to-ten-pound load up and into the boat. He and Joe then work quickly and carefully to free the bird from the net and take hold of its wings and feet so that it doesn't break any bones or get loose and begin spearing whatever leg or hand presents itself. Once Joe has a hold of the bird, I place the towel over its head, and Joe works the cloth underneath his hands until the loon is calm and quiet in his arms. Cory has been trying to keep the light on all of this and stay out of the way. Now, as Joe returns to his seat in the stern with the loon cradled in his arms, we sit and wait until the crew in a second boat nearby is able to catch this bird's mate and the young loons.

Our goal is to capture and band the entire family, and it's best to catch them all at once. In particular, if we catch the adults, we have to take the chicks as well. Though most chicks are four weeks old or more by mid–August, they are unable to defend themselves adequately and could be lost to predators or submit to the numbing cold of Lake Superior. We have to keep the family together. As it turns out, we are surprised to find that these chicks are less than a week old. Consequently, we will not be able to band them because their legs will continue to grow until they are four weeks of age.

Having the entire family, both boats turn toward shore so we can get out and process the birds. Processing involves the taking of blood and feather samples to use in testing for toxins such as mercury. We also weigh the birds, which gives us a clue to the gender (males are, on average, heavier than females). Finally, we band the birds, giving each a standard aluminum band with an identification number and two–to–three colored, plastic bands so we can observe them during the daylight hours to record individual behaviors. Throughout this process, we monitor the birds' stress level by feeling their feet. Loons use these large appendages to maintain their body temperature. Arteries bring blood down to where it can be cooled by the foot's placement in the water, or it can be warmed by placing the foot under a wing. If the feet begin to heat up, we know the bird is becoming stressed and we will let it go. The overriding concern in this operation is the welfare of the birds, and we will forego the data collection if it looks like anything is going wrong with them.

Fortunately, that is not happening here. Everything is going right. We banded this male a year ago, and we check his bands to be sure they are holding up. The female is unbanded, though, and after taking blood and feather samples from both her and her mate, we band her, weigh them both, and release the entire family. Walking out beside the beached boats, Joe and Ken ease the adults down into the water. They are calm, but begin paddling quickly away from shore and into the darkness. Cory and another park employee who have been holding the chicks during the processing, set the fluffy birds down next, and the two quickly move out and begin calling to their parents who wail in reply. Though we cannot see the birds anymore, the sound of the chicks' squealing and the adult's wails are coming closer together with each call. Finally, the two meet, and silence returns.

As we're gathering up the sampling gear and loading it back into the boats, I look out past the last island, through the mouth of this harbor, and into the open waters of the big lake. A light appears at the edge of my vision, and as I watch, it strings itself out along the horizon until the outline of a ship, a large lake freighter, comes into view, white lights marking the highest parts of the superstructure on deck. In the stillness, I can hear the low hum of its engines as it threads the needle between the northeastern tip of Isle Royale and Passage Island, which lies four miles out. It is an awesome and surreal scene.

As the freighter slips into the darkness, we finish loading our gear into the boats and climb aboard. One person gives a shove on each bow, and we are free of the rocks. Firing the engines, we carefully pick our way past the shoals, between the islands, and out into the main channel. Then, turning toward the southwest, we leave the loons, the freighter, and the silence behind and head home.

Making It

Angie Fenton

I held time in my hands and refused to let it go. Time meant packing bologna sandwiches on Hillbilly bread, tossing long, unruly curls into uneven pigtails, throwing on the nearest pair of shorts and T–shirt, mismatched and unlaundered, grabbing a faded, denim bag and high–tailing it to the forest behind our house in Holly for a solitary day of exploration and adventures. I'd lie on the forest floor, reading about Bunny Brown and his Sister Sue, books from my grandmother's childhood shelf. Venturing further, I would stop to skim the surface of the creek that passed through the trees, plotting how to cross it without drenching my first pair of Nikes. A curling vine, knotted in the boughs of a solid tree would often suffice. Once safely on the other side, I would bide my time building huts and houses for the creatures I knew were waiting for me to construct them elaborate abodes.

Angie Fenton lives in Mount Pleasant with three dogs. She received her B. A. and M. A. both in English, from Central Michigan University. She is a full–time English Instructor at Central Michigan University and also teaches Detroit Northern High School students during the summer for the Upward Bound Summer Academy.

When the sun began to drop and no longer streamed down through the woods, I would slowly make my way back. The end of a day merely meant I would be granted another.

Slowly, however, that changed. With increasing velocity, the end of a day meant a loss of time. Gone were the mornings spent on bent knees alongside my siblings, picking snap peas and zucchini, popping fat strawberries into our mouths and drowning thick tomato worms in plastic buckets. We no longer held hands at the dinner table in prayer because supper was grabbed on the run, stuffed into lunch sacks, eaten in the car. Time became an elusive nothing that faded and bleached, dwindling to mere scraps one would chase but never catch.

Seated on a peeling wooden bench, watching people flow by, a professor once told me I must stop saying I don't have time. "Time is the only thing you do have. Now, what you choose to do with it is your choice." I brushed off his words carelessly, insisting I did not have time; I had deadlines and meetings and projects and appointments.

However, when my father called one weekend and left a message on my answering machine, the professor's words came back. Hard. "Hi Ang. This is your dad. I'm driving up from Tennessee tomorrow to see my father. He may not make it through the week. You might want to go see him, but I understand if you don't have time."

I cried soft tears when I replayed his words, ashamed and embarrassed. I didn't want my father to "understand" that I didn't have time to say goodbye to my grandfather. Because I did.

That early Sunday morning, I held my grandfather's hands in my own, caressing yellow skin as delicate as a butterfly's wing, and leaned down to kiss his cheek—to say goodbye—for the last time. And I hoped and prayed I was not too late.

Remember the Alamo

Bruce Phillip Miller

One summer day in 1944, a young married couple left their house near the Army Air Corps base in San Antonio to do some sightseeing. A camera in hand, they stopped every so often to pose for snapshots. After the film was developed, the young woman wrote a

> **Bruce Phillip Miller** lives in Grand Ledge, Michigan. He hopes to be a writer one day.

sentence or two of description on the backs of some pictures and mailed them home to her mother and little sister in Michigan.

The couple became my parents in 1946, but were newly wed the day they took their walk. He was nineteen and she was twenty—just kids. The pictures, a decidedly romantic cache, ended up in a cardboard box along with hundreds of others, a box that found its way to my house after my mother died, still young and too soon. They record a time my otherwise unsentimental mother called the happiest of her life.

Two years after she died I was invited to a conference in San Antonio. I had the idea of trying to find some of the places identified in my mother's fine clear script on the backs of several snapshots. Before I left for San Antonio, I dug through the box and gathered up a few photographs to take with me.

The conference did not start until noon, so after breakfast I put the photographs in my pocket and headed out to the Riverwalk to look for the place in the first picture–City Hall. The path next to the San Antonio River was the same one they had taken, and walking in their footsteps brought to mind Einstein's description of time as a river that you can step into at any spot along the shore. I found City Hall decorated for Christmas but otherwise identical to the building in the photograph.

There was the same raised brick border where my mother had stood, right arm extended like a hitchhiker. On the back she had written, *"As usual, when I'm not ready to have my picture taken, Wayne snaps it."* I asked a passerby to snap my picture, then walked to the exact spot where my mother had stood. I felt like I had just missed them.

My mother was born in 1924, the fourth of six children of Syrian immigrants who came to the United States to find a better life, and settled in Lansing, Michigan, in a small house just west of the Oldsmobile factory. Ransom Eli Olds inhabited a different world a scant mile east of there. My grandfather worked at the foundry that made the street lamps that still line Lansing's streets. He worked there until he contracted tuberculosis and ended up in the sanatorium on Greenlawn Avenue. My aunt tells stories about visiting him there with my mother, the two of them entertaining him by singing songs from movies they saw at the REO Clubhouse. He died at the TB hospital in 1934 when my mother was nine.

I've read that the differences between rich and poor have always existed, but that the distance between them increased in the Depression. Maybe, but figure this: four years after my grandfather died my grandmother and her six kids moved to a house of their own. A man from her church, a small business owner and Knight of Columbus, arranged a loan for her, despite the fact that she lacked a job, marketable skills, education or collateral. My grandmother was bereft of everything but children; she spoke heavily accented English and did not learn how to write her name until 1943 when she was taught by her daughter so she could endorse the paychecks she earned as a floor sweeper at the Olds plant after it was converted to war production. Until that job they got by because the older children worked and because the county social welfare system, along with a chivalrous Knight of Columbus, looked out for widows with children.

My father's mother was sixteen years old when he was born in Plainview, Texas in 1925. Her Cherokee ancestors had walked the Trail of Tears to Oklahoma. Her grandmother married the first Indian agent in the territory, then renounced her rights to land to which she was entitled as a member of the tribe. As luck would have it, the relinquished land held vast oil reserves, and wells there produce to this day.

My paternal grandfather left his family's farm in Wisconsin to find his fortune in the West. He found what passed for fortune driving a truck in the Texas oil fields and playing fiddle on weekends.

My father described his family as Okies, an appellation attached to those unfortunate souls caught in the Dust Bowl, who tumbled along on narrow roads with all their belongings heaped high on jalopies. I have a picture of him at age six with a big smile on his face, standing in a mud rut near a plank sidewalk in a town full of unpainted shacks. I asked him once if his family had been like the Joads in **The Grapes of Wrath**. He shook his head no and told me about walking out of the movie *Tobacco Road*, embarrassed because the audience was laughing at the way he grew up. His family migrated from Texas to Kansas to Torrington, Wyoming, and shortly after his seventeenth birthday he ran away and joined the army. Not long after that his father died.

The old Spanish governor's mansion in San Antonio sits behind City Hall, and I had several pictures of my parents taken there in the walled-off garden behind the house. The garden was closed for renovation, but when I struck up a conversation with a construction worker and showed him a few pictures of my parents taken inside, he let me in and took my picture at the same spot. I showed him a snapshot of my parents embracing in front of a monument commemorating an event from San Antonio's past. There was no writing on the back and I asked him if he knew where it was taken. He told me the monument was at the Alamo, so I headed there.

My parents would not have met if it had not been for the war. My father enlisted in 1943 and learned to fly at Michigan State College in East Lansing. The training route he flew roughly followed the road that goes from the airport to the town where I have lived since 1978, the place my wife and I raised our family. He'd fly out this far, loop back, land and wait at the hangar while his instructor wrote notes about the flight in a small leather–covered log, something else that landed in the box with all the photographs. One day after training, he went with friends to a U.S.O. dance in Lansing, and that was where he met my mother. He was eighteen and she was nineteen; they had a little money in their pockets, a reasonable certainty that tomorrow would come, and absolutely no idea what it might bring. Despite this, or maybe because of it, they married in March of 1944. He was transferred to San Antonio and she went with him, working in a department store near the Alamo while he finished training as an aviator.

His entire class was washed out after D–day. The army figured it wouldn't need more pilots. They marked time together until he was discharged, then returned to Lansing and lived with my grandmother. I was born in November of 1946 and, for reasons that are lost to memory, they separated in 1948. He reentered the army and she found work as a stenographer for the state of Michigan. The army sent him to Japan. Though estranged, they stayed in touch through letters and photographs. When his assignment ended he was sent to a military base in California.

During a Christmas visit with his family in Wyoming he called my mother, asked her to bring me, come to Torrington, and then go back with him to California. Hurried plans were made; we took a cab to a train in the middle of the night. The train lurched into Chicago at daybreak, abandoning us in a cavernous terminal. Groggy–eyed, we boarded a streamliner that catapulted into the Great Plains, arriving in Cheyenne a day later. There I met my father. He tossed me into the air then rubbed my face against the stubble on his. She was twenty–seven, he was twenty–six, I was four and had no memory of him, only pictures.

After his discharge from the army we left California for Wyoming in a new Buick. His mother had married a widower named Bill Jobe, a wheat farmer who did well enough to have his own airplane, an ancient sputtering craft flown by a cowboy from up the road who had a pilot's license but nothing to fly. In that airplane I got a view of what the family calls "the mile square"– the farm in hot, dry eastern Wyoming. "Not the edge of the earth," my uncle likes to say, "but you can see it from there."

One Sunday afternoon in 1952, Bill Jobe took them for a drive, stopping at a house flanked by wheaty stripes that flung themselves out to Laramie Peak.

"This," he told them, "is yours if you stay."

My parents stared at a possible future. The way my father told it, he pictured a silo brimming with grain, cows lowing in a pasture, a pickup in the drive, and a pony for me. My mother said all she saw was an unpainted shack with no electricity or running water and no neighbors nearby. She begged him to take her back to Michigan. She said he told her not to worry, that the last thing he wanted was to be a farmer. He told me he was crestfallen as the pickup, silo and cows disappeared like Brigadoon into the mist. I don't know which version to believe. Maybe both are true, and while I have regrets galore, growing up in Michigan instead of Wyoming is not one of them. Not even counting the pony.

I wonder sometimes if Bill Jobe was warning them off the place, using the Sunday drive to disabuse them of romantic notions he imagined they had about farm life. *This is yours if you stay. This is what your life will be like. Go east, go east!* I don't know.

Still, if time were a river, and I'd had the power that day in San Antonio to step off the shore and into 1944, I'd have taken them aside and gently suggested that when Bill Jobe made the offer a few years down the road, that they give it a try.

Back in Lansing they bought a lot, built a small house, he started college on the G. I. Bill and she returned to work at the state. He also got a night job at Oldsmobile as a security guard, telling my mother and me over dinner that his experience as a peace officer in Japan impressed the man doing the hiring.

The name "peace officer" conjured up a mental picture of him on the battlefield between opposing lines of battling soldiers, untouched by the fusillade, megaphone in hand, urging the enemy with all–American sincerity to put down their weapons and go home to their families. At dinner I asked him if that was what a peace officer did. Holding his head at an angle that bespoke serious listening, and with a faint smile on his face, he said yes, that was it exactly.

My parents separated for good in 1954. They both said it happened this way: he was late coming home from work and she asked where he had been. He said it was none of her business. She told him to get out, and he did. That was that. More exactly, that was the beginning of the lives we led after that. He moved to Arizona. We moved back with my grandmother.

As a kid I spent part of the summer in Wyoming. The mile square of irrigated wheat now boasted a small herd of Blackwatch cattle. We'd drive them down from the north pasture in early summer so the calves could be branded and castrated by the same old boy who flew Bill Jobe's plane years before. Those were good times, though my father stayed away even from there, and I did not see him again until I was in college and journeyed to visit him in Tucson on my own.

In Lansing I went to a school a block away from my mother's office in the capitol. I'd stop to visit her after school, navigating back stairs and passages, talking to people with whom she worked, and then walk home to my grandmother's house, which sat on a tree–lined street that backed up to a city park. Sometimes on rainy summer afternoons, I'd sit in the basement and look at photographs of my parents, nostalgic for a past that was not mine.

I got to the grounds of the Alamo and found the monument in a garden enclosed on one side by the long barrack and the mission on another. Again I had the sense that my parents were nearby. If I waited awhile they might cross Alamo Street, stroll into the garden and pose for a picture, the one I held in my hand. I asked someone to take my picture at the monument. If the two photographs were merged you would see the two of them in an embrace with me watching nearby, old enough to be their father.

Returning to Michigan I had the photograph developed and sent them to my father along with copies of the ones taken in 1944.

I attached a note saying I didn't know if he would enjoy seeing the pictures but hoped he would as much as I did taking them.

The past is usually thought of as a time, but the past can also be a place. San Antonio roused different feelings in my father than my mother. He did not respond to my note and has never said anything to me about the pictures.

There is a Buddhist saying that we walk this temporal plane with an invisible bird on our shoulder, and that every day we should ask the bird, "Is today the day?" The saying is a gentle reminder that the river of time will, one day, flow on without us, that we will be more likely to find contentment if we drift in time's river instead of fighting the current.

Not long ago back in San Antonio, I stopped by the Alamo and spent some time in the garden where the snapshot of my parents was taken. The garden is dominated by a large live oak and a round stone well. The well was in use in 1836 when Santa Anna's force overwhelmed the Texans. Tourists use it as a wishing well, and the money they throw in lands on screen that sits a few feet below the opening. Caretakers at the Alamo retrieve the coins the tourists throw in, taking away the possibility that their wishes will come true.

I stayed a long time at the Alamo, tossed a coin into the well and went back to the hotel.

Paska Willy

F. Gregory Whyte

Willy taught me how to make Paska, and the teaching wasn't easy because, besides being a blockhead, I knew very little about baking, let alone bread. My mother taught me how to cook, but cooking is not baking. Cooking and baking are opposite ends of artistic food preparation. Some of the most beautiful, inviting, inspirational, imaginative, dramatic, and poetic works of art have been created on a dinner plate. When it came to making Paska, Wilma was on a level with Van Gogh, da Vinci, or perhaps, at times, Picasso.

She had the tenacity, determination, and punch of a title–holding prizefighter, and it showed when we made the bread. The bread was her Paska, which is a sweet egg bread made with raisins, real butter, lullabies, marches, Ukrainian anthems, and lots of tender loving

> **F. Gregory Whyte**, a Michigan native, is a Wayne State and University of Detroit graduate. As a Ford Motor Company employee, he received global writing and editing awards. Gregory is presently self–employed as a freelance writer of fictional short stories with a novel in the works.

care. Every Easter, Thanksgiving, and Christmas we made the Paska. It is family tradition. Not that it had to be baked just on those holidays. Truth is, for practice, I occasionally make it on other days, but I freeze those loaves. They are practice loaves to be eaten on ordinary days.

Wilma was a little over five feet tall, on the round side, born February 10, 1917 in the Ukraine, and immigrated to Ohio in her late teens. At times in her life she made Champion spark plugs, operated elevators, and sewed for a living. Eventually she ended up as my ex–mother–in–law. The story between is not relevant, except for meeting her husband John, who, by anyone's definition, was a saint, and the making of the Paska. Seems sort of ironic in a way that I'm the only one left who knows how to make bread the way she did, and now I'm not even a member of the family. Rest assured I was invited to their Holiday dinners, I did accept, I did go, and I made the Paska.

"Gregory, you must start with good fresh ingredients," Willy would say. "Use only wooden spoon." Every time, I started by going to the store and buying Fleischmann's yeast, fresh eggs, Land–o–Lakes Butter, Sun Maid Golden Raisins, Gold Medal Flour, Pioneer Sugar, Carnation Evaporated Milk, Morton Salt, whole milk, and several gallons of spring water. I even bought a fresh container of Crisco. This is really not a commercial or endorsement for these products, it's just what Willy insisted be in her Paska. Once, I tried substituting other brands of evaporated milk and shortening. Clever me. The wooden spoon ended up about a quarter inch from my nose while I was lectured about not changing what goes into "her Paska." Normally at the end of her lecturing, she would reach up, tap the wooden spoon on my head, smile and we went on. There were moments, however, during that lecture when I thought the wooden spoon would end up across my butt! Not easy treatment for a thirty–seven year old student to accept, especially, after she became my ex–mother–in–law. It felt then as if the taps were being administered with just a tiny bit more force and with a slight mischievous revengeful smile.

I don't want you to think because of the holidays that making Paska bread was a religious thing. I really believe it wasn't. Nor do I want you to believe she acted like a German Gestapo Officer. Although at times, it certainly felt that way. I do want you to understand there is a mystery about how this five foot two woman went about making her Paska. You see, I never actually saw her make Paska her way. She helped me to make my bread. I, or anyone else, would never be present when she made her bread. I can't imagine what she could have done differently from how I make it. I create Paska just the way she taught me.

You should know I'm an experienced Professional Engineer with a Master's Degree in business. I have a decent knowledge of measuring, materials, mixing, numbers, temperature, timing, and chemistry. Mix together the same measure of identical ingredients, let it rise for the same length of time in a like environment, bake it at the same temperature, let it cool, and the results should be the same. You'd think it has to be, but…it's never the same!

Please don't tell anyone, but the first time I tried it without Wilma's guidance the loaves didn't rise, were rock hard, and would have made excellent boat anchors! Admittedly, in my younger years, I was sort of a braggart, and I had done a lot of boasting on how I was going to make the Paska, after all how hard could it be? My wife at the time was kind enough not to laugh, but some where between casting anchors and Thanksgiving dinner she leaked word to her Mother. Not much was said until someone related to me by marriage recalled my bragging words.

From Wilma came, "Big smart electrical engineer can't make simple Ukrainian Paska bread. Kill the yeast. In Ukraine if you murder yeast you go to Russian lead mine." Needless to say, that day I ate a lot of crow along with the turkey, several helpings of humble pie, swallowed a big gulp of pride, and asked for Wilma's help. I'm not sorry I did!

The night before we would make the Paska I would soak the raisins in two cups of water removing the stems from the raisins. God help me if I missed a stem. It meant wooden spoon lecture for sure! I heated the evaporated milk, two cups of the raisin water, and two cups of whole milk, being so careful "not to let it bubble." I skimmed the top, and let it cool. I put the yeast in the warm water, added a teaspoon of sugar, and let it ferment by a warm stove. The engineer in me even measured the water temperature. Willy never did. Later, I learned from her to proof the yeast by watching for the yeast to foam or "bubble." Then I took seven cups of flour and sifted it. Regardless of the brand of flour, or what advertising claims were on the sack, flour *had to be sifted* before she allowed it to be used. I then added two tablespoons of sugar, a teaspoon of salt, and put it all together in a very large pot. The pot had to be large since her recipe produces eight to ten loaves of bread sometimes more. In fact, most of Wilma's recipes produce large quantities of food. I often joked and asked if she had been raised to cook for the Ukrainian Army. I took the milk and yeast and mixed it *with a wooden spoon* and put the pot in a warm oven overnight.

The next morning I would have ten "fresh" eggs, salt, two sticks of "real" butter as opposed to margarine, nine cups of sifted flour, sugar, and two cups of raisins without stems ready on the counter. Like colors on an artist's palette, the individual ingredients were arranged semicircle in the order they would enter the pot. All the round enamel pots would be greased with Crisco. The baking pans had to be round, enamel, and greased before she arrived. She never let me make her bread in a standard size bread pan, or Teflon coated one. Once, just to test her, I Criscoed a Teflon bread pan and set it in the middle of the enameled pans. "No, no," she said, and placed the Teflon pan in the sink, filled it with soapy water, lectured on how Paska must be baked in round enameled pans, the wooden spoon tap on the head, and mumbled some Ukrainian words, and we continued.

When Wilma arrived she would begin, not by checking the measured ingredients, but by first pouring each of us a glass of wine and then by removing the pot from the oven, looking, smelling, and sticking her finger in the warm fermented mixture and tasting. The smile on her face would reveal if the mixture passed her inspection. If it passed, we proceeded; if not I started again repeating the process from the previous evening while she sipped her wine, observed what I did, and we waited for fermentation. We began by melting butter and sugar together in the microwave oven. Well, she wasn't totally old fashioned. Then we'd beat the hell out of three eggs (with the wooden spoon of course) and seven separated egg yolks, saving and freezing the whites for God knows what. I still have a large stash of frozen egg whites buried somewhere in the bowels of my freezer. If egg whites were money I'd be a wealthy man!

The flour, salt, egg yolks, and raisins would gradually be added as I started to knead the bread, first by wooden spoon, and then by hand. At Wilma's insistence, the very last thing to be added would be the melted butter and sugar mixture. And, she never measured any ingredient. She'd pick it up with her hand and sprinkle it into the mixture. A handful of flour, a pinch of salt, a few raisins, and stir with the wooden spoon. Sometime we'd have flour left over. At times I'd have to sift more and add it to the dough. One time I even had an egg yolk left over, but she said, "No matter it's good dough." And, of course, after it baked, she was right! At some magical point, based on her "feel" of the dough, she would have me roll it out of the pot and place it on the eighteen inch square piece of granite built into my counter. She would then insist I stop, wash out the large pot, dry it thoroughly, and grease it with Crisco. Then place the pot in the warm oven to "soak."

Now here's where her bread making gets slightly weird, and I'm asking you to keep this part a secret. It could be very embarrassing to a professional like myself if this went public. She would have me talk to the Paska, squeeze it hard with the tips of my fingers, then softly caress the dough, and she'd even insisted I sing as I kneaded the dough with the heels of my hands on the granite. And, when she would take over to demonstrate "how it should be done," she would softly sing a Ukrainian lullaby, or break out in a patriotic Ukrainian march, or anthem. I couldn't understand the words, but then again, it didn't seem to matter. "We are making Paska."

As we approached the end of the kneading process, she would stop me ever so often and feel the dough. When she said it was ready, we'd put a very light coat of "Crisco" oil all over the dough, remove the pot soaking in the oven, and place the dough back into the large pot. We would always cover the pot with a layer of oiled aluminum foil, placing two thin towels, one cross ways from the other, over the foil, and put the pot in a warm spot to rise. Always cross ways. Any other way was verboten!

During the rising time we would enjoy our wine or have a cup of green tea, some cheese and crackers, or cookies, sit at the kitchen table, and talk. At first, I hated green tea, but I wasn't

185

about to tell Wilma. Especially after I stumbled onto a magazine article describing all the antioxidant benefits derived from drinking green tea, and that it had cholesterol–lowering properties.

Before the divorce she would talk about my daughters and ask what they were doing in the school band, how nice they were growing into beautiful young ladies, or she would tell me stories about her life and what it was like growing up in the Ukraine.

After the divorce, she talked mostly about her Church and Ukrainian Cultural Center activities with a little blessing and complaining about her friends. Many of Wilma's closest friends affectionately nicknamed and referred to her as Willy. After John died our conversations were about what a great life her and John had together, how blessed she had been with three daughters, and how, as she aged, disappointing it was not to be able to get out and visit more with friends. As time passed she reflected more on friends who had just died, recalling what nice people they were and the work they had done for the Church and Center. It amazed me, even as Willy approached eighty, she could remember their names, where they were from, how they met their spouses, and many details of their lives including their children's names.

More amazing was that she would share that information with me. You see, right from our first introduction it was clear Wilma never liked me. It was a religious issue, and she was devoutly faithful to her religion. I'm not going to identify the religion, or detail the ongoing treatment I received. It serves no purpose, but it was clear I was not the man they wanted their middle daughter to marry, or their favorite son–in–law out of three. In most terms over the years, I became very successful, but no matter the level of success the feeling of being out of favor never went away except when we made bread. During Paska making I almost became the perfect son–in–law. Almost!

In all the times we made Paska together, she never asked me to change religions, what my religion was like, if I went to church on Sunday, or even if I believed in God. She never asked if her daughter went to church with me, or about problems between her daughter and myself. We missed making Paska together the Easter after the impending divorce was announced. I was shocked several days before the following Thanksgiving when she phoned and said she was coming over to help me make Paska. No request for permission, no question if it was okay, with no explanation why. And she never once asked me anything about the divorce, my relationship with her daughter, or if I was seeing anyone. Maybe I was the son she never had.

When the bread dough had doubled in size she insisted I "punch" down the raised dough with my fist. "You have to show dough who is boss," she would say. What a great way to relieve stress and frustration. I punched Paska dough sometimes as hard as I could. She would laugh and insist we let it rise again for a second punching. Then she would punch it down much like a prizefighter lands that winning blow. Second punch was always hers!

After the second rise in the large pot, I would punch the dough a third time, and then fill each greased bread pan about half full. Mind you, she never measured the amount of dough in the pan; they were just "eyed" half full. We would let the Paska rise in the pans until the dough was a half–inch above the rim, brush the tops of each loaf with a beaten egg and water to give them a slight glaze after baking, and then the pans went into the oven to bake for thirty–five to forty–five minutes at 350 degrees, or until she said they were done. Some times she'd save some dough and put a cross on top of several loaves, a braded twist, or some other design. I was never consulted about the designs; she just showed me how to make a cross or a twisted braid.

Her method of determining if the loaves were done was to open the oven door, pull out the wire rack, tap each loaf with the wooden spoon, and listen. Unfortunately, I never mastered her "tap and listen" technique. When the tapping sound was right the loaves came out. The loaves would cool in their pans and then Wilma would have me turn each loaf out of its pan and inspect it for color, crust thickness, shape, and smell. We admired each loaf of Paska as if it were a crown jewel. I was assigned clean up duty of the enameled pots and kitchen, while she sipped on another glass of wine or cup of green tea and directed cleaning operations, or just sat and read a magazine. Once cleaning was done she would call for her ride home.

At the Holiday dinner table there would be my loaf of Paska, sliced, and placed at her end of the table. And, always to my surprise, she had found time to make her bread, slice it, and ensure it was on a plate at my end of the table. After God was thanked for the bountiful table, and a toast offered by John, the passing of food began. I kept an evil eye on my bread as it passed to see if she would take a slice, and it was clear she had the same spying eye on me. I also kept a watchful eye to see what Paska each of the family members would select——hers or mine. Early on, when the bread–making duel first began, the family was careful to only take a slice of Wilma's Paska and ignored mine. It's still a mystery how I never returned home after a holiday dinner with any of my Paska. As time passed, however, and with Wilma's encouragement, the family members began to select a slice of my Paska as it passed as well, but only after the first passing of her bread.

As we each inspected and tasted each other's Paska, I would glance in Wilma's direction being careful not to let her see me. After she would taste my bread, she would casually look around the table with a strange sort of grin while I tasted hers. Hers was different. It was slightly sweeter, flakier, with a thinner, crisper, and lighter crust. I think the entire family even the grandchildren were observing to see if the teacher was still the master. And she was the master except for the Christmas of 1997.

Wilma was about to turn eighty and it was clear, as we worked together that December morning, her health was beginning to fail. Arthritis was seriously attacking her joints especially her fingers, elbows, and knees. There were other signs like higher blood pressure, loss of hearing, and the Diabetes was worsening, all contributing to higher doses of medication. Her stiff fingers wouldn't let her squeeze the Paska, her elbows wouldn't flex as she kneaded the bread, and the pain in her knees forced her to sit and watch from my kitchen table. As we progressed through the bread making steps, the expression on her face was more of pain than pleasure. When she did touch the Paska dough, there was a noticeable reduction in singing. The telling tale, however, was she allowed me the honor of both the first and second punching. The first and only time that happened.

When Wilma tasted my Paska at that 1997 Christmas table, she didn't smile. Neither did I. We both knew the student had out done the teacher. I also truly believe after tasting her Paska she knew her life's end was not far away. Sort of strange how our declining ability to accomplish certain tasks can predict what's to happen to us in the not too distant future. Especially those activities we have done all our life and love. But, the student's victory was short lived. The following Easter the Master produced what everyone agreed was her best Paska ever. Once I saw that light golden brown color, the exceptionally thin crust, felt the texture, and smelled the bread, I knew. The subtle light sweet taste of the Paska bread trumpeted her victory. I, by the smile on her face, knew she was back and with a vengeance. It was, sadly, the last time she made her beloved Paska.

I missed 1999 Thanksgiving, but made Christmas dinner. A kudo or two was tossed my way for the bread. Most proud though was the silent one from Wilma when her lips curled, and they offered that special smile, as she tasted my Paska. It was her last Paska smile. Wilma died peacefully in her sleep the following March at age eighty–three. I had the honor of being a pallbearer along with her other two son–in–laws and four grandsons. Somehow, I know she's in heaven probably teaching God, or one of his angels how to make her Paska.

I still make the bread every Easter, Thanksgiving, and Christmas. I purchase the ingredients, soak the golden raisins, pick out the stems, sift the flour, proof the yeast, separate the eggs, and mix it all together with the same wooden spoon. I sing Chris Isaak, Phantom Of The Opera, and some of my favorite Jimmy Buffet tunes as I work. I even sip wine or drink green tea as I watch the bread rise, punch it down three times, put the dough in the same round enamel pans, and measure the rise to a half–inch above the pan. I bake it for thirty–five to forty–five minutes and I stick the bread with a toothpick to ensure it's done. I let it cool on the racks, turn out and admire each loaf like it was a precious jewel, and I send one of the jewels, with each of my two daughters, to their mother's and aunt's Holiday table. Yes, every Easter, Thanksgiving, and Christmas I make the Paska...but it's not the same without Willy.

From the Mouths of Babes

Penelope Hudson

I was telling a friend the other day how I seldom realize I am growing older until I look in the mirror or spend time with the grandchildren, the six of whom range in age from four to nine years. Their close scrutiny of me, their Gramma Pennie, and the innocent comments that come from their mouths really hit me where it hurts the most!

The most aging experience occurred a few springs ago when, come to think of it I was even younger, Pop Pop and I visited our daughter, her husband and three of the six grandchildren in Delaware. The weather was rather cold and damp—that special kind of weather created for drinking hot chocolate, playing inane grandkid games (I still detest Monopoly), cuddling on the couch, telling tales and reading stories aloud. On one of those yummy days, the oldest of our grandchildren, Logan, was cuddled especially close to me as we were reading together for the hundredth time the poetry from **Voices of Michigan.** I was so into having fun and bringing the story to life that I was unaware when Logan's hand came out—and with this utterly disgusting expression on her face—touched my double chin, rather as if it might bite, and asked oh so innocently, "What is *that* Gramma Pennie, and why do you have it?"

I took a deep breath, accepted the reality that I was obviously the only one really "into" the story and said, "Well, Logan, this is what is commonly known as a double chin which both men and women seem to develop as a result of the aging process. I suppose weighing more than I should also contributes to

> Penelope (Gramma Pennie) Hudson has recently retired after many years of teaching a variety of age groups, levels and subjects in many different states. She is looking forward to going in search of her karma with her husband and two cats.

my having an, if you will, extra chin. Also it is hereditary in my family which means that all my aunts on my dad's side had them; in fact, they had more chins and bigger chins than mine," and hiding my disappointment quickly turned back to the reading of the book.

And then, still with the wonderful innocence of youth, she looks me straight in my blue eyes with her big dark brown eyes and says, "Oh, I was wondering 'cause you see we've been studying this bird at school...I think it's called a Pelican...and my teacher told us about it and showed us a video of how the Pelican can catch a fish, store it in its neck for quite a long time and then bring it up later to eat. We even visited the Internet to see pictures of what we decided was a pretty ugly bird, the Pelican."

I was speechless, which is rare for me. However, the remainder of the adults in the room (her grandfather, our daughter and her husband) nearly fell off their chairs laughing.

This was not the first time my chin had been the topic of conversation among my grandchildren. But I must say the other grandchildren merely refer to Gramma Pennie's "extra chin" which is a bit more delicate, but nonetheless, disconcerting, hurtful but more important aging!

Gavin, the youngest grandchild called the age spots on my hands chicken pox and asked if I a penis. He wanted me to go home, "but please can your daddy—mind you he is referring to *my* husband, *his* grandfather—stay and play with me?" All of this underscored for me how carefully the young look at us as we age, how inquisitive they are, how they simply express what is on their minds, and how unschooled they are in the area of what we might refer to as *political correctness*.

The three other grandchildren, offspring of our son, live in Indiana. They too know how to unintentionally get to their Gramma Pennie. Without a doubt the funniest age remark that has come my way of late, (and seeing my track record I can rest assured there will be more), and the one I've had the most fun sharing came from the mouth of one of my identical twin granddaughters. I can't tell them apart, so I can't assign the comment to either of the girls, which is probably just as well.

In an effort to seem young and vibrant, I had been wrestling on the floor with the twins. We were doing the usual grandmother/grandchild thing of seeing who could put their toe in their mouth, turn the best summersault, touch their nose with their tongue, dance the "grooviest," make the best under–arm fart, win at "I spy." We were having the best old time, or so I thought when "she," gasping for air from laughing and romping so hard, looked me directly in the eye and asked, "Gramma Pennie, why are your boobs and your belt so close together?" For that one I had no answer.

Enough said, I suppose I should launch a huge diet and exercise program in the effort to rid myself of the pelican neck and go shopping for a bra that might move the boobs back up where they belong; however, I believe I'll go get a cookie and work on a crossword puzzle!

Dragonfly Waltz

Lisbeth A. Lutz

Ray's reflection stares back at itself from an awning of heavy eyelids. Eyes meet eyes, once sun–shot blue, and now grayed as stirred water at the shallows. It seems they must squint without thick lenses propped on his nose, their points indenting his bridge, leaving raw red cups. Eye appointments are few and far in this neck of the north, so Ray's come to adjusting them himself, the irony being he can't see the screw very well without having the damn glasses on.

His fingers fumble as they try to shove the tiny imitation pearl buttons into the small eyelets made stiff with fresh starch. These fingers once nimbly assembled intricate models for city planners; had built an ultra–light plane with just blueprints and skill. Now, shoving a tiny button through a hole is almost too much to ask of them.

> **Lisbeth A. Lutz** won first place in the Kalamazoo Community Literary Awards for her short story in 2000 and had a poem in *Voices of Michigan* Volume III. She is a wild life photographer and currently is meshing her passions into a book of illustrated essays and poems drawn from her summers in the north woods of Michigan, the muse of most of her writing.

Ray's fingers peel off a patch of dried tissue that covers a fresh razor nick. He reaches for a washcloth and gives an extra scrub to a deep cleft by his chin where tobacco juice has left a run off from the corner of his mouth. Chewing is one of the few pleasures he allows himself; that, cigars and his homemade fruit pies. He had to give up fishing and flying. Sold the ultra–light years ago, but still can pass the pilot's exam, by God. Doesn't even bother putting the dock in the water any more, just lets it stay stacked to the left of the yard like a side of old ribs. Ray figures if smoking and chewing haven't killed him yet to just go with it.

He stops to watch his hands as they pass over his chin. The dark patches from the recent cancer burn–offs remind him of the sweet brown trout he used to catch and release in the springtime of his youth. It was easier then to tell the fish from the hand that set it free. His youth is gone and Ray feels winter's breath brushing against his neck.

His juices have all but dried up, like all the toads Carrie caught whenever he'd turn the rowboat over. They loved the damp hollows made by the boat seams. She would carefully pick them out of the cool sand and place them in old pickle jars. But she would forget them, leaving them to set too long in the sun, until they looked like him, with skin turned to leather pulled tight to the bone.

Maude has spent the morning, as most mornings, looking for her glasses. As she scrambles the contents of their lives about her, turning things over and brushing things aside, she keeps up the questions, her litany of confusion:

"Now, who is it getting married again?"

"Susie."

"Now, who is Susie again?"

"Carrie's daughter."

"Now, who is Carrie again?"

"Your daughter."

"That's real nice, isn't it?"

Humming her nameless tune, she'd be gone to him again.

Ray slicks back wisps of hair, frowning at the fresh half–moons over his ears and the sparse rows that form under the pressure of the wet comb. He'd better quit fiddling and knot that burgundy silk in a reasonable facsimile of a tie. He has to leave enough time to dress Maude. It's his concession, the least he can do, as Carrie is too busy helping Susie get dressed.

Maude had her bath right before breakfast. As she spread the frozen strawberry jam on a biscuit, she remembered where the wild strawberries grew at the end of the driveway. She recalled other springs when she had taken her colander and picked the thimble–sized berries, finding enough for jam like she was spreading on her biscuit this morning.

Then, he'd lost her again. The ritual of finding her glasses had begun, occupying her enough to allow him to dress himself in relative peace. But time was running short. There was no more of it to avoid or linger over.

Maude stops her habitual searching as Ray comes through the bedroom door. She looks at him with eyes so liquid, so fawn–like.

"Who the hell are you?"

"Now Maude, it's just me, Ray. Remember, Carrie's not coming this morning, so I got to help get you dressed for the wedding."

Maude cocks her head as her hands nervously fumble to close her gaping bathrobe.

"What wedding? I can't go to a wedding till I find my glasses."

Ray hasn't been under the dress of a woman in a very long time. He's forgotten the order of things; what goes first, and where. She lies like a virgin, her eyes questioning his right, his purpose, as he slips her panty elastic carefully over her waist. She's all pale concave lines and sharp angles. It startles him, but he keeps his momentum going. He has to. She won't lie like this for long before the questions, the litany, will begin again. He hasn't the time or the heart for it.

The afternoon smelled of new pine and moist moss. The sun was ripe, the breeze warm, the lake serene as cut glass. All so unusual for early June. A good omen for Susie's wedding, and, maybe even for him.

The ceremony flowed along very well until the minister, with his soothing voice and trusting eyes, read the part where the words seemed to burn the air around Ray. Those words, spoken in comfort and in all innocence of hope: "in sickness and in health, till death do you part." Ray glanced over at Maude. The glare from the sun bounced off her glasses, obscuring her eyes, the well of all souls. Her mouth was a simple line, devoid of visible emotion or understanding, simply hovered above her tightly folded hands as Ray muttered a hollow "amen."

Floating beneath the stars, the music mingled with an unseasonably warm breeze. Summer, it appears, is spring's suitor, not just come to call, but to stay. The notes assembled themselves into a refrain Ray remembers from times so long ago as to almost be improbable. It was popular during that time of such promise, right after World War II.

Maude, too, remembers. She smiles up at Ray as she firmly takes his hand and leads him away from the crowded reception to the edge of the dock. Ray's hand gently encircles Maude's waist as they float above the lapping water. With grace and trembling tenderness they glide across the worn planks. On the far side of the lake, a loon calls a warbling yodel, adding a haunting depth to the harmony of the notes and the moment.

Ray feels as he once felt while holding an emerging dragonfly in the palm of his hand. The sun had turned its wings of birthday tinsel wrap into rainbows. Its clouded eyes had looked out as if in a vacuum. It was so crushable; so fresh to this world. Its casing lay beside it, split open as a discarded peach pit. Two white threads were left dangling on either side of the gap, signaling that life had evolved. He had suddenly thought of one line from a poem he'd had to memorize for school. "I give you the end of a golden string…"

One Last Trip

Fred Thornburg

There was very little patience left on the drive home. We all were sunburned and tired, and everything had a film of sunscreen and sand on it. The return trip from our week spent swimming and fishing had been put off for as long as possible, to the point of randomly throwing our gear in the back of the truck. The two–hour drive home was spattered with arguments fueled by a lack of sleep and the reality that it was back to work, back to chores. Six loads of laundry awaited our return, as did three hours of lawn mowing, one week of newspapers, one week of mail. Additionally there were coolers to be cleaned, fishing gear to be stowed away, messages to be answered on the answering machine, plus the never–ending attempt to vacuum the sand from the front and back of the truck. The tension was building.

Fred Thornburg has been writing for years for his own satisfaction. Being published in Volumes I and III of the *Voices of Michigan Anthology* has done much to boost Fred's confidence. He is normally a fiction writer, but he felt this was a lesson that needed to be shared.

We stopped at our neighbors, and I sent one of the boys in to retrieve our mail. I gave him that look of urgency: be polite, be quick. I knew we had a large task in front us; I had a plan and a timetable. For the past two hours, as I drove, I went over the list of chores that needed to be done, running through each task and trying to streamline it and time it out. Five minutes to pick up the mail. And that was being generous.

The neighbor lady met my son at the door, and motioned him to come in as her husband retrieved the brown grocery bag filled with eight bundles, each carefully rubber–banded with the individual day's paper and mail, stacked in the bag, in order. OK, he went inside, better give me six minutes here. Her husband brought the bag out and asked me how our vacation was. Lots of people ask such questions; few really care. It's just a formality. Not so with our neighbors. They were genuinely interested in every detail and loved hearing our stories. I felt rude sitting in the truck, leaning out the window, trying to carry on a conversation. I motioned to my wife and other son to get out and head up to the porch for a few minutes, three at the most, to give them a briefing of the fish stories and show them our sunburns.

They invited us in and prodded the boys for their stories. The boys woke up a little as they told about the fish they had caught, the ones that snapped the line because dad left the net on shore, the lures that worked, the ones that didn't, the ones we let go and the ones we ate. Through their conversations I saw my sons become excited by the questions and comments of my neighbors. Soon we were talking about lures and depths, water temps and overcast versus sunny conditions, morning versus night fishing. Funny, as I look back, it seems like it was one of the few conversations I've heard that was not a competition for the boys. They were genuinely interested. Our friends' animated responses and involved concerns injected energy into the stories. The conversation turned specific when we started talking pike.

Our neighbors had always looked after our house, getting our mail and paper for us in the past. On this trip, though, we were hesitant to ask. He was in his seventies, and was a statement of how we should all age. He'd been quick witted and full of energy. If he spotted you on his walks down the road, he'd hold his fist in the air and pump it up and down a few times, the same way a child would if he wanted a trucker to blow his big air horns. No doubt this was his universal wave, carried forward from days past spent as a milk hauler. Some truckers ignore kids when they get the double pump; some look irritated and give it a short blast, like they are all put out. Not my neighbor, he'd be the one laying it on loud and heavy, backed up by a big grin, and pointing at the laughing recipient. I know the enthusiasm he had for life was a by–product of his strong Christian faith. That was his main focus. Our reluctance to bother them to watch our house stemmed from a recent downturn in his health. His strong, purposeful strides were slowing turning into dragging shuffles. His energetic waves were now a hand lifted slightly, barely acknowledging he'd seen you. This was the first summer he hadn't planted a garden. No deep red tomatoes, no crisp green beans, no straight and proud sweet corn. It seems that a mini–stroke had pulled part of the energy out of this zestful man. On this particular day, he had at first appeared overly tired. Doctors were experimenting with various medicines and various doses. Perhaps they should have monitored his response to the word pike.

He motioned us into his mudroom where hanging on the wall, above the washing machine, was a forty–six inch pike. We all came to life as he told the story of catching it. He caught it in Canada during their yearly family fishing trip. The color returned to his face, the spark back in his eyes. For a while. He went on to tell us that this would be the first time he and his wife would miss the trip. He knew, as his family did, that he would never make it back. Just like that his fishing days were over. A moment of frustration hung in the air, but not for too long.

"Hey," he said with renewed energy, "did we ever show you the video of the fifty–four inch pike our son caught? Got a minute?"

What could I say? We had a truck waiting to be unloaded, a week's worth of mail and paper to catch up on, and we were all dead tired. But how could I say no? It wasn't an act of polite obligation; it was the genuine enthusiasm lure that I bit on. I said sure, and we shuffled into the front room and sat on the couch. The boys sat on our laps, sleepy and relaxed, yet intrigued, as our neighbors looked for the tape.

"There, that was the trip. Now fast–forward it. More, more, there. Back it up a little. Right there."

That woke us up and piqued our interest. There was an aluminum rowboat with our neighbor, his two adult sons, and his grandson–in–law in it. By the time the camera had been turned

201

on, his son had been fighting the fish for some time. Our neighbor sat on the edge of his seat as he explained the action. The battle went on, and the excitement showed through their comments. They all knew it was a big fish.

The little aluminum boat was overflowing with excitement. There was no age difference; they were all kids again. The thrill of battling the fish was on all their faces. The pike would take out line and make a run for it, then lie on the bottom. They'd all calm down in the boat, then it would take off again and the boat would erupt with laughs and comments.

As I watched it on TV, I noticed my neighbor reliving the experience with duplicate expressions. As the pike's back broke the surface and the boat full of men got their first glimpse, I could see the excitement in his eyes, on the tape, and in his worn Lazy boy. As it dove under the boat, he moved to the edge of his chair, as if he could look under it and see the fish come up on the other side. By the time the large pike had broken the surface a few times, we were all wide–awake and reenergized.

The anticipation the guys on the boat felt was playing out in the warm front room of our neighbor's house. We were all having a genuinely good time watching them struggle to land this fish. I was having an equally good time watching my neighbor relive the moment. It didn't really matter who was holding the pole. It was as if each guy, as if each of us, were getting the enjoyment of the struggle to land that fish. As the pike grew tired and was reeled close to the boat, we were all on the edge of our seats.

The suspense doubled as he drew near, and they saw the size of the fish compared to the size of their net. "You've got one chance," someone off camera said. "One chance, don't hold it by the handle. Cradle the net with your arms and scoop him up." These guys had been fishing as a team for years, and knew the procedure for landing big ones. In one graceful swoop the fish was in and then suddenly over the edge of the large aluminum net, as it buckled and broke under the fish's weight. They all clapped and cheered; we all clapped and cheered.

Now, some guys that had a forty–six inch pike hanging on their wall would feel threatened by their son upstaging them with a fifty–four inch pike. Not my neighbor. Pride oozed out of his every pore. He knew his trips into remote Canada were over, although his kids and grandkids would continue the tradition. And he showed me there was no better way to end his portion of the tradition. For a few minutes he had been back on that secluded lake. No prescriptions, no doctor's appointments, no diet restrictions, and nobody asking him every five minutes how he felt. Rowing a boat, cleaning fish, carrying gas cans without being scolded. Walking out in the woods or on the beach solo without somebody worrying that he'd been gone too long. He was full of energy with definite plans for the day. That's what I saw in that little snippet of tape. Of all the articles in magazines, the morning talk show segments, the ads on TV and advice columns on how to age, none did more for me than watching it with my family and watching my neighbor's reaction to that five–minute video. As I see him walk by now, a little slower, slightly slumped over with a scant drag in his walk, I know that inside is youthful energy, saved up for one last trip.

Wood Smoke and Whippoorwills

Patricia P. Miller

It's the cabin I most remember, with its logs laid carefully end over end, the heavy pine door, the large stone fireplace and smoke–stained mantel above the wood box. And that delicious smell—old wood, smoky embers, hot coals sparking on the hearth, the pine logs still pungent with turpentine. We vacationed at Lake Hope every summer of my childhood, and always, the smell of burning wood transports me in a moment's time to rainy days spent before that fireplace playing Monopoly with my family. While snuggled in my upper bunk, (a privilege not easily won from my younger brother), that lovely smell filled my head and fueled my youthful dreams.

> **Patricia Miller** was born in Columbus, Ohio and lived primarily in the Great Lakes Region. She has been writing since childhood and has an academic background in environmental protection, English literature, sciences and journalism. She has had a number of travel articles, essays and work–related pieces published in regional magazines and journals.

Our temporary home was wonderful. Its tiny furnished kitchen and plain white sturdy china (hand washed before we used it) stood in stark contrast to our large home and formal belongings. Everything was compact, everything fit like a Pullman car or an airplane bathroom: I loved it. I loved hearing the rain pelting on a mossy, shingled roof. I loved listening by my small bedroom window to an early–morning Whippoorwill whose melodious and repeated call left my Dad grumpy from a long night of broken sleep. I wished fervently that the bird would follow us home, bringing with it some small token of our sunny days and starry nights at the lake when we returned to the reality of our regular lives at home.

Those long ago lake visits seem like a dream within a memory—fleeting in time, yet a clearly focused snapshot of youthful summers that it seemed would last forever...memories fixed by a crystal lens that magnifies experience and ties all together with golden twine. The sensory bits and bites are buried with the innocence of a child whose real memory is short, but whose experiences are long and deeply drawn, even in a child of ten or less. Especially in that child whose imagination was sparked by the world's great literature, lovingly read aloud since toddler hood.

Goethe said, "Where the light is brightest, the shadows are deepest." Memory can illuminate the past with a shining focused ray, but time's passage leaves clouds that shadow experiences and fix the residual memory in a golden, buffed, and burnished haze. "Nothing gold can stay," said Robert Frost. The brightness of reality is dimmed in memory, sometimes mercifully, and pain and loss fall into deeper shadow. It's the natural order of things.

Those few summers seemed eternal to me. I increased my skill base, learning things unknown to me at my landlocked home. I learned to fish standing at my Dad's side, and I baited sharp barbed hooks to entice the small blue gills that lived in Lake Hope. Some took my hook, and I proudly displayed them in now–faded photographs, even while shrieking appropriate little girl noises about slimy worms.

And I learned to swim by splashing wildly in the lake, staggering around on the sandy bottom, pretending to "swim" by walking on my hands in shallow water to impress my mother. She always stayed on shore, anxiously watching my two brothers and me, uncertain of the water environment and suffering a rash from too much sun, being unaccustomed to brilliant sunrays flashing off the lake. My pigtails dripped water down my back; the sand polished my bare feet to summer hardness; the sun burned deep brown tan lines around the white of my swimsuit straps, and I was supremely happy.

And I fell in love. My first hard crush on the handsome lifeguard who taught me to swim was wonderful and exhilarating, but cruel, as are all these premature affairs of the heart. He was much older, strong and kind, and far too sophisticated at fifteen to notice a skinny, obstinate eight–year–old.

After swimming lessons, we treasured the rare treat of choosing a candy bar to eat in the car on the way back to the cabin. My Dad didn't approve of candy or pop, so I am sure it was a bribe on my mother's part to keep us quiet until we were dry and dressed, but it was pure pleasure at the time. I always picked a Clark Bar and one taste of a Clark Bar today, and I'm looking for a sandy frosting on the wrapper and half melted chocolate on my fingers.

After lunch in our cabin where we ate at a small, heavy, wooden table in the kitchen, my Dad would select a book from classic children's literature to read aloud. We lolled around the fire on rainy days, or sprawled on our backs under a tree on sunny days, our eyes searching for ghosts in the cumulus clouds of summer, our ears fixed in fascination on the story of the day. "Improve your mind," was one of Dad's favorite statements, usually uttered when we were, in his opinion, wasting time or watching something on television.

As he read to us on those summer afternoons, our minds ranged far away and we were riding a river raft with Huck Finn, exploring the jungle brought frighteningly alive by Rudyard Kipling, or chasing what passed for villains in those days with the Hardy boys. Sometimes, kids from neighboring cabins joined our charmed circle, chins cupped in small hands, eyes wide, drawn by the ancient art of a story well told.

Evenings in our cabin were a mix of scary stories, popcorn, and games, and more read–aloud books. But, on special nights— those with the right ambiance of full moon, spooky noises, and a soft warm breeze blowing—we were sometimes allowed to go snipe hunting. The fine art and high science of hunting snipe is something most kids learn at camp, and our lake visits were no exception to the ancient ritual of childhood.

Hunting was done in earnest, armed with a paper sack, flashlight, and high anticipation if you were still innocent and naïve; or done with much false enthusiasm, teasing, and scaring the younger children when you came to realize the fool you had been at six or seven. "Oh wa, ty goos, Siam" we chanted as we crept down darkened paths, around behind the cabin, and into the scrub woods out back where we dug night crawlers at dawn. We hunted and chanted, never in our innocence even thinking of what we wanted with a snipe in the first place, or what we would do with one when we caught it, in the second place.

We hiked those same paths in the daylight, bursting with confidence in the sun, forgetting the scary events of the night before. "I never met a path I didn't like," I tell my husband to his fond amusement. Then, as now, paths drew me ever on, curious, guessing where they go and what one might see along the way. A traveler I am, never a tourist; for it's the trip you know, not the destination. As Robert Louis Stevenson said, "It's better to travel hopefully than to arrive."

Now as I stride along into evening, I'm sometimes joined in spirit by Bilbo the Hobbit. He slips over the garden wall, singing softly to himself as he leaves the bright party lights for the darkening road ahead:

"The road goes ever on and on, / Down from the door where it began. / Now far ahead the road has gone, / And I must follow, if I can. / Pursuing it with eager feet, / Until it joins some larger way; / Where many paths and errands meet. / And whither then? I cannot say." Paths of memory lead back—back to where you began. The natural order of things.

On a special evening, once a summer, we piled into the car at dusk and Dad drove to a lookout point high above the lake with a long view down the valley that stretched away in the distance to the south. We watched the fireflies we called lightning bugs ascend in hordes from the weeds by the lake and grassy play areas. Tiny beacons of light in the night served to fire young imaginations and spark spooky tales.

We waited in the coming darkness to hear a long, low whistle and the growing rumble of iron wheels on steel rails. "Here she comes," we would shout to each other. Then we watched in awe and delight as the *Cincinnati Limited* rolled through below our vantage point; its lighted windows offering but a glimpse of uniformed waiters and stylish diners seated at elegant tables with linen and silver, sipping drinks, and eating things with French and Italian names. Train windows reveal a snapshot of lives and days past, brilliant in the darkness and in memory, but fleeting as the summers and innocence of childhood. A filmstrip that passes through the dark, through the mind, and ends in questions, not answers.

The sleek silver train rumbled past, oblivious of us watching at the point. We marveled at the sight of the wondrous train rolling on into the night. We pondered its stops and destination; who were its passengers and where were they going? We knew where we were going, back to our cabin while watching for deer in the road, the high point of the evening behind us now. And then, home to that top bunk.

In the days before "fast food," families took lunch or dinner with them. Ours was the same each year as we left home to drive to the lake: a whole ham roasted in a black metal Dutch oven, great for sandwiches and dinners all week long. It kept well in the car, no refrigeration needed for a few hours, and none to be had either. We had potato chips and white bread, and probably carrot sticks, good for the eyes you know. And sweet purple plums, dripping down our chins and staining our shorts, relished as the meal's sweet treat. And water, lukewarm and unappealing drawn from a thermos jug into small paper cups. It tasted great then and sounds good now. Ham in a Dutch oven takes me back to the cabin still and always.

I made a friend whom I played with many summers at the lake. She was blond and athletic, a year older than I and so was much more interesting to my older brother than I was. Her name was Susie Hopkins and she was the park ranger's daughter. I was jealous that Susie lived at the park where I most wanted to be. She was there all the time. But Susie's playmates changed from week to week, and I rather envied her that experience. She smiles still from brown–toned black and white photos of us in our swimsuits or admiring our bluegills. I wonder if she remembers me and the cabin, and the rest?

As we left the cabin to return home, Dad sternly required us to remove all the linens and fold them carefully, placing them in stacks on the front porch to be picked up before the next people came. I really couldn't imagine anyone else in our cabin, in my bedroom, in that special top bunk. Why, that was MY cabin. But it happened every year and I can still hear my Dad saying, "Fold them nicely I said. You want them to ask us back, don't you?" Of course we did. We folded and stacked with six, ten, and twelve year–old diligence.

Arriving at home meant tons of sandy dirty laundry for my mother to do. We carried it carefully to the outside basement door where every single piece was pulled out, shaken hard, and only then allowed to go inside. "I don't want any bugs in my house," she warned us. "Look in all the pockets." Since there seemed little hope that the Whippoorwill would actually come home with us, I might have settled for a bug or two, or maybe that snipe. Something to fix in time all that the lake, that land of Hope, meant to me.

One of those treasured books read to us was Robert Louis Stevenson's **A Child's Garden of Verses.** I look back at the child I once was, so real, so vivid in my own mind, now long since grown and gone. I see and hear the child at play again and again, an old refrain that plays sweetly and forever in my mind.

"As from the house your mother sees / you playing round the garden trees, / so you may see if you but look / through the windows of this book; / another child far, far away / and in another garden play. / But do not think you can at all, / by knocking on the window, call / that child to hear you. He intent / is all on his play–business bent. / He does not hear, he will not look, / nor yet be lured out of this book. / For long ago, the truth to say, / he has grown up and gone away. / And it is but a child of air / that lingers in the garden there."

It's the natural order of things.

The cabin was a small safe haven, home for a scarce two weeks a year, but the center of my childhood adventures in the wilds of the state park. How sweetly smell inhabits memory; how strongly the long–cold campfires of my youth forged memories never to be forgotten; how it comes back in a flash—a wonder and treasure of deepest remembrance.

The wispy child of air lingers only in the mind; the garden is bare.

A Necessary Car Trip

Tonya S. Lambert

It was dusk, but there was still enough light for me to read from my textbook if I tilted it at just the right angle and held it close to the car window. I knew the light wouldn't hold out much longer, but I was determined to finish that assignment before we got home. I had been infuriated when I learned that we had to make an unexpected trip to the airport to return a rental car for my husband's boss. My evening schedule had been infringed upon, and there I was, scrambling to finish my work in the car. The only thing I wanted to do at home was crawl into bed and sleep soundly, knowing my homework was finished. If it wasn't, I knew

> **Tonya S. Lambert** grew up in Muskegon and has lived in Michigan her entire life. Currently, she lives in Mt. Pleasant with her husband and two sons, and she is a teacher of English and French at Jefferson Middle School in Midland, MI.

I wouldn't sleep. I'd never been able to in the past and there was no way I was getting up early to finish it.

My eyes were getting dry and no amount of rubbing would relieve the itchiness, but I plowed on. Between squints at the book, I would jot down a few sentences in my notebook. I had papers scattered all over the place—on my lap, on the floor, under the armrest, on the dash. I even had one on my husband's lap, but he didn't seem to notice. Fred doesn't notice much when he's driving and there's good music on. At that moment he was lost in some Led Zeppelin tune, left foot keeping time, hands all over the steering wheel in an attempt to drive and play drums at the same time.

Except for the music, it was quiet. I hadn't heard a peep from the backseat in quite a while, which surprised me. I figured they were sleeping and thoughts of them waking up when we got home, raring to go, filled my head for a moment. I knew what they were like fresh off a nap. Sometimes I can hardly keep up. It wasn't something I was looking forward to at ten o'clock at night.

I didn't dare turn around to check on them. I just knew that if Collin saw any movement from me that his preschooler programming would kick in and he'd start on a rampage of questions I could never begin to answer. I'd never finish my work. He must have been reading my mind.

"Momma?" His little voice piped up from behind me.

Fred immediately pulled himself out of Zeppelin Zone and became Daddy again. "Remember, Collin, we promised Mommy we'd be quiet so she could finish her work."

I didn't say anything, but I heard the disappointment in that voice in the backseat. "Oh. Sorry, Momma."

In my heart, I knew I should have just closed shop for the night, but my head told me to hold out for a few more minutes, just a few more. There was only a bit left to do. Feeling guilty, yet driven, I bent back over my papers.

For a few minutes, I became engrossed again in my work. Robert Plant continued to sing and the only other sound was the air whooshing about the car, trying to find a way in around my window. The light continued to fade and I had to angle my book a little more.

"Momma," Collin spoke up again, this time a little more hesitantly. "What's that?" I could hear him tapping on his window.

Frustrated, I put my book down and twisted around in my seat. "What's what, Honey?" I asked impatiently.

He was pointing upwards out his window to the northeast. "That."

I turned back around and looked out my own window, expecting to see the twinkling lights of an airplane or a flock of birds. What I saw instead were the clouds of the sunset. They weren't the full, billowy clouds of the afternoon, but the serene, flat clouds of a quiet evening. Round and flat like the scales on a dragon's belly or the patches on a quilt, they caught the sun's last rays, turning the sky a soft, pale pink. This pink sky thoroughly confused my inquisitive son.

"Oh, that's just the sunset, Sweetie. When the sun goes down, it sometimes makes the clouds look pink." Satisfied with my answer, I went back to work, wondering what question would come next.

"It looks like waves, Mom," he said a minute later. I was surprised that it still held his attention.

Fred finally noticed what we were talking about and joined in. "He's right. It kinda does look like waves in the water."

As I looked up again, our car cleared a stand of trees and we had for the first time an open view of the whole thing. This time I just had to put my book aside. Nearly down, the sun had created the largest patch of colors I've ever seen in the sky. Just above the treetops in the distance was the bright orange I was so used to in sunsets, but above that it blended into a hot red that formed an even larger arc above the orange. I couldn't tell exactly where, but the red became purple and stretched out until, at the highest point in the sky, it faded to pink. So intense and fierce at ground level, the sky seemed so gentle above. It was simply the most beautiful sunset I had ever seen.

"Now it looks like fire, Mom." I could hear the excitement in his voice and felt the rhythm of his little legs bouncing happily on his seat.

"You're right, Collin. It does look like there's a fire." I twisted around again to see Andy in his car seat behind Daddy. "Look, Andy, can you see the pretty sunset?"

Andy squinted up his nose in that two–year–old grin of his and pointed out the window. "Red!" He blurted out, and from that I knew he was enjoying the sunset too.

"Look, Mamma, you're missin' it!"

I obeyed instructions and turned back around. We watched in silence for a minute as we continued to lose sight of the brilliant sun behind patches of trees. It was almost gone.

Fred's voice interrupted my thoughts. "Remember that sunset we saw when we were bringing Father Fritz home from Ohio? He said that there was not an artist on Earth who could duplicate God's work. This sunset reminds me of that."

Finally, I closed my book. I knew what he meant, but this sunset was even more special to me. I had almost missed this one and would have had it not been for the insistence of a four–year–old. In his own way, he had been telling me to slow down and in my heart I knew I needed to or I would miss more than just the sunset. I realized then that this was a car trip I had needed to take. Maybe it was more than just a chance happening that threw me off schedule that night. Maybe it had been meant to happen.

The sun was gone, and it was practically dark. I didn't mind that I'd be getting up early tomorrow. Fred was singing and Andy had fallen asleep, his little blond head nestled against the side of his seat. Collin was now kicking the back of my seat, but I didn't care.

"Hey, Buddy, what book do you want to read when we get home?"

View From a Train

Penny Niemi

Slick steel tracks traverse the backside of
town, where water tower letters coldly
announce the
current destination, and timeworn depot
bricks crumble slowly to nothingness.
Silhouetted against
a late afternoon sun, towering grain elevators
stand their watch. We have arrived through
the back
door of rural America, where life is real; not
perfect, but trying hard, as shabby farm
houses
snuggle grand Victorian mansions, their
postage stamp gardens and lawn patches
stretching out in
gaudy quilts of weedy naturalness. Here
glass–littered alleyways come decorated in
trashcans,
and beaming sunflower faces nod over peeling, broken fences.
Here born–again barns boast fresh
cloaks of red paint and laundry scarecrows flap wildly from
backyard lines.

~~~

Anonymous behind shaded glass, my traveling eyes reach through
windows opened to this
October day's last bright warmth, watching private lives and loves
click on like fast–forwarded
frames of an old home movie. I notice without really connecting,
observe without really feeling,

Penny Niemi is a
nature lover,
writer and retired
dental hygienist.
Her long walks
and backyard
garden in St. Clair
inspire essays and
poetry, and she
has been
published in
*Michigan Out of
Doors* magazine.
Writing is her way
of touching hearts
to share the joy,
wonder and
beauty all around
us.

as the ebb and flow of small town American dreams play out just
beyond my grasp. Yet I cannot
deny that each of these dreams is my dream, too, and that my
journey is an intrinsic part of these
tracks that continue to divide towns and lives.

~~~

Open countryside looms as engines churn: faster, faster, faster. Seas
of raggedy cornstalks streak
past, opening at last to meadows framed softly in crimson sumac.
Delicate Queen Anne's Lace,
regal asters and tawny shredded wheat giants share this grassy
flatness with the sentinel oak.
Majestic, strong, he has persisted through eight hundred seasons,
offering cooling shade to
Chippewa Indian villages; waving leafy salutes as wagons rolled
West; weeping as the woods
disappeared from around his feet. Now alone, but
determined to prevail, he stands guard over a
new breed of forest: pole, wire, pole, wire, pole, wire—Edison's
foot soldiers marching in perfect
rhythm and inviting me to count them like I did when I was seven
and our Studebaker sped toward
grandparents and the Wisconsin border.

~~~

On a distant ribbon of road, cars rush impatiently past each other,
but today I am only an
uninterested observer and not at all a part of their hurry. Treed
ridges swallow the sun as the train
slows to cross a winding river far below. Bordered by seas of
switching cattails, the muddy stream
wanders languidly toward a mysterious somewhere, capturing my
whole attention and pulling my
imagination around each new curve.

~~~

Shadows lengthen; eyelids droop. Soft lights blink on around me,
reflecting new images while
veiling those beyond. I sit quietly, hypnotized by the familiar face in
the glass, pondering dreams
unfulfilled. My destination lies beyond this face, in the bright new
day on the other side of the
darkness. The train rushes on. The journey continues.

The Poet

Linda LaRocque

"Hi, it's me. I'll be sending the poems out in tomorrow's mail. You'll know what to do. We'll need everything as soon as possible. Sorry about the rush. Oh, and there's about one hundred and fifty poems. Love ya. Bye." My machine beeped, signaling the end of Ann's message.

I groaned aloud. "It's that stupid poetry writing contest!"

When Ann, my high school English teacher friend, asked me to judge their all–school poetry writing contest, I agreed. But since I hadn't heard any more about it, I figured they'd scrubbed the whole thing.

"Alright," I grumbled to myself, "I'll judge their contest, but I will never, ever get involved with something like this again!"

Armed now with my new improved attitude, I set about the job of judging the poems. This simple task ended up taking my entire weekend and several evenings, as I read, sorted, and categorized. At last, I had first through fifth place winners, then ten honorable mentions, which consisted of most humorous poem, best romantic poem, best spiritual poem and so on.

However, through it all, the winning submission was obvious. This entry was outstanding. It rhymed, it contained a universal message, it made sense from beginning to end, it flowed easily, and it stirred emotion. It was by far the best of the lot.

An award–winning playwright of more than five plays, **Linda LaRocque's** play, *Revival of Possum Kingdom Church,* opened in the 1999–2000 season of the Detroit Repertory Theatre. Many of her short stories appear in *The Chicken Soup for the Soul* books. Her most recent play, *Joyce's Choices,* was the winner of the Community Theatre Association of Michigan's 2000 Playwriting contest. Linda writes from her South Haven, MI. home.

Being the compulsive personality that I am, I couldn't help but make a positive comment on all of the entries; however, on the first place winner I was generous with sincere praise.

Relieved at last to be finished with the chore of poetry judge, I gathered the submissions together and stuffed them into a red, white and blue priority mailer and sent them off to Ann and her school's contest.

Several weeks went by and this, like so many other once important events in life, was soon forgotten and replaced by new, important events and other deadlines. So it did come as somewhat of a surprise when my friend, Ann, showed up at my door one drizzly Saturday afternoon, in March.

"What on earth are you doing here?" I inquired.

"Oh, I'm visiting Mom for the day, so thought I'd stop by. Besides I've got something for you." I ushered her into my kitchen, and she plopped down at the same ancient table where we'd had countless conversations over the years. She reached inside a shopping bag that had obvious signs of being used before, and brought out a gaily–wrapped package, along with a card. Well, the gaily wrapped package turned out to be a hard cover edition of **Lighthouses of the Great Lakes** and the card was rather generic with its thank you for all you've done kind of message.

"Sit down a minute, please. I've got to talk to you. Okay? I hope I can get through this without crying. You won't believe it. You just won't believe it."

I was really puzzled now.

Taking a fresh tissue from her jacket pocket and wiping her eyes, she began.

"You know the first place winner of the poetry contest was a boy. A junior."

Of course I didn't know because names were not allowed on the poems. They all were numbered instead and then recorded on a master list someplace.

"Of all the students, he was the only one who came to me not once, but several times, to ask if I'd heard anything about the contest."

"So what's the point?" I finally asked.

Apparently the annual poetry writing contest was a popular event at Ann's school. A special assembly was held for the occasion, where the winners were announced starting with honorable mentions, then ending with the first place winner. And all entrants read their works on stage to the entire student body.

Only three other faculty members, the principal, and Ann were aware of the winners, so it was a surprise to everyone when the awards were handed out by Mr. Howe, the principal. In fact, he had to stop several times to allow for applause and cheers. But when it was time for the first place winner to be announced, you could have heard a pin drop.

Imitating the principal, Ann continued, "Ladies and gentlemen, the first place winner is Karl Spears!"

It was then, Ann explained to me, that Karl was considered the school loser by everyone. His father and uncle were both in prison, his older brother was in a juvenile home, his mother was the town mystery woman, and they lived behind the old picture frame company in a place that looked more like a deserted gas station than a house. As for Karl, he was truant much of the time, had no friends, looked like an unmade bed and was considered a slow learner. So when his name was announced as the first place winner, a hush came over the student body. Maybe they thought it was a joke or maybe they had to let the whole situation sink in a bit, but for a moment it was as if the entire auditorium was operating on slow motion. Then, as if someone put things on fast forward, Karl bolted from his seat, and leaping over everyone in his path, piled onto the stage, breathless. Mr. Howe spoke of Karl's achievement in proud fashion and then presented Karl with his award of merit, his scholarship check, and his neatly folded poem.

"He was a sight!" Ann wasn't through with her story yet.

She continued with the account. Karl stood behind the podium. He unfolded his winning poem and slowly and haltingly began to read aloud its contents.

The audience fell silent, and as if on cue, Karl Spears also read the glowing critique I had included.

One of the kids who received an honorable mention stood up first and began to clap, and then one by one the entire student body rose to their feet in complete and total support of Karl's accomplishment. The applause was thunderous; perhaps for the first time in his life, Karl Spears was recognized and accepted.

It has been a long time since that drizzly afternoon in March. Ann continues to teach high school English and as for Karl, well, he stopped being truant and graduated from high school and the last I heard had enlisted in the United States Navy.

Karl Spears doesn't even know me, but I think of him every now and then, like when I'm cleaning shelves and I come across the hard cover edition of **Lighthouses of the Great Lakes,** then I'm quietly reminded of that long ago poetry writing contest where a poor kid from the wrong side of the tracks stood tall and proud and received the greatest of all awards...the respect of his fellow classmates.

"Kids are mean," they say. And perhaps some are. But whenever I hear that, I'm reminded of a high school auditorium, where some pretty good kids encouraged a young boy to believe in himself.

And for that, I dare hope again.

You Will Be Healed

Marsha Jane Orr

When my sister Debra called that July 1997, I cried. She had found a cancerous lump in her left breast and was coming to Boston's Dana–Faber Cancer Institute for care. We hadn't spoken meaningfully to each other in over twenty years. I'd argued with my parents back then and she had taken their side. She was right, but I felt she had deserted me when I needed her most. I had never really forgiven her, even though we had patched things up over the years. The "dead moose" in our corner was simply ignored. But, with both parents gone, her call brought me back to what's truly important in a family: We are there for one another. We have an opportunity to "rub rough stones smooth" and be for one another a healing of our deepest wounds. I was living in Maine at the time but immediately offered to meet her in Boston and stay with her through her arduous six–month recovery regimen.

> **Marsha Jane Orr** has experience in academic, corporate, nonprofit, and international environments. She is trained in organizational behavior and employee relations. Marsha earned her M.S. from the Cornell School of Industrial and Labor Relations and has been an arbitrator for the American Arbitration Association.

I remember meeting her at the airport upon her arrival. It was if God had wiped out all the years of hurt and the lost love between us and had replaced it with our true Selves, vulnerable and loving. We cried. But mostly we were filled with joy that God had—in this most peculiar way—brought us back to each other.

We were scared. But her courage and spirit were more alive than I had seen them since childhood. When we were kids, she had been the neighborhood leader in all our games. Three years older than I was, she climbed trees higher, ran faster, fought harder than any of us in our neighborhood. I idolized her and mimicked many of her attributes. However, years of hard work, a broken marriage, and the deaths of our parents and many of her dearest friends had taken a toll on her. Now, for the first time in many years, I saw her become transformed as God worked a miracle through her.

After getting over the "sticker shock" of rental housing prices, we embraced the excitement of being in Boston, a historical gold mine of our nation's earliest birthing battles. We delighted in its cobblestone walks, its Freedom Trails and commons. We traveled to nearby sites in Concord and Lexington. We visited the Salem Witch Museum and the mansions in Newport, Rhode Island.

We frequently stayed in touch with our older sister, Sandra, who was maintaining the family business on Mackinac Island in Michigan. Coming from the Midwest, where it's a day's journey to get out of the state, we laughed to think that we had traveled through Vermont, New Hampshire, Maine, Massachusetts, and Rhode Island...all in the space of a few hours. It seemed as if every day held a special delight...God's blessing...and we intended to receive it all. Because it appeared that we may have just a short time left together, we became very present and alive. We learned that every moment is precious. It's funny how God calls us to our faith or recalls us or challenges us to deepen it. We are so valuable to God that nothing is spared to call us to our perfection.

Both my sisters, Sandra and Debra, attended Unity Church in Naples, Florida, during their winter season. So when Debra came to Boston, her first insistence was that we find the Unity Church. Being geographically challenged by Boston's winding "cow paths," one–way roads, and often unmarked streets, I ignored her request to find the Unity Church and took her instead to a church I knew. After about three weeks, however, my guilt overcame me, and I finally pulled out the Yellow Pages and telephoned Christ Church Unity of Brookline. God's magic is so complete. The church was a short block from our apartment! We could literally see it when we looked out our window!

On the first day we attended, Reverend Tom was speaking. The sermon was about healing. As if God had acted to deepen our belief and to help us grow in courage and experience true reconciliation, at one point Reverend Tom looked directly at my sister and me. We were sitting several rows back from the pulpit. He said, "You will be healed." We cried. But we already knew it was true. God had brought us back together, and had brought us "the love that surpasses understanding."

It's been four years since that time, and my sister's "clear" reports continue. She has made a number of major life changes. She has sold her business. She dabbles in drawing and other creative expressions. (She took several adult–education art classes in Boston when she was undergoing chemotherapy!) She sees the riches of every day. Indeed, God is alive in her.

A continuing legacy of her choice to come to Boston for care is that twice a year she travels here, often with our older sister, for checkups. We found a treasure in the "three of us." Although laced with some underlying tension we feel while awaiting test results, every trip is an opportunity to be together, to laugh, to remember, to celebrate, to be present to God within one another. I can never again forget the truth of those magnificent words, "For with God nothing shall be impossible." (Luke 1:37)

The Jump

Mary Lee Scott

In March 2000, something happened that changed my life. It wasn't anything you might think terribly radical, like a bout with cancer or a car crash, but to me it was significant. It was no small feat for a thirty six–year–old woman who's scared to death of everything from toads to confrontations to roller coasters. It had a profound effect on me.

It started in Destin, Florida. My husband Mark and I, along with our sons Paul and John, vacation in Destin every spring. We rent a condo on the Gulf and basically live it up: play all day, eat out every night, and catch crabs after dark. It's so relaxing. I wouldn't go to Disney World for a million dollars if I had to give up my quiet week in Destin.

Mary Lee Scott is a 4th grade teacher in Portage, Michigan. She lives in Galesburg with her husband Mark and two sons, Paul and John. She loves reading and writing. She has won several Kalamazoo Gazette writing contests and was included in *Voices of Michigan*, Volumes II and III

Anyway, two years previously, Paul noticed that Destin (which has grown from a lucky fishing village to a busy tourist town in a very short time) had a bungee jump at its little place called "Trax" which specializes in go–carts and video games. I told Paul that he was too young to bungee jump, but that someday I'd do it with him. In retrospect, it wasn't very well thought out.

Unfortunately, Paul has an uncanny memory. Both kids do, especially when it comes to stupid ideas of mine. So the new millennium, with all its hype, rolled in. We went to Destin like clockwork, still stayed at the Coral Reef Club, still ate at restaurants like Captain Dave's. And when we drove by the Trax, there was a huge sign on the bungee jump reading "Special $15!"

Paul immediately picked up on this, reminding me of my inane statement. He was now twelve, which we discovered upon stopping, is the age required for bungee jumping.

I was caught. Since we had just eaten a huge dinner, I convinced Paul that we could not jump tonight. We returned to the condo, Paul bursting with excitement, me feeling absolutely sick to my stomach.

Of course, I dreamed all night about heights. Over and over in my dreams, I fell from cliffs, trees, and Ferris wheels. I woke up in the morning with a vague feeling of dread in my stomach, but I knew exactly what would happen. I would climb to the top and chicken out.

It had happened before. When I was about four, my parents took the family to one of those enormous slides. It was high and wide enough for several people to slide down at once, on burlap sacks. Well, I got to the top, looked down, and cried until my dad came up and walked me back down the long steel staircase. My older brothers were sliding gleefully down, laughing at my infantile behavior. I have never forgotten the slide, or the humiliation I felt at not being able to go down it.

All this was going to change in March 2000. I was going to redeem myself. I was really going to do it.

But deep down inside, I knew I wasn't going to do it.

I felt a little queasy all day, but shook it off. We lay out in the sun, ate lunch in the condo, all the while acting as though everything was normal. I could tell Mark didn't think for a minute that I would go through with it (and I noted that he didn't show any interest in jumping himself). He threw comments at me like, "You'd better wear tennis shoes. Sandals might fall off when you jump." A typical cop, Mark tends to play mind games. I don't think he was being mean; I think he was just trying to make me see what I had gotten myself into.

At 4:00, it was decided that we should leave. Paul and I would bungee jump then we'd all go to dinner. I dressed comfortably—jean bib overall shorts, Reeboks. Paul was excited; I was beginning to get that sick feeling seriously in my stomach. But I wasn't really worried, because I knew what I'd do. I'd back out, as usual.

The Trax didn't look crowded. As Paul and I approached the ticket window, the kid working said, "He's jumping?" When I told him we both were, he did a double take, but to his credit, didn't comment. He asked for my ID, and I filled out forms for the two of us. I had the distinct feeling that I was signing both of our lives away. I handed him two twenties and he gave me a ten back. I slipped it into my wallet, feeling like a prisoner awaiting execution. It began to seem surreal, like I was watching someone else.

We weighed in, and then another guy got us harnesses. The one he put on me was huge, and the first kid said to him, "She's gonna fall out of that!" This did untold wonders for my confidence. Thankfully, they found me a smaller harness.

After we had the straps on, we were instructed to sit on a bench until our turn came. There were several people at the top waiting to jump. Mark took photos constantly, getting on my nerves. Paul and I sat with three college–age boys, who shared a cigarette. Though I've never smoked, I wanted a puff badly. I was dying of anxiety, but felt obligated to be the role model. I desperately wished I'd had a glass or two of wine before leaving the condo.

I'd brought my laptop computer to Florida with me, unable to leave my writing. I was working on a novel, a love story about a quarterback. I thought about Brett Favre. What would he do in this situation? I had no doubt that he would jump. It would be less painful than football, and after all, it would be over in a matter of seconds.

It seemed to be taking forever up there, but when they told our bunch to climb, it was still too soon. All seventy–five feet of the tower was metal. It didn't look too bad from the ground, but about three–fourths of the way up, I got woozy. My legs actually began shaking. They are shaking now as I remember the climb.

On the top platform I looked around. I could see Destin: hotels, restaurants, and across the street, the ocean. When the sea breeze blew, the entire platform swayed gently. Could it fall down? Doubtful. (I hoped.) I said desperately to Paul, "Honey, I don't think I can do this." I meant, "Honey, I can't do this."

He patted my shoulder and said, grinning, "Yes, you can, Mom." I felt so guilty; who was the parent here?

In front of me was a boy smaller than Paul, but probably older. I asked him, "Have you done this before?"

He smiled in a friendly way and replied, "Yes, Ma'am." I love how polite southerners are. I've been teaching in Michigan for thirteen years and no child has ever called me Ma'am.

"Well," I persisted, "how was it?"

He smiled again, benevolently. "It's really fun, honest." I wanted to hug him. Even if it was horrible, he wasn't going to tell me. He casually stepped up to the edge of the platform and jumped after a brief word with the guy working the top.

Then it was my turn. I looked at Paul and the three college kids and said again, "I don't think I can do this." Sorry I wasn't more imaginative, but my brain, along with my body, was starting to freeze up. I approached the guy standing at the edge (he was harnessed, too) and told him urgently, "I can't do this. I need to get down."

Patiently, in the way of someone who hears it all the time, he said, "Yes, you can do this. Don't look down." Too late, I was already looking down at the cushioned mat below; it was dizzying, to say the least.

"I'm going to count three, two, one—bungee, and then you're going to jump," he said authoritatively.

"You're not going to push me, are you?" I asked, panic rising.

He said, "No, I'm not going to push you, but I can't let you stay up here." His voice was firmer now, like a teacher telling a student to get to work. I was aware that he was not over twenty–

five; that in fact no one up here on the platform tonight was over twenty–one but myself. But the commanding tone worked.

I said dutifully, "O.K." I grabbed the cylinder–shaped pillow to hold and waited for his count. At "bungee," I stepped off the metal platform.

The initial fall felt like nothing; it wasn't a big shock. But when the cord stretched all the way down, I felt myself "boing" back up, which was a faster and harder rush than the fall. I didn't scream, but let out a humming sound under my breath. Closing my eyes during the fall, I opened them in surprise at the rebound.

I never worried that the cord would break. My only fear had been that I wouldn't do it. Flooded with relief, after I was lowered into the cushion I just lay there, grinning like an idiot. As I crawled off, the kid working helped me unfasten the harness since I was too flustered. I couldn't stop smiling. Hysterical would be a good word to describe my new condition.

I stood at the bottom and watched Paul jump (naturally he was very brave), and Mark and John met us as we walked through the gate to where the onlookers sat. I spread my arms and declared to all, "I did it!" Who cares, I thought. Mark's parents were there, bursting with pride, and I would never see the rest of the crowd again.

Mark hugged me, and did I see a new respect? John and my in–laws were very supportive, telling Paul and me how brave we'd been. But I didn't feel brave; I felt ecstatic.

We went to dinner at the Back Porch. I had a celebratory glass of rum punch (I saved the glass as a souvenir of the occasion and still have it in the kitchen), and dined on a delicious chicken salad with mandarin oranges and nuts.

My hair, naturally curly anyway, gave a new definition to "frizz" after the jump in the muggy sea air. In photos, I look like I've stuck my finger into a socket. My students laughed when I showed them after we returned from break.

For a few days, I was the talk of Woodland Elementary. I told my students about my experience, not realizing they'd tell every other fourth grader at lunch, and that the news would get to my principal before the first day back was half over. I could tell people were impressed, but surprised. I'm not known as the daring, throw–caution–to–the–wind type. In fact, if you didn't know me, you'd describe me as ordinary, borderline dull. For the most part, I am sensible and organized, dependable, the kind of person who will loan you a cup of sugar or watch your kids while you run an errand.

How did this adventure influence me? It's hard to measure precisely, but it showed when Paul said to me that night in Destin, "Mom, I don't know how to say this, but I really have a new respect for you."

It showed when Mark looked at me across the dinner table with a gleam in his eyes. His admiration was obvious and unexpected.

It showed when John proudly announced to his teacher (and for that matter, anyone we saw for a month), "Did you hear my mom bungee–jumped?"

It showed when I told my parents and brothers and reminded them of the slide incident (of course, everyone else had forgotten it).

But mostly it showed when I looked into the mirror and saw a person who dared to take a risk. I'd become so settled, so careful, I'd lost track of what I could do. I could write stories and enter them in competitions. I could write a novel. I could do anything in the world that I wanted to.

I can.

Poetry

Sam Winsor

Since retiring as an educator, **N. S. Williams** finds she now has time to indulge herself. Consequently, her days and weeks are filled with reading, writing, music, friends and travel. She was raised in Pontiac, MI but currently resides in Rochester, MI, and except for her college years has always lived in Michigan.

Conversation With A Friend

Ah, my friend, we meet again.
Time has allowed no barrier to take seed or grow.
No lulls here, while conversation and friendship
Sail briskly on without trepidation or impediment.
How I've missed your unique coupling and blending of words
That always force contemplation to reach comprehension
And your streams of loquacity
Strung out like lines of laundry hung up to air.
My body forcefully buckles and convulses
At such humorous exchanges.
Can it survive such merriment?
Is comprehension ever truly realized?
Is my perception seen only through my own eyes
Or envisioned, or perhaps reflected, in yours?
Why have you knitted together these precise strands?
What vision enables such unique meaning for you?
Is it possible that such diverse ideas and backgrounds
Do find a common arena in this play on words?
Ah, my friend, what I would give
To experience this conversation from within you.

~~~N. S. Williams

> **Gina Thomas** was reared in Michigan and after traveling through five continents has returned to live in Kalamazoo. Currently she is studying at the graduate level to work in the psychology and holistic health fields, and is working on a book of fiction as well as continuing to write poetry.

Naked Feet

She's the kind of woman
who makes you want to be a woman,
to make the title yours
instead of falling into it by birth.
It's not her hair, exactly,
Medusa tangles flying round her face,
or the sturdy freckled feet
striding naked on the boardwalk.
It's not the way she hikes
the calico bag upon her shoulder
in a brisk, distracted fashion,
pens and paint and paper
threatening to topple and cascade
in artistic flurry under naked feet...

no...

it is that look within her eyes—
Gemini twins hinting at a juicy life,
alluding to tastes of men who she succumbed with according to her
passion,
but who never burned as brightly as that flickering flame within—
a fire which ignites her march upon the boardwalk,
hips that swing in rhythm to the curve upon her lips—
they suggest the memory of solitude
and dreams that bent but never shattered.

You can't escape the feeling
that she has settled like a cat into her limbs,
right down to the
last
indigo
toenail,
and as you pass her on the street
it makes you proud to be called woman
and embrace your naked feet.

~~~ Gina Thomas

Christina Rajala Dembek, who last year had the pleasure of editing *Voices of Michigan, An Anthology of Michigan Authors,* Volume III, now adds her voice to those of her writing comrades. She takes heart from the Art and Must of Writing which always finds new, beautiful, kind ways to bridge inner works to outer words.

The Light and Dark of Romance

I.

"Flambe´," he said gently,
"No," said she, gently,
shaking her napkin,
the movement
a blessing.

Waiting for the order,
the steward moved about—
a lesson on obscurity,
a few tables away.

The couple reclined into lavish shadow.

The man had sable hair
running away from his face—
away, away—in crescents.
She nodded her head in generosity.
He shook his.
What suggestion would the waiter give?
They sighed. No decision.

Should the waiter step in and say—the honeyed cake?
No, no, let them pause;
let them sway.

II.

"Do you suppose he's her beau?"
Marge asked Dave's wife,
while looking at the couple.
"Oh, yes," said Sandra.
feeling uncomfortable in this place.
She fidgeted,
hoping the waiter in his tuxedo
didn't note
her husband roughed in tweed
at the bar.
"Never mind about that," said Marge. "Don't fret."
"I wish I could look like she
does in that fawn–colored lace."
"Around her breasts it adds
so much grace," Marge couldn't help
but add,
and pinched her own thickening.
Sandra watched her husband
watch the woman taste
a black forest cherry.

III.

The lone businessman also
dreamed of the couple:

      Panther–like he catches her eye,
      daring her to stop his firm grasp
      of her bosom.
      He reaches out;
      she plies a hand to his back,
      and closer they draw.

Nibbling her lips
which flush,
he presses
toward her hollow…

"Ahem…Would you like anything more, sir?"
the waiter interrupted.
"No…No," the lone businessman said,
feeling the panther in his bones subside,
always latent there.

IV.

His name, Antonio.
His age, thirty.
He kisses her deftly
in the dim light
certain nights
after dinner,
nothing more. She stands
in the door, a blond minnow
going into her home's dark cave.
He feels like a prowler,
and could be.
"Be careful, Leila," he says,
as she closes the door.

V.

Leila looks at her hands' shake,
draws off her coat, her shoes,
and feels the cold floor.

In the living room one light is on,
a false greeting she planned

before the night began.
There's no one here—
unless she thinks, and thinking
he comes back.

Biting her lip
while going upstairs,
to an image of him in the dark,
she muses,
"I must stay away,
because
I could pray to you,
which is unfair."

VI.

Nonchalantly, Antonio slips
down the stairs,
and follows
an old echo
of his footsteps
downtown.

His night shadow comes
and goes by the lamps.

Under one he inhales a smoke,
and is content that no one observes,
and no one walks late,
as he does.
For it is in these hours
and on these vacant roads
that his thoughts come to him
like cats out of alleys.

Dawn,
Antonio watches the harbor gulls rise,
and reflects that they are like
the steam of his longing
never caught,
distilled.

~~~Christina Rajala Dembek

Language has always fascinated **Margrit Schlatter.** She has been an avid reader all her life and has always wanted to write. About a year and a half ago, Margrit picked up a pen, composed her first poem and has been writing ever since. Her native language is German, and she grew up in Switzerland. Margrit immigrated to the United States in 1976.

Leader of the Parade

It is his rightful place
to head the Lilac Parade,
his people lived off this land
before history washed onto shore.
  Down main street
He gracefully rides his horse
spine erect, he acknowledges faces
from many different tribes.
  His head crowned with feathers
in red, white and blue
to honor the Chippewa nation
whose glowing hearths dwell
along the Straights of Mackinac.
  They call him Chief,
his native features
marked by time and the sun
tell stories from long ago,
about people with peaceful hearts
and The Great Spirit
 who lived in their souls.
  Prayers from the ancient drum
resonate in his presence,
today he has no choice
and follows a different beat
but from across centuries

reverberates the rhythm from the drum.

Does his spirit fly with eagles,
and his soul chant with content?
I wonder what moves across his field of vision,
as I watch him ride
                    toward the evening sun.

~~~Margrit Schlatter

Eric Martin was born and reared in the small town of Parma outside Jackson, MI. While at Lumen Christi School, Eric was privileged enough to have a few poems published in the school writing magazine *The Corona* (1997). Eric is a recent graduate of Northern Michigan University in Marquette.

Lady Gitche Gumme

As an eighteen year old boy
Raised in the heart of Lower Michigan
I sought out a state education,
In a quiet little city on the South Shore
Of our Northern Sea.

That's when I saw her—
She became my first love.
I was an awkward, ignorant virgin
And she seduced me from her broad silica beaches
She let me stalk her entranced from isolated cliffs.

Finally she beckoned me to come closer
From out behind my hiding place.
She spread out her surf for me
I desperately plunged into her—
Yearning to drink her cold, clear spirit.

I visited her regularly after that.
And she never failed to listen,
Whether I was at my best or worst.
I'd always find my way to her.
And she'd smile when she saw me.

It comforted me to see how alike we were.
I've witnessed her tempests rage in November,

And then watched her nurture children playfully in August.
I've seen her icy veil in January—
When all she desired was solitude,
Even then she welcomed me
For she loves me too.

She let me get drunk and then sick
And her waves never scolded.
She watched patiently while I broke down and cried
And she stretched out her tides to hold me.
I both prayed and sinned on the edge of her shore,
Whatever I was in the mood for.

I swam naked with a girl—
Who at the time was my love forever.
She welcomed us both unhesitantly
And quickly disarmed my girlfriend,
With one of her cool caresses.
We were consumed by her ebony water
Our souls redeemed by her orgasmic baptism—
A starlight manage et trois in the lee of mountains.
While bull legged Ontario who was never asked to join
Watched us from over her shoulder.

 I told another girl that I couldn't love her anymore
On the sheltered beaches of Marquette harbor.
The girl wept incessantly, I looked for an escape.
She just laughed and she drove her white horses ashore
Offering me to ride into her sunset.

I also held a woman I shouldn't have—
We sat together awestruck as she protested over the breakwall.
Terrified I vowed never to enrage her again,
Ask Mr. Lightfoot he will tell you.

Yes, even I make her jealous.
But her spite is just mere show
Compared to the envy she stirs in me,
For I am not her only lover—
I have caught the moon staring
And I know that he pines for her.

She calls up to the clouds for him at midnight,
And the thin veil of gray parts on cue for his entrance,
His smile shimmers admiringly on her surface.
She opens up her depths and shows him secrets—
She would never waste on me.
Then she laughs indifferently and basks in his pale warmth.

Only her love immeasurable could quench his cosmic burning,
As I look on jilted and scorned.
I know they're plotting for a secret rendezvous
Away from her various other admirers,
When he will finally dip below her vast horizon
Two forces entangled in a mythical embrace
Just moments before the dawn.

~~~Eric Martin

Evocative words and images are **Cecilia A. Winston Floren's**
palette, issuing from God through the heart and mind,
spreading out in shimmering rings, connecting us all together.

Serious Defoliator

Hanging from my finger by a gleaming thread,
appearing out of nowhere, a half–inch worm must have hitched
a ride as I walked the dogs this morning in the field.
It becomes a brief distraction from the ongoing horrors
in lower Manhattan.

It descends gracefully to the white page on my desk,
disconnects from its silk and begins to hump and straighten,
looping along with the prolegs on its hind and front segments.
The table lamp throws a larger shadow of the worm
and they proceed together.

This is the caterpillar of a geometrid moth,
deceptively camouflaged to look like a twig —
a pretender—like the terrorists who blended in so well—
a larval earth–measurer, shape–shifting from black button hole,
to wish bone to croquet wicket on the march, or an eight when
hunched—multiple personae, many disguises.

It stops, rears up, leans and waves around,
then locks to a 45 degree angle,
a tiny, stiff line with inky shadow, unwavering,
wrinkly, dark and thin, like ET's neck.

I watch. And wonder
that even on paper it knows what to do.
This tiny wiggly isn't, as it appears,
scanning for something,

testing the air for pheromones or
receiving tremors from ground zero.
It's just freezing up to stay unnoticed.

"Don't be afraid," I murmur. " I do not eat worms."
As though reassured, it begins once more, inching away
to the corner of the page, then onto the sharp edge
where it hooks with little feet and starts yawing to the right,
then stiffening to become part of this white tree—
trying to blend in.

It's harder to see against the deep brown of the desk.
The phone rings. I answer, and talk for quite a while,
grieving aloud with a friend over our frightening, lacerated world.

I do not see my visitor again.
It has gone as softly as it came, wandering off
to some other part of the house,
oblivious to me, or the cats or the dogs,
or anything to do with Allah,
or even September eleventh.

~~~Cecilia A. Winston Floren

Cathy Scoda is a Michigan native born and reared in Wyandotte, MI. After a few years in Texas, Cathy and her husband returned to Michigan and settled in Westland. She has written poems since she was twelve years old and usually writes in order to free thoughts from her mind.

The Life of a Year

January is icy winds and frosty faces,
Brilliant blue skies,
And the sun's glare reflecting off
Ice crystal snow banks.

January is the great–grandfather of all months.
Wizened and far more serious than giggling June,
He blows cold breaths to rattle shingles
And shake the traffic lights—
And then sends piles of snow to bring
A downy quiet to the city.
"Hu–u–ushhhh!!" blows the wind
As the last flake lands on a soft white hill.

January's roaring has gone to bed.
In its place is temporary peace—
To be shattered soon enough
By cries of snowmen–building children.

***

Hearts and flowers adorn the dress of February.
She prefers shades of pink and red,
But—in fits of jealousy—
Has been known to wear green.

February is perky

255

As she tosses off winter's coat
In anticipation of the spring
That she knows is still weeks away.

February weaves crowns of flowers and ivy
And parades through the town as though it were her kingdom.
She alights on the city like a bird of love
And croons old–fashioned melodies of broken hearts
That are on the mend.

February is a rose–filled celebration,
Sweetened by heart–shaped candies of all flavors.
February whispers secret messages to new loves
And wipes the tears of the broken–hearted.

***

March is January's indecisive nephew.
He cannot decide if he should allow a thaw
Or permit the snow to continue falling.
Like a petulant child he acts according to his mood.
When he has a tantrum,
Icy cold sleet pelts the street—and any person
Brave enough to venture out.
On a good day, he might let the sun break
Through the thick, gray clouds.

March is slushy mud…
With sunny afternoons too warm for boots
And frosty mornings too cold to go without them.

March is wild cloud formations
Being tossed about by wicked winds.
March is umbrellas blown the wrong way
By those same winds…whose screaming laughter is heard
Once the umbrella is useless and its owner is soaked.

256

March is also quiet and contemplative.
Soft gray skies permit peaceful thoughts.
Mud brings to mind planting…tilling the soil with hopeful plans.

March bridges the seasons—
And cannot make up his mind
Which one he prefers.

***

April is either soggy or sun–kissed,
Depending on her mood.
Her laughter bubbles into crystal raindrops
That splash into transparent puddles.

Ducks swim on a newly thawed lake while
Lilacs and honeysuckle burst into scented bloom
To quietly announce April's arrival.

April is March's older cousin.
She's been known to compete with him
To see who can send more rain
And pelt more rooftops with hail!

April laughs,
For she knows her rains are welcomed by farmers
While her cousin's are merely endured.

April is fresh blades of grass
Poking their heads out of the moist soil
And youthful saplings reaching skyward
Toward the brilliant sun.

April is a new beginning…
A rebirth of one's spirit.

***

May wears a green cloak of hope.
Joyous is her laughter,
And mirth is the hat she dons for her stroll
Amid the dewy grass.
Daffodils nod at the lady whose sunny, smiling eyes
Caress them with warmth.
Nesting birds sing merrily of her crystal clear blue sky.
Feathering cirrus clouds visit May's sky,
Followed by puffy cumulus that send rejuvenating showers
To the thirsty ground below.

May is springtime's favorite daughter—
Bringing tulips of red, pink, and yellow
And new leaves stretching in the sun
On branches that wave in the afternoon breeze.

May is the earth turned inside–out and upside–down
By ploughs in the fields and shovels in the suburban yard.
May is the promise of new opportunities
Which await discovery…
Chances waiting to be taken.

May is a brave step forward.
She is optimism cloaked in serenity.

***

As May's cloak of green
Gives way to June's blooms,
Specks of fragrant colors
Appear on the grassy landscape.

Yellow sunflowers adorn hillsides and lawns.
Red tulips greet visitors at door fronts.

Lavender lilacs share their heady aroma
With nectar–gathering bees
And bouquet–clipping gardeners.

The mourning dove's cry
Greets the dawn
And the sun stretches his rays
Across the sky in a golden hug.

June's melody is the
Laughter of children
Who have begun summer vacation…
Riding bikes on trails,
Reading comic books,
Building sandcastles,
And slurping popsicles.

June is a celebration
Of no routines.
Every day holds an adventure.
The unexpected awaits.

***

July is a freedom parade
Marching to the drumbeat
That you can feel in your chest.

July tastes like cherry snow–cones
And pink cotton candy at fairs.
July is the sticky–sweet coolness
Of watermelon juice
Running down your chin.
July tastes like fresh corn–on–the–cob.

July is red, white, and blue

Waving in the wind.
July sounds like the oohs and aahs
Of children
Watching fireworks
Explode the nighttime
Into brilliant arrays of color.

July is a youth—
Exuberant and unpredictable.

***

August is the droning buzz of cicadas in the trees.
It is the winking lights of fireflies
Playing hide–n–seek at nightfall
And the scent of new leather shoes
Bought in anticipation
Of school's first days.

August is the fading shrieks of children
As they run one last time
Through the cold water of the sprinkler.
August is a teen pleading to stay up later—
Just once more.

August is the last bonfire
Where smoke curls rise up to the sky
And gooey marshmallows are eaten before bedtime.
August is ice cream that melts too fast.

August is the woolen blanket of humidity
Draped over the town.

August is restlessness.

***

September is a pony–tailed girl
Skipping off to school on that exciting first day.
September tastes like chalk dust
Swallowed by children
Who are clapping erasers.

September is green leaves
Tinged with red and yellow.
September is sunny with cool breezes
That melt in your mouth when you breathe.
September tastes like a crispy, crunchy, juicy apple…
Tanging your tongue in a tantalizing way.

September is the chattering squabble of squirrels
As they fight over acorns on the oak trees' branches.
September is finding the shiny treasure
Beneath the chestnut tree.

September is honeybees
Drinking the last of summer's nectar
And cider mills where the air itself
Is saturated with the mingled perfumes
Of tart and sweet apples.
Leaves and soil blend together
Forming an earthy, moist scent
That lingers for hours.

September is the scent of new copies,
Blue ink, and black number two pencils.

September tastes like new beginnings—
Fresh and crisp.

***
October is September's wild aunt.

Cool and breezy,
She flits about
Chasing the season's last honeybees
And tossing leaves away from the raker's bag.

October is the black cat's smooth fur
And glowing emerald green eyes.
She is the crackle of fallen leaves
Beneath the trick–or–treaters' feet.
She is the full moon's glow—
Guarding harvests and lighting the way
For Homecoming kings and queens.
Jack–o–lanterns' grins reflect October's smile.
Her mood is joyous—
With a carefree attitude.

October is the first mug of apple cider
And a mouth filled with cinnamon doughnuts.
October ages quickly—
And so enjoys her fun times,
For she knows they will soon end.

October is change.

***

November is the great–uncle
Of October.
Far wiser and more weathered,
He has no time for childhood games
Of spooks and costumes.
His is the time of preparation.
His furrowed brow relaxes
As he watches his pets scurry and store
In preparation for winter,
And he nods approvingly

At their stash of provisions.

November's winds invite the leaves
To fall like rain.
Shower do they upon all passersby.
Soon the leaves swirl in
Circular dances across walkways
And hardening soil.

The first frost visits in November,
Leaving starry designs on windowpanes.
Winds are so steely cold
That they must be as gray as the sky.
These winds warn walkers,
"Hurry home to the warmth of the hearth!"

November smells like
Spicy pumpkin and sweet potato pies.
November gathers families together
To give thanks for all blessings.

***

December is snow–soaked mittens
And bootprints in fresh snow.
December is a happy–go–lucky youth—
Head adorned by a ski cap—
Racing down a snow–covered hill.

December is sledding and skiing
And snowballs being tossed,
Followed by drinking a mug of hot chocolate.

December is evergreen;
Pine perfume floats through the air.

Bayberry candlelight flickers
And the spicy aroma welcomes guests in from the cold.

December is the hushed whispers
Of secret surprises.
Moms and dads hide packages
From curious eyes.

December tastes like homemade sugar cookies
And peppermint canes
Eaten by children with sparkling eyes
And rosy cheeks.

December sparkles with Christmas lights
On trees, houses, and churches.
In the sky the stars shine and twinkle brilliantly
In the cold midnight blue sky.

December is a promise fulfilled.

~~~Cathy Scoda

Melissa Croghan is part of six generations on Mackinac Island and feels her work is strongly influenced by the spirit and ethos of living on an Island in Michigan that lends itself to strange leaps of faith. **Communion** was first published in *The Massachusetts Review*. Melissa works as an oil painter, and is employed by the Farmington School District as their poet–in–residence.

Communion

Could be there's a lot I don't know.
I do know I have a hatch in my house
that leads outside. Under the hatch
there are some stairs, and then at the bottom
a delicate trellis so lovely it is deserving
of roses. Next to the trellis is a red wagon
I keep in case a neighborhood child should stop by.
Lately nothing has bloomed, neither the roses or
the children.
Something else I don't know is how it is that
I have found another hatch in my house.
Last night I opened it up and went through.
It seemed I was searching for you, my dear friend, but
then I took a turn and was in a damp shallow valley,
almost a muddy font, almost wet enough to get all wet.
I got through it, and was searching for you, still, but
I was up too high, I'd found an old wagon and climbed
in it and it took me to where I used to live in
the country, right up to those hills that lift above the
lower fields, and I didn't want anyone to pull the wagon
so it went by itself. I came to a wonderful field, trees
tipped with a copper light, branches like silver silos,
a few splayed ends, and everything shot from behind
with a dark sun, the earth made over into a kind of
stark coriander. But this place I was in kept heaping

and piling higher until I knew I couldn't reach you
and that made me sad but you were so far away and I was
busy anyway, busy grazing in a green and white clerestory.
I was at an altar eating roses.

~~~Melissa Croghan

Lorabeth Fitzgerald of Grand Ledge and Mackinac Island, MI was graduated from The College of William and Mary in Virginia where she majored in English. She worked on the *Hillsdale Daily News* before pursuing a career in New York where she did editorial work for *Esquire* and *Coronet* magazines. Lorabeth has edited three books for the Grand Ledge Area Historical Society.

Rosebud

I dip into the cluttered closet
To withdraw pressed prom rosebuds.
They disperse and flutter floorward,
Artifacts of another me.

Who was she preening and flowing
In blue, net–skirted splendor wearing
Pink rosebuds as a badge of honor?
Who smiled and said goodnight to the chaperone?

A plumb line links her to me.
It shimmers and fades, stands in sharp delineation,
Or ravels and hangs in loops and festoons,
Then seems all but to break clean.

A plummet … some arcane anchor
Twirls and bobs at the end as if
A snub–nosed fish dawdles playfully
Now taking a massive swipe, then a nudge.

It must exude some bitter protection
Some persevering, life–giving element,
This anchor that waves aimlessly as a dried rosebud
Lending me a certain perpendicularity.

~~~Lorabeth Fitzgerald

Dianna L. Zimmerman lives in Albuquerque NM, is a graduate student in Creative Writing at the University of New Mexico and the mother of beautiful twins. She has been writing poetry since she was a child. Her strong connection to mid–Michigan, having grown up there, is reflected in much of her writing.

White Sheets

after a poem by Gail Mazur

I stood next to the hospital bed
in Saginaw, Michigan. I lied
with a weighted tongue about recovery,

My brother was dying. He'd had headaches
and a lump under his arm, misdiagnosed,
and we both sat mutely toward the wall–mount TV.

We had walked through life on thick calves
inherited from an ancestral German farmer,
distant crop picker. Those sheets

were too white in an already white room:
I wanted to paint them, dye them,
puke on them, anything to cut the sheen

and rough starchiness. We slumped like
runners after a marathon, together and alone
in our fear, descended into this stale room

with monitors that show heart rate, breathing,
other things that you don't think
about doing until a time like this.

Voices of Michigan

We looked out the window to a perfect blue
Sky. I wanted him to tell me his dreams but
he had a tube stuffed harshly down his throat.

I confessed my sins, I wiped our tears,
I realized, this is my place isn't it,
to hold his hand, reassure him to the end.

~~~Dianna L. Zimmerman

Writing enables **Jeannie Milakovich** to deal with elements of life she can't let go of. Through it, she copes with her questions about and frustrations with life. Jeannie lives in Ironwood with her husband and two of her three children.

Chasing Windmills

Tell me where you go
When a mother's only child,
Young, foolhardy, demonstrates his valor,
But struggles futilely to rise above the surface
Of a watery grave.

Tell me where you go
When another child,
Fragile arms crossed above an unprotected head,
Cries out desperately for help
And no one answers.

Tell me where you go
When the old man,
Devoid of fortune and will,
Freezes to death in his cardboard home
In a deserted back alley of the city.

Believers said I'd find you under the steepled tower
Clanging salvation on a Sunday morn.
I see finely feathered pigeons
Prance haughtily down the aisle
Cooing loud affirmations of an ambiguous belief.
I find you not.

Perhaps you only appear in isolated fragments—
A few eighth notes in a whole concerto,
One perfect high C in a cacophony of raised voices,
A prodigy in a myriad of hopefuls.
Perhaps you don't exist at all—

Shadow, fantasy, nebulous border of a dream,
I search for you;
Logic whispers, "Abandon your search."
I remain—a modern Quixote chasing windmills
In the human heart.

~~~Jeannie Milakovich

Kay MacDonald writes with a Labrador at her feet and a Poodle in her lap. The dogs and Kay's husband are her only company on their quiet river. Kay grooms and trains dogs but since her short story was published in *Voices of Michigan, An Anthology of Michigan Authors* Volume III, she prefers to say she is a writer.

Card Dreams

Her fingers spend away the afternoons
shuffling, dealing, laying down the cards
while out of doors the sun lays a pattern
through the new bright leaves around the place
where she lives in papered rooms and flashes
from a fading television set.
The cards are friends that speak of games once played
with ladies laughing and cups of tea.
She loves the cards. Smooth and warm, each new deal
a chance at luck and new adventure.
And the television applauds and cheers
the clever tricky tactics that fill
her days with might be's that come along in
numbers laid on numbers and black kings
that welcome queens with something akin to
the love that she remembers from days
before the cards became her constant friends.....
When she was the flame–haired queen of hearts.

~~~Kay MacDonald

John R. Alberts performs his poetry in auditoriums as well as intimate settings. His work has appeared in several journals and in Sunday editions of metropolitan newspapers. He has enjoyed performing his work to live music and with dancers.

I Am the Cat

you think is lost.
The one *you* call
Tabitha, or Jasper, or Phoebe, or Spats,
or just
cat.

I am the cat who,
  you named with an –itty
  or an atty
  to make it handy
  or suit your fancy
  when summoning your
  domestic
  the good house–mouser
  who, tail at attention
  scampers for treats,
  or strokes,
  or praise,
  or as your conceit allows you...
  shelter from the grim of damp,
  of the bone–seep cold.
I now demur.
I'll be myself awhile.

Cry your gray cries.
Inflect reproachful sighs.

Thunder vile invectives.
By all means, bawl, if that's your style.
This cat will be herself awhile.

Your 'kitty' won't answer the knock at her door.
She's taken her phone off the hook.
She's in a brown study and shan't be disturbed.
So nice that you've come but please go.
She's being herself awhile.

I am the cat
you think is lost.
Peer under the porch,
climb up to the attic,

descend cellar deep
where I may lie,
not asleep,
behind cool jars
of thoughtful tomatoes,
enjoying being myself
... for awhile.

No matter your weeping
my eyes won't widen
my ears won't twitch.
I'm being myself—
for awhile.

Who asks after puss–cat
with such pleading,
such needing?

~~~John R. Alberts

Katherine Ha was born in the thumb of Michigan in a small
farming community. She feels that experience shaped her life as a
writer. She is a teacher of English, focusing on writing, for the
Portage Public Schools. She is married with two daughters,
coaches volleyball, and is a fellow of the Third Coast Writing
Project.

For the Fairest Goddess

I have stolen the Golden Apple,

that poisonous gift–curse Eris
bestowed on generations of women.

Aphrodite kept it in a velvet–lined case
near her bedside,
the last thing she looked at before bedtime.
Next to it, a framed photo
of the day she won her prize.

I snuck in under cover of false darkness.
She lay on the bed, drugged,
bandages on her face,
remnants of the latest plastic surgery
on the aging beauty queen.

The years had been cruel,
and the sacred apple had chipped.
Gold flecks falling away,
the iridescent surface beneath
revealed warped images of scalpels,
diet pills, and beauty crowns.

The bottom was burnt black
from years of exposure

to the flames of vanity
created centuries ago,
claiming Helen as the first
dry–kindled martyr.
The pyre grew—
scarring bodies
of women worldwide.
The prize

was heavy;
I struggled under
slightly hunched shoulders
going into dressing rooms,
beauty salons,
standing on doctor's office scales,
watching Christina Aguilera videos,
and playing with Barbies.
I took the weight from them—
relieved the tired At-lasses.
They stood,
still crouching,
waiting for the return of the weight,
not knowing how to exist without it.

I carry the apple to Hephaestus,
take his anvil and sledgehammer,
orange with inner fire.
The strength of generations
fills me.
We create a reckoning
for the poisonous fruit.

The hammer strikes
and rotted skin breaks
into razor–sharp shards

that shatter the glass shelves
of Estee Lauder counters everywhere.
Brainwashed priestesses in
The Temples of the Apple
awaken—
no longer
holding their bottles of perfume,
posing on catwalks,
primping for the camera,
or driving cotton–candy pink
Mary–Kay Cadillacs
down the freeway.

I have freed Aphrodite
and the masses.
They hate me for it.

~~~Katherine Ha

Margaret von Steinen, a freelance writer, lives in Kalamazoo with her husband, Randy and two sons, Ryan and Drew. She is currently working on a M. F. A. in creative writing at Western Michigan University. Her poetry has appeared in *Wild Stars, Moonlighting: A Collection of Kalamazoo Voices* and the *Kalamazoo Gazette*.

On the Day Before My 41st Birthday

All the blackbirds in the county pegged
the branches of the trees across the street,
their chattering the dry–hinge squeak
of a thousand screen doors, ajar, fanning

in the breeze. Maybe talking about Florida,
made me think of Hitchcock's, *The Birds,*
and how I used to be frightened of all
that flew, crept, or crawled, back when

I measured courage by the size of the spider
or snake coddled or killed. Grandfather
chopped off chicken heads and flamed
garden spiders as they swung head–down

on their spiral webs. One winter, he hunted
a rat that moved into his store and came
out only in the after–hours dark, taking first
to the bread on the low shelf in front of the meat

counter, later doing the cookie aisle across
the store, chewing off the corners of vanilla
wafers and gingersnap bags. Every morning,
we swept up that rat's mess before opening,

and every night Grandfather set out the skull
and crossbones marked boxes, and I never was
far from his or Grandmother's side until spring
when he found the cookie–fat rat dead at the foot

of his butcher's saw. That summer, Father taught
me to thread a thin worm over a barbed hook,
catch a bluegill, a keeper if it was as big as his
hand. But I never could bring myself to slice

the fish behind its neon–blue ear flap or run
a knife down its belly, like Father, who pushed
out the guts with a tar–stained thumb. Just last
week, I stood here listening to oak leaves scuttle

across the asphalt, parched and bony as the back
of Grandmother's hand, looking at the stunned,
black squirrel lying under the oak that my son, Ryan,
had knocked from a branch with a soccer ball.

I'm sorry, mom, its just something I've wanted to do
since I was five, he said. I felt my nerves reverse
their current, my eyes puddle, because some say
it might have been teenagers who bludgeoned

the elderly couple and their daughter on Q Avenue last
month, their bodies bloody rags, scarlet splashed
on counters, cabinets and walls. And now the old
man's plot of zinnias he used to cull and sell

in one–dollar bouquets are curling their petals,
and I'm stuck in September with our yard's
oldest maple, cool–green–calm on the north side,
a red–hot cluster of tongues on the south.

~~~Margaret von Steinen

> **Nancy Gump Ceslinski** wanted to be anything but a "Gump" until
> Forrest Gump brought honor to her goofy name. Her mother, a
> teacher, inspired her to write instead of talking so much. Nancy's
> story about Vietnam was published in *Looking Over My Shoulder*.
> She met her husband, Ed, in a local Cadillac bookstore.

Life Story in a Hundred Words

I wanted to be a cowgirl,
Riding my steed across the prairie.
Instead I became: Vietnam wife waiting
For war to end,
Wanderer of the nation's park
Campgrounds,
Searching for dreams after the war.
Tent–woman, tipi dweller,
Earth Mother of seven babies,
Teacher,
Single parent
Watching Michigan winters
Turn to daffodils,
Churning up sun fed
Summer soil to plant
The smiles of children
In my backyard.
Now, an artist,
I rest and paint pictures
With words
Of those dream days.
Now, riding my steed across the prairie:
Grandma feeding cowgirl books
To children riding on my knee.

~~~Nancy Gump Cieslinski

Emily Meier is the product of a Michigan summer love affair. Her work has appeared in *The Smart Girl's Guide to College*, *The Grosse Pointe News* and *Voices of Michigan, An Anthology of Michigan Authors*, Volume III.

My Age

I meet a friend for a drink.
Pinstripe suit, dark grey
He wears his choices well—
Business school, glass office on the 32nd floor.
His success, obvious.

"What do *you* do?"
the bartender asks me.
I shrug.
He nods, not caring that I have no answer.
A man's music fills the space.

People my age are making decisions
career moves, having babies without the tsk tsk
or hint of mistake.
People *my* age are planning
grad school, dissertations, 30 year mortgages
I'm *not* like people my age.

Order up a second round.
I lose myself again
in another person's story

And the piano man winks,
fills the awkward silence playing
For Emily, wherever I may find her.

~~~Emily Meier

Kelie Callahan has lived in Michigan her entire life. She is a graduate of the University of Michigan–Dearborn where one of her poems was published in *Lyceum*, the University's literary and fine arts journal. She currently teaches in a Detroit middle school.

Sun

He caresses my shoulders,
kisses my back and my cheeks.
My skin blushes darkly at his attentions.

He warms me from my skin to my core,
makes me sing and clap for joy.
I know I would wither without him.

The sun is my adulterous lover,
coveting all he sees even as he smiles on me.
He will take whomever he wishes while I watch.

I cannot help but share him.
He will not hold himself for one alone.
His charms and rages are too bountiful to restrict.

Many days I've felt myself slighted by him.
He admires himself behind the clouds for days.
His long weeks of absence leave me aching for his return.

Not just my lover but my father also,
he gave me life when he wrestled with my starry mother.
At twilight their truce was my creation.

At my dawn he claimed me as his acolyte,
and initiated me to the pleasures of the afternoon.

Daily I look forward to our communions.

At times stealthy night calls to my soul,
beguiling me with her powers of silence and finality.
My lover's creations are all that keep me here.

~~~ Kelie Callahan

Beryl Bonney–Conklin grew up in Michigan when winters were fierce and summers seemed long and hot. She now lives in Southern Illinois in summer, Florida in winter. She writes for the sheer beauty of the words and the feelings they present to her and to her reader. She learned early to paint with brushes in oils and with words in poetry. Her poetry has become the journal of her life.

Michigan Winter Ritual

The sun breaks in sharp rays
off an early morning snow,
to glitter against my eyes
and jump start my brain,
as I inhale air so cold
my nose becomes a crystal cave.

The beckoning sun
is nothing but a mirage of heat,
as it moves through thick air
while my fingers gloved and clumsy
scrape at frosted windows,
and internal circulation
searches in slow motion
for life and warmth.

I curse the cold
while my breath falls silent
crunched
beneath my boots.

~~~Beryl Bonney–Conklin

A former fellow of the Third Coast Writing Project, **C. J. Gilbert** knows that poetry hides inside everyday objects, lurks behind almost–forgotten memories, and will spring into her head at the least convenient times. When not writing, she teaches English and Acting at Battle Creek Central and walks with her husband.

Sunday Afternoons

my memories of Grandma Kay
are screwed tight into a medicine bottle
the dark gold plastic kind
with a snap–on white lid
before childproofing was the rage

I remember
those bottles, filled with pennies
heavy, jangly in our hands
each time we visited
one for me
one for my sister

I remember
those bottles, filled with pills
big, little, white, red
peeking out through receipts, old
newspapers, junk mail, and magazines
scattered across her heavy mahogany table

that table dominated,
fixed, immovable in an apartment
awash in sea–greens and aqua–blues
carpet, couch, floor–length fluttering drapes all
reflecting the light from outside into this
aquarium

perched on the couch,
my Sunday shoes, black and shiny,
crossed neatly at the ankles
I would watch
my grandmother,
my mother,
their sighs,
tight lips,
upright posture.

I don't remember their words,
only the rhythm of the conversation,
like the tennis warm–ups of my later years
volleys, gentle, kind, floating back
and forth
until a sharp backhand
spins over the net
to test the reflexes of the opponent
on the other side

Grandma's voice, never raised
softly clucked at my mother
and my mother would smile broadly,
gaily, like the time she broke her big toe
but didn't want us to know
how badly it hurt

eventually, Grandma's serve
slipped past the defenses
then Mother's words would miss
a beat, then come out clumped together,
louder, as if having to push their way out
past a pill or a piece of food
trapped in a dry throat

I would pass the medicine bottle pennies
from one hand
to the other hand
weighing them
waiting for the polite
goodbyes

~~~ C. J. Gilbert

Youth

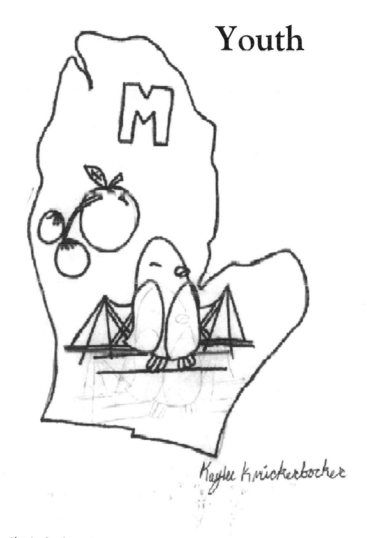

Kaylee Knickerbocker

Surprise Awakening

Laurie Lijewski

Last night, when I couldn't fall asleep, I softly turned on my CD player and listened to "Jaded." The radio announcer signed off to go to commercial, so I clicked off the radio and picked up my new book, **Harry Potter and the Chamber of Secrets.** After about ten pages, I saw a sudden, bright light go flying across my bedroom window outside. I decided at that time to go out there, but before I left, I turned off my alarm clock that read 2:32 a.m. April 19, 2001.

Laurie Lijewski lives in Midland, MI and wrote this story when she was fifteen. She is now sixteen and has just completed her sophomore year. She has enjoyed writing and revising fictional stories since she was in the second grade.

When I crept outside, my breath met with the cool night air and made a fog, which looked like a train when they blow their whistles. I turned my attention toward the forest behind our barn that was full of life. As I approached the forest, I saw the rabbits scurry into the dark woods and a mother deer with her two baby fawns. When the deer saw me, the fawns dashed to their mother's side who began running toward the forest. As I slowly walked closer to the fence, I gazed at the bright shining moon and I could see the craters and that were indented into its crust. The clear starry sky right beyond the moon caught my eye and hypnotized me. My gaze was fixated on the stars—that were burning brightly light years away—because they seemed so near to me, but yet so far.

A soft sound then pierced the empty silence in which I had been engulfed. My eyes darted toward the fence where a large shadowy figure stood. My heart started to beat faster, hoping that it wasn't a prowler. As the figure came closer to me, I felt the urge to scream rising up my throat, but to my relief, it was only my neighbor's horse. I let out a long sigh and looked deep into the beautiful creature's eyes knowing that it wouldn't run away. I walked over to the majestic creature and softly said, "May I ride you?" and the horse turned its side to face me.

I climbed up on the fence and hopped onto the horse's back. When the horse started to trot, I noticed that along with the natural wildness of this animal, there was also peacefulness. While we trotted down the old, unpaved, country road, I had time to observe the captivating scenery around me that was illuminated by the moon. We passed the Smith's house (the owner of the horse), and I noticed that the fence to the pasture had been broken. That must have been how this magnificent horse had gotten free. I knew that the Smith's wouldn't mind my riding their horse because I have known them since I was a small girl.

We then passed the old General Store with the roof of rotting shingles that was caving in. The door was boarded up and graffiti was drawn over the whole building. A light flew onto the road from the window up above; a firefly lit up the darkness that surrounded me. At that moment, from the pit of my stomach, I knew that it was time to move on.

The horse and I then began our journey down the road again. The cool night air brushed the hair off my shoulder as we progressed down the road. As the air got damper, I knew that we were approaching my favorite place ever, the Sassville Swamp. I pulled the horse to the side of the road and came to a stop. The air was filled with the music of the animals. Their songs floated through my mind with ease as they erased all of my worries. It was so peaceful being surrounded by animals. The frogs were croaking while sitting on the moldy, rotten logs, the crickets were chirping their nightly lullaby, and the mosquitoes were buzzing in my ear telling me that they were hungry. The swamp made me feel like I was at home and comfortable. A star then shot across the sky, like a bullet through thin air.

The horse whinnied like a sick old man and my instincts told me to keep going. I closed my sleepy eyes for a moment and knew I couldn't fall asleep just yet. Slowly, the horse proceeded back onto the road without even having to be told. This gave me a feeling that I was being taken care of and that the horse could sense my feelings.

While we traveled down the road, memories flowed through my head; the old tree house overflowed with many memories. All the memories of when my friends and I had sleepovers, filled with tales of truth or dare and midnight snacks, exploded inside my head. The hill that we were approaching brought back the best memories of all. This was the place where the winter snowfalls provided my brother and me with the most fun. I remember our sleds zooming down the hill with my brother on one and me on the other while our dog was trying to chase us down the slick path. I also recalled the first snowflake of the winter falling on my little red nose in late fall when I was only five years old. The snowflake was cold and left a drop of water on my nose as my body heat caused it to melt.

I was in deep thought until I heard the bird that signals morning the lark. At that moment, I knew I would have to be home soon, or my parents would awake and find out I was gone. I pulled the horse around in a circle until we were on the road again. The horse galloped down the dusty drive as the birds started to awake and sing their wake up call to the world. I started to ease up on the horse's gallop, when I realized that the morning air was becoming quite damp. I figured that it was just the morning dew, until I noticed something strange, about twenty feet ahead of me.

At that time, I started to slow the horse down to a slow trot, noticing an eerie, iridescent, glow, sweeping across the road in front of the swamp. It only rose about five feet off the ground, but it was below the tops of the cattails that were almost covered by this mysterious fog. About five feet from this hazy blanket of what I thought to be fog, I stopped the horse. It whinnied as it came to an abrupt halt. Something about the swamp was different. At first, I couldn't quite tell what it was, but then it hit me. I realized that there were no animals or insects in the area. There were no croaking frogs, no singing crickets, and no buzzing mosquitoes in my ear. The horse whinnied again and at that split–second, I knew that there was something odd about this mysterious, glowing fog that was rising off of the swamp. I held my breath to hear nothing but dead silence.

I started the horse back out on a slow trot, but hesitated for a moment before entering this sparkling, white fog. I just wanted to leave because I was becoming a little scared and my hands were starting to tremble. The horse was still very hesitant at first to enter, but then after a small nudge from my foot, we continued on cautiously through this unusual and glistening white fog. My skin tingled and all I could see all around me was a bright, white light, that made me feel I was inside of a gigantic snowball. The hairs on my arm were standing up as we progressed through the mirrors of light making my eyes hurt. I couldn't wait to get to the other side because at this moment I was ready to cry from the glare of the light.

About ten seconds later, we finally reached the other side. The air felt warmer and not as damp. I was happy and relieved to have that over with. When I looked toward the East, I noticed the pink clouds of morning were rising over the dark horizon. Dawn would be coming soon. But before we went on, I gazed back toward the swamp as the horse began to speed up. To my surprise, the fog had vanished. I felt a chill run down my spine, from my neck to my legs. Spinning around as quickly as I could, I ordered to the horse to go faster.

We raced down the road trying to beat the rising, pastel colored clouds. As we neared the Smith's house, I slowed the horse down and jumped down to the ground. I walked through the wet, dew–dropped grass, while guiding the horse by holding on to its mane. I showed the horse into the closest empty stall then closed the door behind it. I started to look toward my home, when I turned around and looked at the stall once more before leaving. It seemed as if the great creature was saying goodbye to me, because of the bright gleam in its big, brown eyes. The horse then turned away and was hidden by the stall wall.

My legs sprinted down the dusty road, until I came upon my own driveway. Out of breath from running, I paused for a moment and glanced at the horizon again and noticed the bright morning sun gleaming, playing peek–a–boo over the horizon. After gathering my breath, I had forced my tired legs to dash up the drive to the doorstop. I then stretched out my long, cold arm, and picked up the newspaper. Moving quickly, my cold fingers turned the handle of the front door, only to startle me when the handle would not turn. To make sure that I wasn't mistaken, I turned the knob two more times. Thinking to myself of how strange this was because when I had left, I left the door unlocked. I pondered momentarily about who could have locked the door, then tucked the paper under my arm and bent down to the spare key that my family kept underneath the "Welcome" mat.

I unlocked the deadbolt, stuck the key back under the wet mat, and tiptoed to the kitchen table. I couldn't wait to read the comics because it was the first thing I did each morning after I put my slippers on. I quietly pulled out the kitchen chair and sat down in hope of resting for a few moments while reading the comics.

Lakeford Daily Newspaper
$.35 per issue www.LDN.com Monday, April 19, 2002

I read the date twice and thought that it was very strange the editor of the paper missed correcting the year on the date. Isn't it their job to catch errors like that and fix them? Thinking nothing of it, I turned to the comic section, while getting very anxious to read my favorite comic strip Ziggy, but to my surprise, there weren't any comics on the page. Instead in its place, there was a whole page dedicated to one article. What could be so important to take up a whole page of the local newspaper is what I thought to myself. The big headline printed across the top of the page caught my eye and I couldn't help reading it. It stated, in bold letters:

One–Year Anniversary of Missing Girl.

Right next to it was a picture that made me feel as if I were seeing my reflection in mirror. It was a photograph of me.

The Dragon and the Jaguar

Holly Ann Steinmetz

Once upon a time there was a great and powerful dragon. She ran the lands claiming her territory. She drove out all that tried to stop her. No one really knew her name. Some called her Red Dragon. Others called her Demon, but most knew her as Claw.

Holly Ann Steinmetz has been writing stories and books since the age of four. She wrote this story at thirteen. She enjoys writing stories for school and stories for her personal pleasure. Holly is currently in the ninth grade at Luther L. Wright High School in Ironwood, MI.

One day Claw was taking over a forest when all of a sudden the shadows began to move. Claw stopped pillaging and watched them move. One by one the shadows disappeared. The biggest shadow, however, leaped in front of her and what actually stood in front of her was no shadow, but a five foot long white jaguar. The jaguar was a beautiful cat covered in spots.

"What be you beast!" asked Claw savagely. The jaguar stood before her twitching its tail back and forth behind her. "What be you beast?" cried Claw louder. Claw stomped the ground and thrashed back and forth with her tail and wings, but the jaguar said nothing.

They stood there in a staring deadlock for hours until the jaguar asked, "Why do you come? Why do you destroy us and our homes?"

Claw replied, "I am gaining more territory for the ruling creature."

"Who is this ruling creature?" asked the jaguar.

"I am!" replied Claw. "Now leave or I will be forced to destroy you and the forest!"

She stood silent for a moment then replied, "This is our home. We forest dwellers have lived here for centuries."

Claw replied shyly, "So you and the creatures of this forest can find a new home."

With that the jaguar smiled and said, "If you try to take this land you will pay dearly; you will lose your most precious gift."

"I have no possessions you stupid cat!" Claw hissed. "Nothing is dear to me!"

The jaguar knew Claw was lying. "You are scared!" sneered the jaguar. "You once had two precious gifts. The villagers took one and the other is hidden away. If you do not stop your rampage you will lose your second gift by sundown."

Claw was shocked, "Where did you hear this?"

"I know what you think of; I know you mourn the loss of another." The jaguar said wisely. "Now go to your hole in the ground and tend to the 'needs' of your business there."

With that Claw charged at the jaguar but missed for the jaguar leaped on top of a rock ledge. "For that you will suffer," hissed the jaguar up on the ledge. I gave you a warning and now you will pay. By sundown the villagers will come to your home and destroy it in a rock slide, crushing your gift of life." With that a flash of light engulfed the jaguar and she disappeared.

"No, stop this fate that will take my cave and what is inside it!" Claw cried. "Please stop this!" Claw was alone again. I have little time she thought. She leaped off of the ridge and took off.

She saw many sights below her. She saw burning cities, dead cattle, people cursing and throwing rocks at her as she flew. They have all the right to be mad at me, Claw thought bitterly. I destroyed their lives. I will save a life and then leave here forever.

It was getting close to sundown. She was a ways off from her cave when she heard a crash. A rockslide. Fearful, she hurried into a nosedive straight at the side of the mountain. What she saw made her move even faster. The villagers that she stole from a few days before were dislodging rocks with sticks, trying to collapse her cave. She dove into her cave. Then came a loud crash and the villagers were cheering. A boulder came rolling down the mountain with a huge rockslide behind it...she was trapped!

It was dark, very dark! Then came a new noise...silence! The villagers are gone, thought Claw. I might be able to move these rocks," she said. It took her awhile, but she worked a boulder over the edge. She took in the fresh air with delight. Then she saw it. A small crushed wing protruding out from under a rock. Claw was horrified.

"Come to mommy, Gold Foot." Claw called over and over hoping that the little dragon was just hiding. To her dismay, he was under the rock. When she finally moved the rock, her sorrow was confirmed. Gold Foot was crushed. She bent down and gingerly picked up her baby dragon. She held him in her arms and wept.

"I wish I had spent more time with you." Claw sobbed. "I was too busy destroying, rather than being with you," Claw snarled at herself. "Mommy always loved you Gold Foot," Claw reassured the baby dragon. That night Claw brought the body into the woods and buried it. As she dug she sang:

"Shut your eyes little one, soon you sleep
and dream of flying. Someday soon you will
take to wing flying away from mommy
forever. My little one, so small forever.
I will miss you flying on my back. I'll never
see you fly from home. You little sweet heart,
you will never be forgotten. Wherever you may
go, wherever you may fly, your mother's love
will be with you forever. My little baby don't cry.
You will soon sleep."

Claw was exhausted after digging the grave. She fell onto her side and slept in the soft grass. She heard something but when she opened her eyes she found that she was locked inside a cage. People were crowding around the cage and laughing at her. She hung her head in shame. Then the people separated. A large cart pulled by an oxen went through the crowd. On the cart was a cage like hers, but a little bigger. Inside the cage was another dragon, a blue–green one with bigger wings and a longer tail. It was Riach, Gold Foot's father. Riach had rescued her many times, but this time she failed to save her true love.

A man approached the cage with a long serrated sword. He climbed on top of the cage and raised the sword ready to jam it into Riach. Without warning he dropped the sword and, "No!" screamed Claw. She sat straight up in the grass next to Gold Foot's grave. It was only a dream, Claw reassured herself. A dream about the night Riach had really died. The jaguar was right. I have lost my two most precious gifts, Gold Foot and Riach. I have nothing now to live for, Claw thought sadly. I should have stayed to die with Riach instead of breaking out of my cage and flying away. I have nothing, Claw thought.

Over the next few days she did some thinking, but she grew weary of thinking and living, so she stole a chain with an iron lock and got the biggest boulder she could find. She dragged the boulder, lock and chain to the deepest lake. She got the boulder in position on a cliff overlooking the lake then chained herself to the boulder.

"Is this how it ends?" came a familiar voice from the forest. "There is another choice."

"Who's there?" called Claw. Out from the trees stepped a white five–foot long jaguar. "You!" hissed Claw. If you wouldn't have passed that fate, my baby dragon would still be alive."

"I did not pass your young one's fate," said the jaguar. "No one can change fate."

"You, if I ever get my talons on you, you will be chopped veggies when I am through with you!" hissed Claw louder. Forgetting that she was chained to the boulder, she lunged at the jaguar. "Argh!" snarled Claw with surprise.

"Calm down!" comforted the jaguar. "I did not make this fate. I just knew of it."

"What are you?" Claw asked. With that the jaguar stepped back. "That is of no concern to you," said the jaguar. "It is the information I possess that will ease your pain."

"What is that?" asked Claw. With a flash of light the lock and chains fell away from the rock and released Claw.

"Over the great mountain range, past the Red River, around the great forest, past the broken rocks and then on the hill beyond seagull cliff, you will find happiness again," advised the jaguar. "By flight you should be there in four weeks."

"Thank you," Claw said sullenly. "But this means leaving my home forever."

"If you stay here you will lose your life, " advised the jaguar. "Go now," called the jaguar.

Claw jumped off of the cliff. And called back, "What is your name"?

"Ashala," called the jaguar. "Now go."

It took her several days to reach the great mountain range. Claw spent the night on a cliff. In the morning she ate a dead deer and headed off to the Red River. She could see it clearly from the sky. It looked like a red vain running on the skin of the earth. She camped on the shore of the river. It took her several more days to get to the great forest. She landed in the forest for the night and nearly crashed into one of the big red wood trees. It took her six more days to get to the broken rocks. She couldn't land because a village was under the rocks and they did not like dragons. So she kept on. Five days later, she flew over seagull cliff. The seagulls started pecking at her as she flew over the ocean. Then she saw it, a great hill. "Yes, I've made it!" cried Claw happily.

She decided to camp in the forest for the rest of the day and wait for night. Claw curled up on a patch of moss and went to sleep. When she awakened it was dark. She saw the stars, moon and the northern lights swirling in the sky. She got up and caught dinner before she was ready to go. "I will find happiness!" Claw thought. She ran through the woods toward the hill. She was so close. But then memories came flooding back. The night Riach died and when Gold Foot died. "Fight the memories!" Claw snarled to herself. She cleared her mind of all thought except of what she would find on the hill. All of a sudden she heard voices from the village. She crept to the edge of the village staying out of sight.

The villagers were in the town square. There was a large cage in the middle of the square. Inside, a large silver colored creature moved uneasily back and forth. Claw saw that it was a dragon...a very large male dragon. "No, they're going to kill him," and then she did something that could have killed her and the silver dragon. She flew above the cage and hoisted it into the air with all of her might. When the silver dragon found that he was being lifted he looked up. He saw a beautiful red female dragon trying as hard as she could to save him. He wasted no time. For as much room that he had in his cage he flapped his wings and they were off. He looked up again and was love struck.

Claw set the cage down on top of the hill. She bashed open the cage with a rock. He stepped out regally and knelt down in front of her. He gazed up at her through golden eyes.

"Winged beauty," he said, "I am Valar. May I have your talon in marriage?"

"Yes," Claw said. "Now I will find happiness. You have proven worthy and our child will need a father." Many weeks after the wedding by the waterfall, the two dragons decided they would protect the village. Valar did the hunting and protecting because pregnancy left Claw weak. Valar heard the rumor that in return for protecting the village, the villagers were going to do something unthinkable...banish them!

"What?" cried Claw, "we have protected them, how could they?" Claw tried to stand up, but Valar stopped her.

"Calm down. I have arranged to talk with the village elders."

"They won't listen!" cried Claw.

"Be calm," Valar quieted her, "for Gold Foot's sake."

The elders' decision shocked the dragons. "You must leave our land forever, or we will kill you and your wife," cried the elders. "Dragons are dangerous!"

"We cannot leave." Valar cried. "My wife is weak."

"If you don't leave, you and your wife will perish," the elder said. Valar returned home with the news.

"I told you they wouldn't listen," Claw said. "I know of a secret valley of dragons that we can fly to."

In the morning, they took off without even a word from the villagers. They made it to the valley of dragons where they settled down to live and raise their new dragon baby that they named Gold Foot. They lived happily ever after.

Moral: life is hard, but never give up. All problems work themselves out in the end and there is always another choice.

The Championship Game

Christy Ewers

One day the Joneses got a phone call and it was a basketball coach. He asked if Mary, the Jones' daughter, wanted to play basketball. Mrs. Jones asked Mary and Mary asked her mom if she could call the coach back. Mary talked it over with her mom and dad and she decided to give it a try.

She asked her dad to teach her about basketball. So her dad taught her everything he knew

The first few games she didn't score many points but after she practiced a few more times with her dad she began to score the most points on her team.

Her team made it to the championship game. She asked her dad to come and he said, "Yes, but I have to come from work so can I be a little late?" Mary said "Sure dad, but only a little late."

On her dad's way to the basketball game he got in a car accident and he had to be rushed to the hospital. At the basketball game Mary wasn't doing so well because she kept looking in the stands for her dad.

After the game, Mary asked her mom if she knew where dad was. Her mom answered, "No, I don't." So her mom tried his cell phone, but no one answered. So her mom called the police and the officer at the phone checked and said that Mr. Jones was rushed to the St. Luke's Hospital because he was in a car accident. So Mary and Mrs. Jones went to the hospital to see Mr. Jones.

> **Christy Ewers** wrote her short story this past summer when she was eleven years old. She and her two brothers, Steve and Brian, live in St. Louis, Missouri where Christy attends Holy Infant School in Baldwin. She enjoys softball, soccer, basketball, swimming, reading and writing. One day she hopes to be an author and illustrator. She and her family vacationed on Mackinac Island

When they got to the front desk, they asked the lady what room Mr. Jones was in. She said he was in room 216 on the second floor.

Mary and Mrs. Jones ran to the room as fast as they could. They ran down the hall to the stairs, up the stairs and down the hall to room 216. When they got to the room they saw that Mr. Jones was in a full body cast.

Mary got worried so she tried to talk to her dad. Her dad was sleeping so he didn't answer her. So Mary got *really* worried and she started to cry. When Mary was crying her dad woke up and asked if Mary had won. Mary was so happy her dad was alive she didn't care if she had won or lost but she told her dad that her team had lost. Then her dad asked if Mary had done well and Mary replied, "No, I didn't do that well because I was worried about you." Her dad then said, "Thank you for worrying about me."

By the time her dad was out of all his casts, basketball season was ready to start again. Her dad made a promise that year. The promise was that if Mary made it to the championship game that year he would skip work to make sure that he could watch the whole game.

Well that year they did indeed make it to the championship game and Mr. Jones saw the whole game. Mary's team won, thirty to twenty–two and after every basket Mary scored she would look in the stands and give her dad a thumbs up!!!!

Genie In The Toy Room

Kylie R. Clark

The youngest cook that ever lived is Kylie Clark. Her specialties are Cheese Pizza Towers, Cookies and Cream Pyramid, and her dessert Crokembush. She works at Adventureland, the restaurant. She makes $1 million dollars a day.

One day, her brothers and sisters came to visit. She gave them free Cheese Pizza Towers. They loved it so much that they gave her a magic ring. She could have three wishes from the ring. Kylie rubbed her ring and a genie popped out.

Kylie R. Clark has spent summers on Beaver Island, Michigan since she was three years old. *Genie In the Toy Room* was written on Beaver Island when she was eight years old. She lives in Iowa and just completed the third grade; she was in the S.O.A.R. program.

The genie's name was Elvira Solis. Kylie wished that her home were a Toyland. **POOF!** Her house became a huge Toyland with no boy toys at all...just the way she liked it.

The genie popped back into her ring. Kylie started to play with her new toys when someone tapped her on the back. It was one of her new toys. Barbie started talking to her. Then all her toys came out and all started talking to her. She got scared, so she rubbed the ring and wished that all the toys would go away. They went away using her second wish.

Then she said, "I wish I had a dog that can speak." **POOF!** A dog appeared. "Hola! Hola! Como esta usted?" And Kylie said, "Oh no! I meant to say an English–speaking dog! Well, I have no more wishes, so I might as well learn Spanish."

A Light on the Horizon

Kara Kuchapsky

A seagull cried as it flew overhead while a warm, gentle breeze played with my dark curls. I sat on the rocky shore of sparkling Lake Huron with my head in my hands and cried until my eyes stung. I wasn't accustomed to being surrounded by nature but was secluded by tall birch trees and miles upon miles of beautiful blue water, which sparkled like diamonds where the sun hit it.

Horse–like animals with soft, black noses, (Daddy calls them deer), leapt through the forest and little squirrels would scurry around looking for food. Every morning we would see fresh new animal tracks. The wind carried crisp, fresh smells and talks in silent whispers. The sound that overtook all other sounds was the soft crash of the waves on the shore and birds singing songs in the morning. Occasionally, a passing ship would blast its horn to the secluded lighthouse in which I lived.

Kara Kuchapsky wrote this piece when she was in eleventh grade and age sixteen. She got the inspiration for it over the summer when she was up north at her cottage near the Old Presque Isle lighthouse. This past school year she was a senior at Our Lady of the Lake High School and turned eighteen in March.

My family and I moved from New York to Michigan so my father could be the lighthouse keeper of the new Presque Isle lighthouse that was just built a year ago, in 1870. There was no town, no family, no school, and worst of all no friends. I missed all my friends at school in New York, and that is why I cried until my eyes stung.

The sun sank low on the horizon, casting shadows on the trees, making everything seem larger than life when I finally got sick of crying and dried my eyes. I decided to take a walk until the puffiness and redness went away. My walk led me a mile down the road to the smaller, old lighthouse, built in 1840. The old lighthouse was all alone sitting at the edge of the woods. It hadn't been lived in for over twenty years. There were no toys in the yard or laundry hanging on the clothesline. The lighthouse was run–down, the paint was chipping and the bricks were crumbling while the grass grew over my knees.

The sun was ready to go to sleep for the night when I decided to go up to the top of the lighthouse to watch it depart, but the door was locked. I went over to the cottage and found the same. I don't know what made me do this, but I picked up a large rock and threw it right through the window. The glass shattered and a gust of musty, old air blew at my face. I scrambled through the window and shivered as I realized how cold the little cottage was. After all, it was July. Luckily, there was a key on the table. As I reached the top of the lighthouse the sun had almost set. It cast a variety of pinks, oranges, and reds across the sky all mixed together like a finger painting. A strip of yellow–gold sun reflected in the water to where I was standing, making me look like I was in a spotlight. As I turned to go down the stairs after the sunset, a glow floating on the rocky shore caught my eye.

Everything was so quiet and peaceful as I slowly turned around to look down. The only sound that could be heard was the gentle, omnipresent, soft rolling in and out of the waves under the moonless black sky. I looked down and saw a faint, iridescent light floating on the rocks near the shore. As the light grew closer, I realized it was a girl my age with dark, raven hair just like mine. Her skin was a pure white, almost transparent. The white, lacy dress she wore billowed in the wind while the waves that rolled in and out swallowed up her bare feet. The most remarkable characteristic about this girl was that she was wrapped in a soft glow although there was no moon or lantern in her hand. She threw a quick glance at me that sent the hairs on my back up and disappeared into the forest. I stood staring for a few minutes at where she walked before I snapped out of my trance and ran home.

As I reached home, I decided to go back the next day to clean up the glass and not tell anyone what I had done or where I went.

The next morning after breakfast, I told my mother I was going to skip stones on the shore. Once out of her sight, I ran as fast as I could to the old lighthouse. When I came into the little clearing where the cottage rested, I stopped dead in my tracks to find all the glass was picked up and the window repaired without a crack. I turned around to find the door to the tower open when I knew for a fact I locked it the night before. Slowly, I ascended the steep steps and looked out over the lake. I turned quickly as I heard a giggle and found the same girl I saw last night right in front of me. She laughed again as my mouth fell open.

"You know, it's not nice to stare," she laughed.

"Where did you come from?" I asked in disbelief.

"You're not the only one who lives in this neck of the woods." she replied, "My name is Amilee Porter and I live about a mile away."

"I'm Hannah, but weren't you here last night?" I asked, overjoyed with happiness to finally find someone to be friends with.

"Yes, but that's a long story. I had a fight with my dad." she said sadly, "Come on, I'll show you some things."

Amilee grabbed my hand and we were off, running around the forest and having the best afternoon I've had in a long time. The whole afternoon, we built forts and houses out of dead tree branches and evergreen boughs. If we got hot under the bright sun that peaked through the multitude of green leaves, we would jump in the lake for a swim and spend hours playing in snow–tipped waves. By the end of the day, I knew Amilee and I would be best friends.

When I got home later that night, I felt weak and dizzy. My mother felt my forehead and blamed my fever on my swimming excursions earlier in the day. She said I had to stay in bed until I got better which disappointed me because I was unable to see Amilee.

In the middle of the night a faint tapping woke me up. Amilee was standing with the shadows outside my window. As I opened it up, a cold gust of air blew on my face sending me into a fit of coughing.

"What are you doing here and why do you always have that glow around you?" I asked between coughs.

"I had another fight with my dad and I have a lantern, see," she said holding it up, "I'm sleeping at the old lighthouse tonight, you want to come with me?"

"No, I'm sick," I replied.

"Oh, I see," she whispered in an almost pleased voice, "I'll see you later then."

~ The Next Morning ~

"Ma, do you know why they built a new lighthouse?" I asked.

"They needed a new one and no one wanted to work the old one," she replied with a sigh.

"Why wouldn't anyone work the old one?"

"Something terrible happened, that's all you need to know," she feverishly replied.

"Please, pretty please tell me," I whined.

"A little girl was beaten by her father and jumped off the tower because of it," my Ma said. She was not in the mood to argue. "Don't ever go near there."

"Yes, Ma," I replied.

As soon as mother left to do her washing, I jumped out of bed. I planned to go to the old lighthouse to scare Amilee with what my mother just told me. I dressed quickly and sneaked into the woods. As I ran, sweat started to drip down my forehead and back, but when I got to the old lighthouse, I caught a chill and shivered.

"Amilee, Amilee," I yelled, " I have something important to tell you."

I tripped as I ran up the tower steps because of my weakness and dizziness. When I reached the top, Amilee wasn't there; there was no sign of her anywhere.

"I knew you would be getting here soon," Amilee said from behind me.

"Why do you always scare me like that?" I gasped as I spun around. "I have something to tell you."

"What?" Amilee asked with a smile, "Hey, aren't you sick?"

"Yes, its worse today, in fact it just got worse, but I have to tell you something. The last light keeper's daughter jumped off this tower after her father drove her to it because he would hurt her," I said. "Can you believe something so terrible could happen?"

"Yes, as a matter of fact I could." she replied quietly.

"I wonder...is it is haunted?" I said as I sat down. I was feeling weak. I leaned my back against the thin metal railing and closed my eyes because my eyelids were unbearably heavy. The wind picked up and carried the fragrance of rain. The sky was darkening as black rain clouds gathered in the distance. I could hear thunder laughing from the west. The waves started to crash viciously into the shore sending blankets of spray into the air.

"Did you know the girl?" I asked. "Maybe we'd better go to my house, because it looks like it is going to storm in a while."

"No, I like the rain and thunder," Amilee quietly replied holding her head down.

"Did you know the girl?" I asked again.

"You could say I did," Amilee replied looking off at the oncoming storm.

"What was her name?"

"Amilee, her name was Amilee," she said. I crinkled my forehead, not understanding what Amilee was saying. A gust of wind blew from behind and sent shivers through my body making me cough.

"I better go home now, I don't want to get any sicker," I said shakily, struggling to get up.

"No, you're not going home, not ever." Amilee sneered.

"What are you talking about?"

"I'm the girl that jumped, I'm not alive. I'm dead, soon you will be too," Amilee replied.

"What's gotten into you? I'm not going anywhere," I said starting to get scared.

"You're not sick because you went swimming. You're sick because I'm taking all the energy from you for myself so I will become human again." Amilee taunted.

"That's impossible," I shrieked, feeling myself become weaker.

"No it's not and I will do it. I'm doing it now," Amilee laughed, "I'll take your place in your family and you'll become the ghost."

"No, please don't." I cried, "I don't understand. Why are you doing this?"

"Being dead didn't solve my problems and wasn't as fun as I thought it would be," Amilee replied, "Now you get to be dead."

"How is that possible?" I asked hysterically.

"I told you, by getting you to like me, I take your energy, ultimately your life. You put energy into the friendship because it means so much to you. I take that energy and give myself life," Amilee said in a matter of fact voice.

I started to cry frantically because I had no idea what to do. I felt myself get weaker by the minute, but did not know how to stop Amilee. She had her ghostly powers and my energy. I saw color rise in her cheeks as that iridescent glow disappeared from her and encircled me.

"I have to stop her, I have to be strong," I told myself, "If she is almost human, she can still die." With all the strength and courage I could find within myself, I threw myself at Amilee and forced her over the iron rail. Rain had started to pour down out of the clouds making Amilee slip and fall to the lake below. I fell back exhausted, having no idea if my plan succeeded or failed.

When I woke up, I was in my bedroom with my Mother sitting next to my bed.

"Ma, what happened?" I asked in a hoarse whisper.

"Hannah...you had pneumonia. We found you three days ago at the top of the old lighthouse," she replied, taking my hand.

"Oh Ma, I'm so sorry," I said, crying.

"That doesn't matter. You are okay and alive, that's all that matters," she said with a smile.

My Ma was right. Nothing about Amilee mattered now. She didn't take my life. I don't know what happened to her, nor must I tell anyone what did happen. What matters now is that I am alive and for that I am thankful.

* * *

Hannah stayed at the two lighthouses for the rest of her life. The night after she died, a strange light appeared in the old lighthouse. It is no longer in use because all the electricity to the tower and the light bulb has been taken out. The light goes on every night but cannot be explained. Many people say that Hannah has stayed at the old lighthouse to warn people of the possible danger within the lighthouse's walls. She protects people from Amilee's ghost should it ever return. While some see the light as scary and dangerous, others look at it as a sign of protection and comfort. Whatever people believe, the mysterious ghost light is there and comes on every night sending chills down the backs of spectators to this spectacular, unexplained light.

Jack Russell Terrified on Mackinac Island

Amy Geer

"Roxy! Roxy get back here!" I screamed so frantically when my dog slipped out of her lead, and was running after some animal. Roxy was my dog, a Jack Russell Terrier. She had a beautiful white body with a tan spot over her left ear. The Jack Russell Terrier is a great breed of dog; however; they love to explore, which means they require a lot of work. That was just what I was doing: taking her for a run.

I live on Mackinac Island in Michigan, which is a widely known tourist trap. It's a very beautiful place to live year–round however, because I get to go through the state park area during the seasons. A weird part about living here is that there are no automobiles on the island. I am fourteen years old and my father owns a medium–sized inn for the tourists. I help around the inn, especially during the summer because that's when we really get a lot of business. My Dad didn't want a dog at first, but he likes it now because the tourists like it.

> **Amy Geer** is fifteen and in the tenth grade. She was fourteen years old when she wrote the story. Amy enjoys skating, biking and running track. She also likes to read, write, sketch, act and listen to music. She really wants a Jack Russell Terrier like the one in the story, but her mom is allergic to dogs ☹.

Anyway, I was taking my dog for a run on that particular day. It was late July 2001, near sunset time, and the bridge looked especially beautiful that night. When she got away, I knew I couldn't let her out of my eyesight, so I ran quickly. She ran to the Devil's Kitchen, which is a well–known cave carved out of limestone. When I caught up with her, I noticed an odd black hole in the cave. The sunset was radiating a bright beam of light right over the small hole; otherwise, I may have never seen it.

"That's funny" I thought, "I don't remember that being there before."

I figured Roxy must have gone in the opening chasing after the creature she was pursuing. I knelt down and called her name several times. After about a minute lapsed, I heard distant barking emanating from the cavity. I put my head in the hollow and waited for my eyes to adjust. It seemed the hole was actually a long tunnel. It was just big enough for a human. I crawled about a foot into the hole and bellowed out Roxy's name. That put me in a real dilemma. I knew if I left to get a flashlight, Roxy might emerge and go off looking for me. However, if I crawled in the cavity I wouldn't be able to see in front of me, and I had no clue what else was down there.

I picked the latter of the two choices, and inched slowly into the burrow. My hands sunk into soft earth, and I knew I was going to be very dirty. I crawled for less than five minutes when I saw a faint light ahead. I knew that was impossible because the sun was to my back. I continued crawling toward the light and when I came out of the hole and looked around I saw what appeared to be the exact spot where I had started. The odd part of it all was that Roxy was sitting on a boulder and looking at me as if she were an angel. I approached her and she didn't even squirm when I put the leash on her.

I looked back at the Devil's kitchen and there was no sign of an opening anymore! I was very puzzled by this. I sat down on the rock and thought about what had just happened. I had followed my dog into an unusual hole in the Devil's kitchen, and it came out on the other side in the exact same spot. There was no hole remaining. Nobody would ever believe me. I wasn't so sure I even believed myself! I had to be hallucinating or something. However, when I looked down at myself, there was dirt all over me. In addition, I realized something else was different. There was no paved road for the bikers! When I had gone in the tunnel, it was there, and now, it was gone! There was only forest and dirt out until the beach. I was beginning to get a little scared. There had to be some logical explanation. Then I thought I was going loony when I heard a rifle shot far off in the distance. And that was only the beginning!

The Jack Russell Terrier is a relatively small breed, so I picked up Roxy and began to carry her toward the city. When I got to a point, I looked out at the lake, and something I had not realized before astounded me. There was no Mackinac Bridge! It was just lake and water! It all looked so naked! I could also see many canoes, boats, and other crafts. However, these were no ordinary canoes, boats, or ships. They reminded me of vessels I had seen drawings of when we studied Michigan History. This had to be some kind of joke! That was the only explanation. But even that was not quite right. There was no Shepler's, Star line, or Arnold ferries, or yachts, sailboats, or even skidoos. There was just a bunch of ancient looking vessels in the water. Then the rifle shots began to be a regular thing.

Suddenly I felt Roxy go tense. I whirled around but there was nobody there. The hairs on the back of Roxy's neck were standing up and she uttered a low growl.

"Who's there?" I cried out in sheer terror. I heard a branch snap, and there was a boy not much older than I was. He was leaning against a tree. He had a small nose and a splattering of freckles that set off his abysmal green eyes. He had dressed up in a beat–up, red soldier outfit, with a scary looking rifle. It looked like those Revolutionary War relics I had seen in museums. I had seen many a reenactment in my day, and so I knew he was only a guy hired to dress up and act out a battle. It had to be another mile to get to the remodeled Fort Mackinac so it was odd that he was so far out there, but I quickly forgot about that.

"It is only I," he said in a heavy British accent. "My name is Benjamin Shaw. You may call me Benjamin. Now I must ask you three questions in return. Who are you, what are you doing on British territory, and why are you wearing those ugly clothes?"

"Oh please," I said, "I know you are just a reenactor. You don't have to pull the old routine on me. I live here. And personally, I think you're wearing much uglier clothes than I am. Now that we have got that settled, I need to talk to you from one native to another. There's some weird stuff going on around here. First, the paved road is gone, and second the bridge is gone, and third there are all these rifle shots, and also I was at the Devil's Kitchen and—"

"What are you talking about?" he barged in. "I am not a native of this strange land. I was born in London. I do know that we are under attack. The Yanks are trying to shell our Fort but the walls are too high. However, what are this "paved road" and bridge you speak of? If you weren't a woman I would shoot you right now."

"I told you already! You don't have to put on the whole show! Well, if you won't answer my questions, I'll head back into town and find someone who will." I said snippily, and began to saunter in to the direction of the main city.

"Wait! Please don't go! If they find out I let some unusual girl get as far as the fort I'll be severely punished! I'll even tell you why I was following you!" he begged. I turned around and studied his pleading face. He was somewhat cute, and what did I have to lose?

"Alright, but you've got some explaining to do." I informed him. He laughed and said:

"Okay. Before we do anything else, we have to get back to my mate's hideout because someone might be able to see us from here. We don't want to upset the Indians. Follow me." He turned powerfully and began heading through the woodland towards the center of the island. I followed close behind. Nothing he said could possibly be true. Or could it?

We hiked along at a rapid pace until we came upon what appeared to be some sort of shelter. Multiple deceased logs had been hauled to one spot where they leaned on each other for support. Smoke was rising up through an opening at the top, but it was a slender line that curled into thin air. It was not enough to notice unless you were looking right at it. Benjamin got down and crawled through a void in the logs. Then I followed with Roxy in

326

my arms. The inside of the refuge was remarkably larger than it appeared from the outside. There was another man sitting by a very small fire in the middle. He was dressed similar to Benjamin and he stopped tending to the fire and looked up when we crawled in, but had said nothing. He was very tan, and his hair was charcoal black. His big brown eyes looked as if they had seen the world, and they weren't amused with it.

"I can't take this any longer! What is this? What is going on?" I cried out.

"Calm down!" Benjamin ordered, his green eyes dancing. "Let me explain. I assume you know it's 1814. Maybe you haven't been here in a while, and if not I then I must tell you that we, the British, now control Fort Mackinac." I decided I better just go along with his crazy notions and keep my mouth shut. Boy, my Dad would never believe this one!

"This man's name is Thomas Burns. He is mute so you might be wasting your time talking to him. We've both been outcasts from the moment we arrived on this tiny island. Let me tell you my story. As I've already informed you, I was born in London. Your little dog there reminds me of a terrier I once saw in a foxhunt. That's why I was following you. What breed is she?" he questioned.

"She's a Jack Russell Terrier. How could a terrier be in a foxhunt? I thought they only used hounds." I answered.

"Well, being a woman, I guess you've never had the pleasure of a good foxhunt. A terrier man always accompanies the hunt. He carries the terrier on his horse, and when the vixen disappears into her burrow, the terrier is sent down the hole. The terrier's job is to convince the vixen to come back out of her den, and when the terrier does it's job, the hunt resumes." He informed me.

"That must be why Roxy loves holes so much." I thought. By this time, Roxy had fallen asleep.

"I'll continue." He said. "When I transferred to this island to serve at the Fort, everyone else but Thomas has already been here for at least a month. I was much younger than the other men were, but I had to help around the kitchen and barracks where my mother works. I quickly made friends with Thomas, and we stuck together. The lieutenant here had no use for us, and we were rejected by the men. When the Yanks began to attack the fort, we both ran to this shelter. We are planning to cross the lake after the attack is over, and find work at a Blacksmith. No one has even noticed we are gone with all the concentration on stamping out the rebel force. We hate all this war anyway, and wish it were over. I just hope my mother isn't worried. I befriended a prominent Indian who brings us food. The Indians are our allies, and our Indian will appear whenever I use a whistle. I may give you a whistle if I decide you need it. You are very lucky I found you; a guard would've shot you. Now that I have told my story, you must tell yours. I am especially interested in your odd clothing." When Benjamin finished his story I knew I had really gone back on time! I decided to be truthful.

"I believe your story is true Benjamin. However, I am a Patriot. Please don't harm me. I know you may find this hard to believe, but I'm from the future!" I said, hoping for the best. He narrowed his eyes.

"I will not injure you. Although I don't hate Yanks like everyone at the Fort does, you must prove yourself true." He demanded. I searched my pockets for evidence. I had two quarters, a stick of gum, and my cell phone. I showed him all these things. The cell fascinated him, which he punched numbers on for a long time. I then described to him how the Devil's kitchen looked at sunset when I had traveled through it. He was convinced.

"I always wondered if it was possible. Moreover, these artifacts make sense. But we must get you wearing something more natural looking. You can stay the night here, but tomorrow we have to try get you back to where you came from. Now, please, make yourself comfortable. It will be a long night."

The earth was harder than rock, but I was so tired when I lay down, I fell asleep instantly. I awoke to Roxy licking my face the next morning. Light streamed in through cracks in the shelter. I was sore all over. The first thing I noticed was that it was very humid. Benjamin was nowhere to be found. I had to use the bathroom very bad. I saw that Thomas was eating berries. When he saw me staring, he offered me some. They were blackberries, and very delicious. I also fed some to Roxy. I recalled that the English use the word "privy" for bathroom so I tried my hand communicating with Thomas.

"Is there uh… a privy around here somewhere?" I interrogated. He frowned and pointed at a coat Benjamin had been wearing.

"Oh. Benjamin? Is he around? May I go outside?" I wasn't getting anywhere. Thomas just shook his head. I didn't know what he meant.

"Well, I won't be gone long." I said. I grabbed Roxy by her leash and we went outside. It was very foggy and muggy out. I could barely see more than five feet away. I discovered a thicket and relieved myself. All the time, I couldn't quite tell whether someone was there or not. I hurried back to the hideout with the unshakeable feeling that somebody was watching me. Benjamin soon returned with a stack of clothes and food.

"You will have to wear these." He told me. They were Indian deerskin pants and a rabbit–skin shirt. They were very primitively cut, but I guess they were the best Benjamin could do. I put them on over my clothes and in an instant I was sweating. Benjamin also passed me a clay figure of some kind.

"It's the whistle I was telling you about. Use it only in dire need. Some of the Indians don't know we are staying here and they would kill us if they found out. Just be cautious." He instructed. I put it in the pocket of my shorts.

"We may be here for a while. The fog has just settled in."

For the long hours that passed after that, Benjamin told me stories about London. We talked quietly. I also tasted a very hard biscuit. Benjamin passed me a jug to soften the biscuit with water. I tipped the jug so water would pour out, but none flowed.

"Looks like we're out of water." Benjamin observed.

"What'll we do?" I asked.

"Well, I need to talk to the Indian to ask when he thinks the fog will clear. This may set us back a bit. Thomas and I were planning to leave within several days, but if the fog lasts, we can't. It's too dangerous to travel with the fog. The attack will also be put off until the fog clears. You and I will go out and Thomas will stay here with your dog. I'll stay at a clearing and wait for you there. You must take this jug and fill it with water from the lake. Hurry, and be silent about it." He ordered. I didn't really want to leave Roxy behind, but what choice did I have?

Benjamin and I left the hideout and when we got to the clearing he was talking about, we went our separate ways. I could hear the rolling of the waves within ten minutes, although I could only see trees and mist. I crept through the foliage. Then I heard a shout coming from my right. I froze in place.

"Alexander! Come here!" a deep voice called out. The voice didn't belong to a British man. I figured it must be an Indian's voice.

"What is it?" a tenor British voice said.

"White was here, look." The Indian said. After a pause, I heard the Brit. say:

"Good work. Keep searching. I know that damn Benjamin is around here somewhere. He wouldn't dare brave this fog. Let's head back to the fort."

I don't know what the Indian found, but apparently Benjamin needed to be more careful about what he left lying around. I was terrified. I stayed motionless for a while, until the only thing I could hear was my pounding heart and the waves lapping against the shore. Then I began to move very slowly through the shrubbery. I finally approached the lake, knelt quickly down, and filled the jug. Once more, I couldn't shake the feeling that somebody was watching me. I hustled back to the clearing and met up with Benjamin. Once we were back in the retreat, I said:

"Benjamin! There are men looking for you! I heard and Indian and a British man! They found something and I think they may discover this shelter soon."

"Yes, it's true. The Indian I met with told me that several Indians were looking for me. I can't risk this much longer. The Indian said that the fog showed no signs of retreat and that we may be here for a long time, perhaps several days. I won't lie. This could be very dangerous for you. If anyone discovers that we are here, Thomas and I might be killed, for running away and harboring a Yank like you. No matter what, never let anyone see you. You'll have to stay here until the fog clears, but not a second longer. When it's time, we'll have to rush you to where I found you, and look for the hole. Thomas and I have a canoe lined up." He declared.

The rest of the day was hot, muggy, and very boring. I tried to eat another biscuit but I got sick to my stomach. Roxy was longing for the outdoors, but we couldn't even risk it. I found myself sweating and the heat became unbearable. I remember closing my eyes, and resting. I don't know what happened after that.

What I do remember was cool water on my face, and I opened my eyes. Thomas had been pouring water on my face. I felt like I'd been asleep forever. I realized I had passed out, maybe from the heat, or the biscuit, or something in the water. It was so unsanitary in there, I didn't even know.

"How many days have I been unconscious Thomas?" I managed to whisper. He held up four fingers. I was shocked. Roxy was at Thomas's side. Apparently, he had taken care of her.

"Where is Benjamin?" Thomas showed me Benjamin's newly bloodstained coat.

"Is he alive?" Thomas nodded vigorously. The blood must have meant he tried to escape. That was the Benjamin I had barely known, but grown to like.

"Did the Indians get him?" he nodded again.

"Did they take him to the fort?" a final nod.

331

"I guess it's just us now." He shook his head at that. He pointed at the door and made a motion to get up. So I stood up. He held a finger to his lips. I picked up Roxy and we crawled outside. All the fog was gone. Thomas moved stealthily. I heard gunshots and screamed. Thomas made a motion for me to stay out of sight, and then took a whistle similar to the one Benjamin had given and blew hard. It sounded like a bird of some kind. Within five minutes, an Indian approached Thomas, but he couldn't see me. He was dressed with a simple loincloth and was streaked with mud. His face showing a wise, aging man, with sharp cheekbones and proud, dark eyes.

"I need skins you took. You are alone now. No more help. Too much work for me and not enough pay from you. Canoe at place agreed. Leave skins there. Yankees are attacking. Go now." The Indian demanded, and as quick as he appeared was gone.

Thomas and I left the bush. The gunshots were closer. Roxy was trembling. I heard a bloodcurdling scream, and could then hear the beach once more. I could sense we were near the Devil's Kitchen. We continued on, and then I saw it ahead. Thomas stopped me. He pointed to himself, and then toward the gunshots. Next he pointed at me, and then the Devil's Kitchen. I nodded, I would pretty much be out in the open, and Thomas was on his own.

"Thanks," I whispered, and he was gone. I hovered near the edge of the forest and watched a man go by. I decided he might not see me once he was past, so I ran as fast as I could toward the Devil's kitchen. Out of the corner of my eye, I saw the man moving quickly and I screamed. A bullet whizzed past my ear. Roxy jumped out of my arms. The hole was there again! I have never been that relieved in all my life. I dove for it and another bullet sounded off. Roxy was way ahead of me. When I was all the way in, I looked back. There was only blackness. The hole had closed up! And, the Indian skins I was wearing had vanished! I didn't care. I crawled along at a breakneck speed and when I emerged, I saw the paved road! I ran to it and knelt down to kiss it. A biking tourist passed by and shot me a crazed look. Here I was, dirty, torn up, and kissing a road. I laughed so hard I cried and rolled over. I looked at the Devil's Kitchen. There was no hole! Was I crazy? I thought so until I felt a lump in my pocket. It was the clay whistle Benjamin had given me!

When Roxy and I burst in the door at the inn, my Dad was surprised to see us so dirty. From then on, I would not be chasing my dog down any strange holes. I went straight to my room and took a shower, and it never felt so good in all my life.

Note: The Battle of Fort Mackinac took place in 1814. The British won, but surrendered the Fort the following year. The characters in this story are purely fictional.

Candy of Life

Gregory Jewell

When I awoke for the first time, I saw nothing. The nothingness permeated to my innards and I could stand it only so long. Then I felt a hole ripped into my being and I felt objects being poured inside me. I could feel my insides shaking inside me whenever I moved. Whenever I moved, someone came over and shook me up, but I did not care because that intensified my contentment because I could feel the free–floating candy inside me.

> **Gregory Jewell** wrote this piece in the twelfth grade at age seventeen while attending Creston High School in Grand Rapids, MI. He has had no previous writing experience outside of high school.

They moved me down the conveyer belt and stuck strings and hooks inside me. Every once in a while, I could see what they were doing to me because I saw the others like me. They all had beautiful colors on them, but none of them shook like I did. I felt sorry for them because of their mindlessness that I had escaped, but I also felt lonely. I had no one to talk to besides my unblinking companions. The makers merely pushed buttons and more like me were created.

The conveyer took me higher and higher until I feared that I would fall and spill the happiness inside me. Then I did fall, but I fell down a chute into more darkness. I felt a rumbling and then movement. I saw none of where I was to go.

Eventually, my companions and I were unloaded into a huge building where many brightly colored objects resided. Every once in a while, a thing like the makers would come by and pick one of my companions up and exchange some paper for them. Every time, I was not chosen.

I wept bitterly into the darkness at night. One time, I caught a glimpse of myself. Unlike the others, I was black and white striped. I had no flashy colors on myself. More and more of those like me passed onto the world in which I longed to go. I was the only one left. Still no one came for me.

One day, a young boy and his mom came into what I realized was my prison. They looked for the brightly colored ones, but could not find one. They searched the whole place, passing by me again and again. I remained still because I had no hope of their taking me. They left the store and I never saw them again.

Many days crept by. Newer and more colorful companions came and went. Finally, a poor couple came in. They looked extremely happy together but had not enough paper to bargain for the others. They looked at me with a look that said, "It will do." I almost jumped into their arms while they looked at me, but that might have scared them away from me.

When I left the prison that day, I felt overjoyed. They hung me up for all to see. Many people came by and looked at me with greedy eyes. Others started mock swinging at me in anticipation. The couple shooed them away and I loved them.

My time came. Everyone looked so happy and rich. Even the couple shone in their white gown and suit. Everyone received a blindfold and, in turn, they swung at me with a stick. Most missed, but when one connected, the crowd cheered. I felt good for them. I brought them a joy that would not have happened had I not been there. Each contact with that stick brought me more and more joy because I felt alive.

A small child was next. He had a hardy swing and I cracked in the middle. All my innards came tumbling out and everyone rushed to retrieve them before anyone else. Some ate what I had called mine, but I found pleasure in the activity around me. I started fading from their world. I could not live without myself, and in my last feelings, I felt total elation.

Untitled

Gabrielle Russon

The sun disappeared slowly under the horizon; an array of vibrant colors had darkened and was slowly turning a shade of midnight blue. In the twilight, the figure quietly shut the front door and walked on the sidewalk, away from the neighborhood. She shivered. Although it was only September, the nights had begun to be chilly.

A dog barked, and the girl looked up for a moment. She stared at the brown collie that eyed her cautiously from a screened in porch. It reminded her of Shallow, her boyfriend's dog. Ex–boyfriend's dog was more correct, she thought.

The girl ignored the dog and kept walking past her neighborhood; the sidewalk ended, but she continued to drag her feet on the road. Small drops of rain sprinkled from the sky and glazed the girl, but she felt absolute nothing. Nothingness. She was numb.

Gabrielle Russon just completed her junior year at Mattawan High School. She was sixteen years old when she wrote *Untitled*. She is a member of the Mattawan Varsity Basketball team and also plays softball for her school team. Gabrielle loves hanging out with her friends, watching movies, traveling to foreign places, and playing sports. Her family plays an important part in her life, and she can't wait to graduate in 2003!

Minutes later, it began to rain harder. She ran now for she couldn't turn back. Her house was no longer her home; it was a battleground for her parents who had announced to their daughter that they were on the verge of divorce. The girl wasn't stupid; she knew about her father's phone calls. It wasn't normal to speak in a muffled tone and then quickly hang up when someone was approaching. But it didn't matter to the girl. Nothing really

337

surprised her anymore. The numbness had swallowed her up; the girl didn't feel like crying.

As she sprinted up the road, flashbacks of Shallow popped into her mind. Dereck. Dereck had broken up with her.

"You never smile anymore, Jessalyn," he had said to her as they sat together in her backyard on the swing set. They rocked back and forth on the swings, and she had stared straight ahead. He couldn't make eye contact with her. "I know you're not happy, and now I'm not happy either. I guess I just can't make you happy," he was babbling now. "I'm going to go now, I guess." He got up from the swings and started walking toward the house.

"I'm all alone." The words had surprised her; she didn't really mean to say them out loud to Dereck. "You can never understand me."

Dereck stopped walking, and he looked back at her. "Goodbye." Then he turned around and walked away from her. He drove off in his car and disappeared down the street, leaving her to swing on the swings. It had been a week ago, and he hadn't even called once. The girl was definitely alone now.

The girl stopped running. She finally was there, her sanctuary. The wooden bridge overlooked the deep river. There was a white bench on one side of the bridge with a large sign next to it that read *GOLDENVIEW PARK DISTRICT*. She remembered when the Park District had put the bench there to encourage the community to admire the beauty of the outdoors. She had never seen anyone by the river, sitting on the bench. Perhaps that's why the river was her special spot where she would go to be away from the pressures of school, her parents, life.

The figure in the night solemnly looked at the river. She pulled herself up and sat on the top of the bridge. Rain swallowed her up, and she sat shivering in her wet clothes. As she sat watching the wind blow the river into waves, a strange thing happened. At first, it was a just one tear. Then there were two. Soon the girl began to sob as her gray eyes flooded. A sudden sense of relief rushed over her, maybe I'm not numb, she thought. She held her face in her hands as she thought about the end to her first teenage romance. Where will I spend Christmas next year, she thought, remembering her parent's break up.

Jessalyn sat on the bridge crying for what seemed to be hours. Her brown hair was drenched and stuck to her face. It felt like the entire Mississippi River had invaded her tennis shoes, but none of that mattered now. Jessalyn stared into the water. Slowly she lowered herself off the bridge and climbed back down to land and walked home.

When she finally reached her house in her neighborhood, she was greeted by the familiar light of her house. Her mother anxiously opened the door and stared at her daughter, obviously surprised to be confronted with a water rat. "Jessalyn, where have you been?" she exclaimed, pulling her child inside. "Why didn't you tell me where you went?" Mrs. Harrisburg rushed to the kitchen and returned with a handful of towels.

Jessalyn sat in her bedroom in dry clothes with three kitchen towels wrapped around her thick wet mass of curly hair. Her hands trembled as she reached for her pink telephone. Taking a deep breath, she mustered up the courage to dial the numbers. "Hello," she meekly said when the voice answered. "Dereck, I miss you...." and the tears began to pour down her cheeks. She swallowed her tears, realizing that she finally wasn't numb anymore.

Ireland's Farewell

Sara Anne Aycock

The sun was a child playing merrily on the dewy wet grass. The different shades of green clashed together like glistening swords. The day was calm and sweet. The only noise came from the soft patter of the rain. As I got out of the car, I was astounded by the simplicity of it all.

As I looked to the side, I gazed at a body of water that wound itself around like a snake that encircled Ireland.

I returned to my other side and was astounded by the power that the mountains had.

The mountains were giants ready to strike down any trespassers.

There were myths about fairies and leprechauns who lived there. I know why Ireland was where they chose to live.

As I thought about leaving, I was struck with sadness. I peered down at the flower—covered meadow. It was a carnival of beauty and time. I never wanted to leave Ireland's embrace, but the time was drawing near. As I turned toward the car and was ready to say a final farewell, I saw a bird whistling like it was saying, "goodbye."

On board the plane, I looked out as we flew by white shapeless clouds. I looked down and Ireland was slipping away like a grain between my fingers.

Sara Anne Aycock is twelve years old and in the seventh grade at Ring Lardner Middle School. She has lived in Niles, Michigan all of her life with her parents Jamie and Glenn Aycock and her brother, Collin. Writing poetry and stories are a passion of Sara's, as is reading. She was eleven years old when she wrote this story that was inspired by a holiday in Ireland in March 2001.

Sweat and Potatoes

Nicole Walawander

Farming runs in my blood. My grandfather was raised on a farm in the "Old World" of rural Poland. His grandfather was also raised on a farm, as was his grandfather's father, and so on. Coming from a suburban upbringing in Michigan, it was always difficult, but fascinating, for me to imagine life on a farm in the "Mother Country." My ancestors, whom I grew to admire so much from the stories of them my grandfather told me, had lived off the land by sweating in fields. Why should I be so different?

> **Nicole Walawander** is from Shelby Township, MI and is currently sixteen years old and a high school senior at the Academy of the Sacred Heart in Bloomfield Hills, MI. She looks forward to attending college where she plans to further her pursuit of becoming a successful writer.

Since the age of seven, I have spent the summers on my great grandfather's farm, located in northern Poland. My great aunt, Ciocia, and her husband, Wujek now own and operate the farm with their children and their children's children. It was the close–knit, intimate family I knew and loved through my grandfather's stories, and once a year I could belong to it.

Though everyone around me was busy working, I spent my days on the farm in complete leisure. While my cousins would clean out the pig stalls, I would take a shower. As they milked the cows, I walked to the market to get ice cream. Don't get me wrong; it wasn't as if I was a spoiled brat. In fact, I wanted to work. To me, it was the ultimate symbol of belonging to my family. But, it seemed as if I was more of a nuisance than help.

For instance, when I was ten years old, Ciocia asked me to pick a basket of raspberries from the garden, for dessert that evening. Naturally, I considered my job to be of utmost importance: this was my opportunity to prove that I, too, was fully capable of doing farm work. It took me nearly two hours to fill that tiny basket. Taking into the count all the time I wasted on avoiding bees buzzing around the delicate fruit, this was not bad timing. After I placed the last berry in the basket, I let out a sigh of relief, and triumphantly marched back to the farmhouse.

Unfortunately, on my way back, Box, the farm dog (I still swear it was a wolf), began an enraged barking at me from the inside of his kennel. Frightened, I dropped the raspberries and scampered out of sight from wolf dog. It was only until seeking refuge behind a shed that I realized my fatal mistake; I left the raspberries! Ciocia must have seen this pitiful episode and came running. It was too late. The chickens had swarmed over the mass of raspberries. All traces of them were gone in less then a minute.

I was ashamed. My one chance to prove myself, and I blew it. Ciocia didn't seem to mind, though. In fact, I think she was rather amused. She knew how embarrassed I was and tried to console me, "*Dziewciena, to nic.*" But my shame returned that night at dinner, as everyone seemed to linger around the table, seemingly, as if they still needed more time to resign themselves to the fact that there would be no dessert that evening.

Three years later, for no apparent reason, the family finally deemed me worthy (or perhaps brave enough) to participate in "real" farm work...helping harvest the *ziemniaki* (potatoes). This is no small consolation when one realizes the significance potatoes play in the Polish diet. The vegetable is eaten at all three meals. It is boiled and fried. It is cut up in pieces or mashed, served in soups and stews, prepared with dill and butter, used as a meal in itself—in essence, it is given a place of honor at the dinner table. Most importantly, during World War II, when food was scarce in the country, the potato was Poland's sustenance. It is the reason why I am alive today.

After the midday meal on the potato–harvesting day, *Wujek* (my uncle) took my hand and proceeded to feel my palm with his rough thumb. "Ah!" he exclaimed with a wink, "Just like a baby's! Don't worry though, the potatoes will take care of that."

Before leaving for the field, Ciocia, with an expression of both amusement and pity, handed me a pair of white latex gloves. She seemed to have taken Wujek's words more seriously than I did. I took the gloves, thanked her, and then rushed to the tractor to join the rest of the potato pickers, my cousins.

My four semi-familiar cousins already sat inside the tractor's wagon, acknowledging me with their distinctive Polish eyes of exhaustion, cheerfulness, and insight. I had not seen them in over two years. The discomfort was evident. Szymek and Tomek smiled bashfully, while Emilia tucked a piece of hair into her kerchief, and Joanna quietly greeted me with, "*Czesc, Nicole.*"
They were not the only ones feeling somewhat uncomfortable. Being the only one with gloves, latex at that, I felt incredibly out of place. It was bad enough to have an accent, but gloves too? I quickly shoved them in my back pocket while hoping none of my cousins noticed.

As the tractor began to move, Joanna smiled again, and in no time the five of us were gabbing cheerfully. The tractor crossed multicolored fields, a small bridge, and train tracks before arriving at the potato field. My cousins and I spoke of school, airplanes, and Michael Jordan. Szymek showed me his lucky stone, and Emilia told me about her best friend. We sang songs and laughed loudly. I felt as if I belonged.

Just then, Wujek stopped the tractor, and teasingly told us to stop playing and get to work. Ciocia distributed wicker baskets to each of us and assigned a row of potatoes to harvest. The day was hot and sunny, and I could hear the birds singing passionately to one another. Surely, this was the kind of day which filled my grandfather's memories. This is the kind of day he often spoke of while recounting his childhood. As an infant he would spend this kind of day lying on top of a bed of straw between two rows of potatoes, watching his mother work nearby.

I worked hard, placing potato after potato into my basket while reflecting on these thoughts, and soon my basket was filled. Looking up to see if anyone had noticed my victory, I was filled with embarrassment with what I saw. The others had filled their baskets numerous times already, whereas I had only filled mine once. What kind of farmer was I? Surely not a good one, first the raspberries and now I could not even keep up with my cousins! So I began to hasten my pace.

I can't brag that I filled more baskets than anyone else. After hours of labor, a sore back, and blistered hands, I probably picked the fewest. Surprisingly, I didn't feel discouraged. To the contrary, I returned to the farmhouse with an overwhelming feeling of achievement and belonging. In those few hours, I developed a deeper love and understanding of my ancestors. I had sweat in the same soil as did my father, grandfather, and great–grandfather. I had earned my place in my family.

My Grandma and Grandpa

Savannah

My Grandma and Grandpa teach me Spanish.
I like Spanish because it is fun to learn.
They read me stories, and it is fun to learn how to read.

Savannah Garland is a second grader at Keeler Elementary School in Redford, MI. She wrote this piece in the first grade and became a member of "Readers' Theatre." She has read her work at her classes' "Authors' Tea." Savannah also enjoys ballet, Brownie Scouts and computers.

Suki Meier is twelve years old and just completed the sixth grade at East Grand Rapids Middle School. She enjoys writing poems and short stories and has been fortunate enough to have teachers who share the love of the written word. Her poem was written while she was studying early immigration to America. Suki also enjoys swimming, basketball and equestrienne sports.

I See You Annie

I see you Annie,
Out in your field,
Plowing your new farmland
And planting your new crops,
Making a living.
Your hands are blistered
And your face brown,
With dirt and soot
From your busy day.
Your dirty blonde hair
Knotted and filled with tangled masses.
Your straw hat covered in leaves,
And your basket filled with lunch.
You have a picture of your father
When he was a young farmer
Just like you.
You have two tears in your eyes:
One of happiness,
The other of sadness.
You've come to America,
A free country,
Yet you have left your family and friends behind,
But you know that everything will be fine
When it works itself out in the end.
Time has passed and night has come.
You say goodnight to the stars,

But know in your heart
That in a way
You really said goodnight to your family and friends.
And in a way,
They said goodnight back to you.
I see you Annie,
With a tear in your eyes,
And a smile on your face.
You have come to America for freedom.

~~~Suki Meier

Shannon E. Hascall is twelve years old and in the seventh grade at Brimley Area Schools. She has been interested in writing for a couple of years. She had one poem published in the *Anthology of Poetry* which came out last August.

A Weeping Willow

There is a willow,
a weeping willow,
that lives,
in my back yard.

I say one day,
"don't cry, weeping willow."
He weeps some more,
yet does not reply.

"Please! Don't cry!"
I ask once more.

For the weeping willow,
is very wise and truly,
does not speak out,
against one.

~~~Shannon E. Hascall

Seventeen–year–old **Maureen E. Hanley**, a junior at Hopkins High School, wrote *Brush of Hope* at the age of seventeen in tenth grade. She lives on a small farm in Dorr with her parents, three siblings, and assorted animals. Maureen won her first writing contest at the age of ten in a state 4–H essay competition. In the Allegan County Fair, she earned Best of Show for Creative Writing in 1997, 1998 and 2000. Currently she is the body–copy editor of her school yearbook, *The Reflector*.

Brush of Hope

Drip Drop.
A silent tear
Unseen by the busied,
Disdained by the angered,
Slips slowly down a flushed face
Followed in quick succession
By drops of the same pain.
Pain born of loneliness, of being
Always present, yet always absent.

Drip Drop.
A silent tear
Brushed away by a friendly hand
That longs to ease the heartache.
The silence has broken, and
Pain is no longer falling,
No longer disdained,
It is now seen.
It is now heard.

~~~Maureen E. Hanley

Danielle Lynne Seitz is sixteen years old and just completed her freshman year at Mattawan High School in Michigan. She loves to write, sing, act and play sports with her favorite sport being hockey. She considers writing as a lifetime career.

Winter's Glory

Snowflakes fall with a pattern of grace.
All the marvelous angels dance in place.
Crystalline flakes are blown against your face.
You're blessed with an angel's kiss.
One of peace and everlasting prophecy.
The snow, like shooting stars in the sky,
stands as a majestic mass both white and fair.
Jack Frost's touch has made delicate designs,
Upon your window frames so gloriously.
The Sun shines down on Earth as though in vain.
My Alaskan paradise be forever chilled.
Heaven's tapestry now full of stars,
Fills my heart with the strength of love,
Which melts the cold,
That shackles my winter heart

~~~Danielle Lynne Seitz

Appendix

TONY Snyder

Artists

Marta Olson is a lifetime summer resident of northern Michigan. She has enjoyed photography since a young child and more recently turned her creative expression to painting. Watercolor and oil are her favorite media. Although she develops her skills with occasional workshops, she is primarily self–taught and loves the process of experimenting on her own with new techniques and approaches. She enjoys studying the works of the masters, as well as contemporary painters, for fresh inspiration for her art.

She has received honors in Michigan juried shows in Hillsdale and Petoskey and her work can be found in the Victorian Summer shop on Mackinac and on her web page at www.mackinac.com/art/olson. She also exhibits regularly in three annual Mackinac Island Artists' Guild shows on the island.

In her own words, "Painting is a way for me to express my love of the natural world. Trying to capture the spirituality and seasons of the north is a delightful process for me. The light here is always changing and it is a wonderful challenge to teach myself to see its effect on the water, sky, and trees."

Marta's professional background includes work in education, hotel management, and the personal computer industry. She received a B.A. in Liberal Arts from the University of Michigan and an M.B.A. from Michigan State University and recently taught business at Jackson Community College. She, her husband Peter, and two daughters moved to the Harbor Springs area in 2001 where she paints, provides freelance business consulting, and develops commercial websites. Marta can be reached at olsonma5@msu.edu.

Robert Roebuck, the graphic designer for the covers of Volume II, III and IV, hails from Talladega, Alabama, but considers Atlanta, Georgia his home where he has lived for over twelve years.

Professionally Robert has been a graphic designer for almost twelve years, but he has always been an artist at heart. He won his first coloring contest at age five at the Woolworth's department store in Talladega. The grand prize for his mastery of color schemes and keeping well within the lines was a $50.00 shopping spree during the Christmas season. Right then and there, Robert knew that the world of art and design was calling his name.

Robert graduated from the Art Institute of Atlanta and now works for an international publishing company where he has honed his computer design skills on a Macintosh, his weapon of choice. He also owns a small design company, Identity. There he designs products ranging from brochures, posters and CD/menu/book covers to magazine ads, flyers and corporate identities for a wide range of clients.

Misha Dodge, age fifteen, is a newcomer to Michigan, but more importantly, to America. He was raised in Vlekovechnoye, an orphanage in Krasnodar, Russia. Following a year of trials and delays, Terry and Linda Dodge of South Boardman, Michigan adopted Misha and a girl, Anya, and brought them to Michigan. Misha is still learning the customs and language of the United States, but he is able to communicate quite well now. His drawing and sense of humor know no language barrier.

Tyler Finkel has lived on Mackinac Island, Michigan his entire thirteen years and just completed the eighth grade at Mackinac Island Public School. He feels privileged to help represent Mackinac Island (all 5.5 square miles of it) as an artistic place and is honored to know that his art is actually good enough to be part of something bigger than a wall of the art room.

Kaylee Knickerbocker lives in Grand Haven, Michigan with her mom and two brothers. Her favorite hobby is drawing animals.

Tony Snyder just completed the fourth grade in Kentwood, Michigan and is ten years old. In his free time he likes to email his friends and family, cook and play with his cat and dog. At school he likes to take tests, and he likes to read!

Sam Winsor lives on Mackinac Island, Michigan and just completed the seventh grade at Mackinac Island Public School. He enjoys painting pictures of landscapes. He's been working with oils for only two years but feels he is getting quite good. Sam loves Mackinac Island, loves to paint and dreams of one day becoming a famous painter who makes millions of dollars. His favorite hobby is doing tricks with his bike. In the summer, when the weather is warm, he loves to entertain Island visitors by jumping his bike off the coal dock into the chilling waters of Lake Huron.

The Editors

This year, for the first, time we used a team of three editors, **Michelle Cowell, Jeaneene Nooney** and **Michael Patterson.**

Michelle Cowell lives in Atlanta, Georgia though Michigan was her home throughout her childhood years. Michelle has a Bachelor of Arts in Creative Writing from the University of Colorado at Boulder and currently works in publishing when she is not spending time writing or cavorting with her honey (who just happens to be the cover designer for **Voices of Michigan**, Volumes II, III and IV.)

Michelle's future plans include the creation of a literary sounding board for young adults. For more information on this exciting project, please contact her at mrc@toast.com.

Michelle's contributions to the Anthology go beyond editing, as she as been the creator behind most of the quarterly newsletters provided **Voices of Michigan** authors, readers and significant others.

Jeaneene L. Nooney is a freelance writer who lives in Kalkaska County, Michigan with her husband John, and three children. She's been interested in writing since she was a child. Her formal education includes college writing, literature, and genealogy courses and study through Writer's Digest books, workshops, and the American Christian Writers seminars. Publishing credits include feature stories in The Leader and The Kalamazoo Gazette, Plane and Pilot, various organizational newsletters and in poetry in Volume I of **Voices Of Michigan**. She was a Poetry Reader for Volume II. She has taught creative writing workshops for junior high and high school students, and is a member of Stories.Com.

Jeaneene's been active as a genealogist and a Vice President of the Kalkaska Genealogical Society. The society's major recent accomplishment is an 800–page volume entitled Big Trout, Black Gold: A History of Kalkaska County, for which she served as a copy editor. Jeaneene enjoys the editorial process and honing her own and others' writing to the finest possible edge.

She is currently working to complete and publish her novel set in a small northern Michigan town. It's the story of a prodigal son who returns from a successful career in Detroit to his hometown where the grief–ghosts of his brother's accidental death confront him and force a dramatic change in his artificial emotional moorings.

Michael Patterson was born and reared in Toledo, Ohio. For many poor young blacks, like Michael, living in the shadow of Motown was a challenge. Detroit was slick, fast and glamorous. Young blacks tried to dress, dance and live like the pimps and gangsters that periodically came through Toledo in their long, luxurious cars. In 1972, Michael moved to Detroit, and for six months lived a life as raw, cold and brutal as the winds blowing over the Detroit River in February. Those six months were an eye opener. Michael realized his so–called heroes were nothing more than vicious predators, and he did not want to be like them. So, he moved and enrolled in the University of Toledo where through the years he received two Associate degrees, a Bachelor of Arts in Communications and a Master of Arts in English in 1989. Since that time he has taught in Ohio at the University of Toledo and Perrysburg Technical School. In Georgia, Michael has been on faculty at Morris Brown University, Georgia Military College and currently he is an instructor in the Department of English at Fort Valley State University in Fort Valley, Georgia.

Volume IV Contest Readers

Julia (Judy) Bartholomay was a freelance writer and teacher in the Chicago area before retiring to Florida in 1984. She attended Vassar College as a Classics major but withdrew during World War II to marry Henry Bartholomay, an Air Force Navigator–Bombardier. Twenty six years and five grandchildren later, she received her B.A. degree in English from Lake Forest College where she was elected to Phi Beta Kappa, graduated with honors and was awarded the MacPherson Prize for Excellence in English. A year later she earned teacher accreditation in secondary English but never made a career of teaching. Over the years, Judy has had the opportunity to know and to work with some of the outstanding poets of our time. Her book, *The Shield of Perseus; The Vision and Imagination of Howard Nemerov,* (poet laureate, 1988–89) was published in 1972. As a member of the Winneka Fortnightly Writing Group, she presented a monograph on the poet Isabella Gardner that is in the group's archives at the Newberry Library and also among the Gardner papers at Washington University. Judy is the past president and continues to be an honorary member of the Modern Poetry Association that publishes *Poetry* magazine. She is currently enjoying her seven grandchildren and working on her genealogy.

Joan Schmeichel, writing under the name **Joan Roth**, lives in Kewadin, Michigan with her husband Neill. Before retirement she was a development officer at the University of Michigan. Her writing background includes consumer information pieces for Detroit's old WXYZ Action Bureau as well as free–lance advertising copy. Joan's fiction credits include *One Day In a Swamp*, published in D.C. Heath and Company's children's reader *My Best Bear Hug.* Other stories, also published by D.C. Heath under the Callamore Educational label and included in their *Reading and Thinking Strategies* series for grades 3–4, 5–6, and 7–8, include *Fine–Feathered Dinner Guests, Nothing Good Ever Comes*

From Helping a Hawk, The Frog Who Sang Soprano; and a number of adaptations of fables and fairy tales. Joan's children's book, **Charlie Jump–Up**, self–published in 1982, was carried at Community News and Little Professor bookstores in Ann Arbor. Joan has also completed several book–length manuscripts for young people, at this time unpublished.

Glen Young is a teacher of high school English and journalism in Petoskey, Michigan. A long time summer resident of Mackinac Island, Glen's poetry appears in Volumes II and III of **Voices of Michigan.** His column *Literate Matters* appears regularly in the *Petoskey News Review*, and his profile of two of Mackinac's most historic hotels and their owners appears in the 2002 issue of *Mackinac Living* magazine.

Carol Douglas grew up on the shores of Blue Mountain Lake in the Adirondacks of northern New York State. Fishing, boating, camping, hiking, swimming caused summer days to fly by. Skiing, skating, sledding, walking on frozen crusted snow hurried winter along. Reading these selections with familiar images of campfires, lightning bugs and motorboats called up many childhood memories. As dean of faculty at University Liggett School in Grosse Pointe, Michigan, Carol has taught writing to high school juniors for the last seventeen years. An avid reader of both fiction and non–fiction, especially contemporary American works, Carol is delighted to encourage those intent up on following in the footsteps of Michigan's proud tradition of writers.

Deborah K. Frontiera grew up in Lake Linden, Michigan. She teaches kindergarten in Houston, Texas and spends her summers in a cottage near Lake Linden. She frequently gives workshops on various aspects of writing to teachers, students and other writers. She has judged poetry contests for the Houston Writers League and was coordinator for their student–writing contest for two years. Her poems have appeared in a Houston Literary Magazine, *The Talker, Texas Voices*, newsletter of the Texas Council of Teachers of English, **Voices of Michigan,** Volume II, and in a self–published chap book, *Through My Eyes*. She has also published fiction—*The Chronicles of Henry Roach–Dairier* (www.Iuniverse.com) non–fiction, and has signed a contract with New Concepts Publishing for a children's picture book series known as e–books.

Stefanie Lassiter teaches writing at Lansing Community College and Eastern Michigan University. She earned her M.A. in Literature at Eastern Michigan University and her B.A. in Writing at Grand Valley State University. She has published a few short stories, and has recently completed work on a 19th century romance featuring Mackinac Island and Grayling, Michigan. AmericaHouse Publishers has published **Choices of the Heart** and it will be released August 2002. Stefanie is married and has a son.

Tracey Koperski grew up in Greenville, Michigan. As a child and young adult she was lucky to have her parents take her to all the wonderful places in Michigan and around the United States. She graduated from Central Michigan University. Tracey now works in the advertising sales department of The Grand Rapids Press. She lives in East Grand Rapids and is married, with two daughters. She loves to read, garden, sail, ski, work with Girl Scouts and live life!

Francis M. "Bud" Mansfield, a septuagenarian, is a life–long resident of Sault Ste Marie, Michigan. Bud has been married fifty two years and is the proud father of eight highly satisfactory children and other assorted offspring. He retired in 1998 as the Executive Director of the Sault Area Chamber of Commerce. Bud wrote a whimsical Chamber of Commerce newspaper column for ten years for the *Sault Evening News* Sunday edition. He has revised selected columns and compiled them into a book published under the charming name of **The Chamber Pot.** He is nearing completion of a book he explains as being part fact, part fiction (faction, maybe?) about a chronic, frustrating bowel condition called Crohn's disease that he has tolerated for 35 years.

Mary Rupe is a graduate of the Institute of Children's Literature and the Long Ridge Writers Group. Her first published story was included in **Voices of Michigan,** Volume III. She lives in

Union, Michigan with her husband, Frank. Finding time to write isn't always easy, but she captures ideas as they come to her...standing in line, waiting in traffic or enjoying a lakeside sunset from their pier.

Peter Olson was born in Denver, Colorado, but has summered on Mackinac Island since 1990. He divides his time between Harbor Springs, Michigan and Mackinac Island where he works as a paramedic for Allied EMS–LifeLink. Until May 2000, he directed the English Department at Hillsdale College, and has published academic articles on Euripides, Ezra Pound, Lorca, Mallarme, and Derek Walcott among others. Peter's poetry appears in Volume III of *Voices of Michigan.*

Sharon Frost was the assistant editor of *Voices of Michigan, An Anthology of Michigan Authors,* Volume III. Poetry holds an essential form of communication in Sharon's heart, and she was honored to read all of the poetry offered in Volume IV. Sharon is committed to being a "bridge" of harmony and peace in the community. She recognizes the arts to be a universal form to heal pain and to celebrate joy. She is a core member of Visions of Peace Drum and Dance Company and VSA arts of Michigan–Char–Em (Promoting the Creative Power in People with Disabilities). Sharon is an Occupational Therapist, and is currently studying Massage Therapy. She and her husband own a log cottage rental business on Lake Charlevoix. Sharon loves her family, friends and community.

Gary Cusack, the third of three children, was born and reared in a strong Irish–Catholic family in Lansing, Michigan. He attended Catholic schools in the Lansing area but eventually joined the Army at seventeen along with Elvis Presley at Fort Hood. After leaving the Army, Gary spent six years in pursuit of a college degree, but never succeeded, as he persisted in changing his major and his school every few weeks. He has coursework from Michigan State, Lake Superior State, Lansing Community College and North Central Michigan College to name just a few. In 1967 he went to work on Mackinac Island, Michigan as a bartender because a good friend said to him, "Mackinac Island is a great place to make money, have fun and meet lots of single young ladies." On this Island he did indeed meet and eventually marry Anna Mary Denneny. Together they have reared five daughters and are the proud grandparents of eleven grandchildren. Gary and Anna Mary live in Petoskey.

Joan Johnson Richards was born, reared and graduated from High School in White Cloud, Michigan. She earned a Bachelor Degree from Central Michigan University and a Master Degree from Michigan State University. Jo taught art in the East Lansing Public Schools until retirement. Currently she and husband Don live near Bath, Michigan.

Nancy Martin was born and reared in Brookfield, Illinois. Her love of reading began at the age of seven when she discovered the public library and the summer reading program. Now the grandmother of eight, she is still reading children's books, biographies, historical novels, other fiction and especially books on the history of Great Britain. She is also interested in genealogy, scrap booking and ephemeron. Nancy has written seven articles for *Miniature Collector and Contemporary Doll* magazines with her most recent article being about antique Dennison paper dolls. She and husband Coby have just moved to an eighteen acre farm and have two horses, two ponies, three goats and two cats. They love their Highlander Farm!

George A. Corba, a lifelong Michigan resident and bibliophile, attended the Ohio Institute of Technology and has spent his last ten years employed as an engineering technician in broadcast television. When at liberty from his duties at work and home, he is an avid reader and quadline sport—kite flier. He lives in Vienna Township, Michigan where he helps care for his elderly father.

Pam Meier was born in St. Johns, Michigan and has lived in the Grand Rapids area since the age of two. She earned a Bachelor of Arts degree from Albion College, a Master of Music Education degree from Northern Michigan University and a

Master of Management degree from Aquinas College. She is the Vice President/General Manager at D.C. Martin and Son Scales, Inc. where she has been employed for the past fifteen years. Pam has been a Girl Scout Leader for the last seven years and enjoys music, horseback riding, and of course, reading! Pam and her husband, Chip, have three daughters.

Joy L. Brown, a mid–Michigan resident, has been married twenty years to John Thomas Brown Jr. Joy is the daughter of Robert and Florence Corba, and she has three brothers. Her work as a cosmetologist, parts clerk, secretary, and family caregiver has put her in observation of the human condition. Joy, a self–proclaimed word junkie, reads constantly!

Voices of Michigan

Permission was granted by the following authors for publication of their listed work in this fourth volume of *Voices of Michigan, An Anthology of Michigan Authors.*

Youth authors:

Sara Anne Aycock	*Ireland's Farewell*
Kylie R. Clark	*Genie in the Toy Room*
Christy Ewers	*The Championship Game*
Savannah Garland	*My Grandma and Grandpa*
Amy Geer	*Jack Russell Terrified on Mackinac Island*
Maureen E. Hanley	*Brush of Hope*
Kara Kuchapsky	*A Light on the Horizon*
Shannon E. Haskell	*A Weeping Willow*
Gregory Jewell	*Candy of Life*
Laurie Lijewski	*Surprise Awakening*
Gabrielle Russon	*Untitled*
Suki Meier	*I See You Annie*
Danielle Lynne Seitz	*Winter's Glory*
Holly Ann Steinmetz	*The Dragon and the Jaguar*
Nicole Walawander	*Sweat and Potatoes*

Other authors:

John R. Alberts	*I Am the Cat*
Linda Barlekamp	*Halloween Witches*
Beryl Bonney–Conklin	*Michigan Winter Ritual*
Kelie Callahan	*Sun*
Imogene A. Callander	*Traverse City Two Step*
Nancy Gump Cieslinski	*Life Story in a Hundred Words*
Cheryl Ann Clark	*Lemonade and Paint*
Melissa Erwin Croghan	*Communion*
Douglas C. Dosson	*Pickerel Creek Hunt*
Angie Fenton	*Making It*
Lorabeth Fitzgerald	*Rosebuds*
C. J. Gilbert	*Sunday Afternoons*
Theodore J. Gostomski	*Ships in the Night*
Katherine Ha	*For the Fairest Goddess*
Penelope Hudson	*From the Mouths of Babes*
Sandra Jo Jackson	*The Lilac Painting*

Kathryn Fritz Kniep	*Parallel Walker*
Linda LaRocque	*The Poet*
Tonya S. Lambert	*A Necessary Car Trip*
Roger Leslie	*Against the Pitch of a Winter Sky*
Lisbeth Lutz	*Dragonfly Waltz*
Kay MacDonald	*Card Dreams*
Eric Martin	*Lady Gitchee Gumme*
William R. McTaggart	*The Race*
Emily Meier	*My Age*
Jeannie Milakovich	*Chasing Windmills*
Bruce Phillip Miller	*Remember the Alamo*
Patricia P. Miller	*Woodsmoke and Whippoorwills*
Megan J. Murray	*My Lake Journal*
Lori Nelson	*Snowy Night*
Penny J. Niemi	*View From a Train*
Jennifer Niemur	*The Message of Manitou*
Marsha Orr	*You Will Be Healed*
Christina Rajala–Dembek	*The Light and Dark of Romance*
Joan Roth	*A New Year for Laura*
Glen Rothe	*The Lion*
Margrit Schlatter	*Leader of the Parade*
Cathy Scoda	*The Life of a Year*
Mark Scott	*Hunt of a Lifetime*
Mary Lee Scott	*The Jump*
Addison Thomas	*Onus*
Gina Thomas	*Naked Feet*
Fred Thornburg	*One Last Trip*
Marti Towne	*Surrender*
Mike VanBuren	*One Desert Night*
Margaret von Steinen	*On the Day Before My 40th Birthday*
Janet West–Teskey	*Unlikely Friends*
F. Gregory Whyte	*Paska Willy*
N. S. Williams	*Conversation With A Friend*
Cecilia Winston Floren	*Serious Defoliator*
Dianna L. Zimmerman	*White Sheets*

Contest Information

Voices of Michigan, An Anthology of Michigan Authors, is the product of a statewide–refereed writing contest. Michigan writers are encouraged to submit poems, short stories or works of non–fiction to the contest. A panel of judges reads each of the entries and determines which are to be included in the anthology.

The entries need not be about Michigan, and the writer need not currently live in Michigan. For more in–depth information about the contest and the anthology, visit the *Voices* website: www.voicesofmi.com, contact the publishers via email at macjanes@juno.com, write the publishers at *Voices of Michigan*, #5017, 413 Walnut Street, Green Cove Springs, Florida 32043–3443or call the publishers at 478–542–1642 or 906–847–3802.

The four volumes of the anthology may be purchased directly from the publisher's website, email or snail mail address. Additionally, the books are available at bookstores and gift shops throughout Michigan or the websites: amazon.com or barnes&noble.com.

Ordering Information

Keep in mind that if books are ordered directly from the publisher, the money stays within—and helps improve—the contest and the Anthology. Additionally, orders are handled more quickly through the publisher, plus there is no sales tax.

Volume I	ISBN	0–9667363–0–3	$15.95
Volume II	ISBN	0–9667363–1–1	$15.95
Volume III	ISBN	0–9667363–3–8	$18.95
Volume IV	ISBN	0–9667363–4–6	$18.95

**Shipping and handling: $6.00 up to three books. If you order four books or more, the publisher will pay the shipping and handling.

~~~

Order from your publisher: MackinacJane's Publishing Company:
> **Phone**: 1–478–542–1642,
> **E–mail**: macjanes@juno.com,
> **Web site**: www.voicesofmi.com
> **Snail mail**:
> > *Voices of Michigan* #5017
> > 413 Walnut Street
> > Green Cove Springs, Florida 32043–3443

You may use MasterCard or Visa, check, cash or money order.

Books are also available through your local bookstore, Michigan gift shops, www.amazon.com and www.barnes&noble.com.